SOCIETY AS SERVICE/SERVICE AS SOCIETY

A Bordieuan Presence through Voices of Alice Springs

SOCIETY AS SERVICE/SERVICE AS SOCIETY

A Bordieuan Presence through Voices of Alice Springs

By Richard Michael Head

COMMON GROUND

First published in 2020
as part of the New Directions in the Humanities Book Imprint
http://doi.org/10.18848/978-1-86335-223-9/CGP

Common Ground Publishing
2001 South First Street. Suite 202
University of Illinois Research Park
Champaign, IL
61821

Library of Congress Cataloging-in-Publication Data

Names: Head, Richard Michael, author.
Title: Society as service/service as society : a Bordieuan presence through
   voices of Alice Springs / Richard Michael Head.
Other titles: Service as society
Description: Champaign : Common Ground Research Networks, 2020. | Includes
   bibliographical references. | Summary: "Alice Springs has been a
   traditional service provider for central Australia and continues to be.
   Its remote character has created a place of 'pure' serviceability.
   'Pure' in the sense that it has no traditional primary production to
   fall back on (mining, farmland, manufacturing, sea port) to provide a
   sense of why it exists, as other settlements seem to possess explaining
   their initial and ongoing presence. Its existence is a question of
   service, which drives the local economy. These geographical factors
   provide a place rich in 'serviceable' research material, a valuable tool
   to gauge society. Bourdieuan theories assist with service and society
   understanding"-- Provided by publisher.
Identifiers: LCCN 2020033902 (print) | LCCN 2020033903 (ebook) | ISBN
   9780949313003 (hardback) | ISBN 9781863352222 (paperback) | ISBN
   9781863352239 (adobe pdf)
Subjects: LCSH: Human services--Australia--Alice Springs (N.T.) | Alice
   Springs (N.T.)--Social conditions. | Bourdieu, Pierre, 1930-2002.
Classification: LCC HV474.A5 H43 2020 (print) | LCC HV474.A5 (ebook) |
   DDC 306.3099429/1--dc23
LC record available at https://lccn.loc.gov/2020033902
LC ebook record available at https://lccn.loc.gov/2020033903

Cover Image: The front cover image is a hand drawing of the central business area of Alice Springs
            looking down from above
Cover Image Credit: Kayla Head

Acknowledgements

To all those who dwell in Alice Springs which kindly gave their time by helping to contribute to the 'servicing' of the book.

Book dedicated to Kayla and Jessica Head

Table of Contents

Introduction

Servicing the Book

The Singular/Multiplicity of the Sovereignty of Society

As Service defines Society and Society defines Service, the narrative begins with an engagement of the abstract/concrete thing termed society...

Human settlements express an array of characteristics reflective of their cultural and historical legacies. The plural of legacy is emphasised since a mono profile of human representation does not adequately inform of what human performance is about. In a world of multiplicity, culture, society, history, time, space, and place, a singular interpretation is 'out of place'. However, a singular interpretation is simultaneously 'in of place', since both the multiple and singular of life perspective drives human performance. The singular can be thought of as one individual's needs, wants and desires, within an ongoing will to create life as one's place. This is an idealised place that others accede to, and/or resist, depending on their strength of will and material position in life. Everyone has potential to be singular, but whether this potential is realised, wholly, partially or not at all, is when the clash of singulars come into play. The multiple is when like-minded singulars join, in a loose to tight commonality, to achieve and sustain control over as much place as possible. Place within this context is geographically both physical and human. Physical, in which the control and ownership of land and its resources are perceived, depending on cultural filters, of what is useful and acceptable. Also, other humans living within that physicality experience degrees of control and manipulation. This is where the human geography of place connects with the physical, since humans are coerced into going along with the designed physical schematic. A paradox is that many individuals do not even realise coercion is taking place, and taken the place of their 'one place'.

Coercion or force is at its most effective in pushing or pulling the will of others in intended directions, if these others do not realise this stimulus is taking place. Also, this force of non-force is enhanced in its effectiveness by those doing the forcing not knowing they are doing so. This is because the regularity of the performance, perhaps through generations, is seen as natural, so is not questioned or it is not seen at all as it is so interwoven in the framework of the cultural network. One must stop playing the game of cultural life for a time, creating a sense of cultural vacation, to begin noticing the unnoticeable. This is the unnoticeable of unseen, but felt, forces driving society along particular ways of being that hold it together in an intentional shapeless shape. The shape is the inner core of society along the latter's time and space journey. These forces are the driver of power relations in a perpetual motion of intention to control geographical physicals and humans within their sphere(s) of influence in the protective core. Two assumptions are raised; firstly, that there is more than one singular/mutual multiple presence in the inner core, for example, various religions, big business interests, political organisations, military, and individuals, working for their own interests, and secondly, since the core is protected, an implication is of perceived threats (imaginative or concrete) from singular and multiple presence in the outer core.

The shapeless is the space of society that is perceived by all in its visible form, implying that the shape is invisible, or more precisely the actions and intentions (the agenda) of those within the shape are invisible, and only public faces are seen. The shapeless can be regarded as the ongoing transformations in the way humans live, work, and play. The shapeless cannot be still for even a moment to create a substantive shape, as new ideas, or the converting of 'older' ideas, enters the fray of society, producing a consequent reaction in the consumers of these ideas. Consumers can be from the inner core and without. The inner 'manages' these ideas and sells them on (both economically and ideologically), and without to adapt to them, willingly or not. The inner would also adapt to new ideas, as no one singular or multiple is isolated completely from society, since being part of society. A rippling cause and effect results, creating fresher cause and effects and so on. The point is that the shape, although experiencing its own series of movements, retains a timeless quality and quantity of power considerations, so appears rigid in its 'core' agenda of being, whereas the shapeless is the product of the shape. This is where continuous fluidity takes place, sometimes imperceptible other times marked, but always moving. It is this ongoing movement that produces and reproduces opportunities to create economic and cultural capital, and maintain the insubstantial status quo of core inner and core outer. Insubstantial, for too vigorous a movement and change of the outer, can upset the assumed stability of the inner. Adding to threats from without are threats from within, as the loose conglomeration of inner core members would be in constant interplay of one up(hu)manship with each other, since each is vying for a larger slice of the power pie.

So, the shapeless shape of society can occasionally become shapeless as the outer core rebels against the inner. Or an imbalance of the inner members occurs, in which a singular, or an inner inner group of multiples, retains too much power. The potential of the inner inner (implying an elite group inside the inner) produces further stratification of power distribution, and perhaps is an advanced concentration of power in fewer hands or interests. It is conceivable that fewer hands or interests can further 'simplify' the ways humans think, act, and behave, to the greater advantage of the former. Further 'simplify' implies that the discourse and hence narrative of the inner core was, and is, the ideology that all humans follow by varying resistances. The inner core follows a path that encourages distancing from compound ways of living, and opportunities to think for oneself against its restrictive chains of construction. Hence, narrow forms of perception are encouraged, simplified forms that hide the complexity of the dominant narrative designed for the masses to conform to its reality. Paradoxically, perhaps the dominant narrative is actually simple and straight forward when getting and retaining power, since the most efficient way of doing this is the selling of simplicity to the mass market of human consumption. Part of which is to ensure that the mass market has been trained as consumers.

The inner and outer core 'imaginary' or 'real' is vague and indistinct, and deliberately so. Perceived boundaries between them may only exist in the form of the manipulator and manipulated, driven from the spaces of organisations, who experience structural and post-structural ways of being and doing. There will be movement of workers flowing from the outer core into the functional workings of the organisation's inner core to maintain and ensure its existence. A hierarchal structure differentiated by degrees of salary, decision making, specialist skills and experience, and attitude to the organisation. The majority, at the end of the working day (or night), returns to the outer core. The minority founders, owners, shareholders, and key stakeholders retain weightier intimacy with their respective core organisations and cannot, without difficulty, remove themselves from it. Indeed, even if they wished to, they need to consider that this state of being defines them, ensuring so-called special status in the political and economic rough and tumble of societal survivability. Therefore, leverage to maintain and manipulate advantage over the competition, assumed or actual, would always be welcome, and it would be difficult for a 'privileged' singular to walk away from that. Considering this difficulty faced by the privileged singular minority, and the obligations of the majority returning into the fray of the organisational environment daily, it can be realised that the societal system claims ownership over all.

One may think that she or he 'owns' an organisation or is charged with running it from the urging of remote 'owners', if achieving executive positions, but perhaps it is the other way around. The owner or their senior agents are owned by what defines them. If this 'what' suddenly evaporated, they would become directionless, rudderless, grasping for threads that society still may offer them. They seek for meaning and order out of the disorder being experienced. This would be especially galling for those used to maintaining and creating what the order is, to not have that power and influence any longer. Alternatively, the majority already 'owned' by how the structure of society operates, may experience less of a wrench if their particular 'what' is withdrawn. Although this may not necessarily be the case, as all may suffer identity crisis as ownership is taken away, at whatever level of society one regards themselves to be. It may be a social irony that those with the least to lose in terms of so-called societal capital, tentatively the homeless, long term unemployed, discriminated groups and cultures, will be the ones least affected by societal cruelties and exclusions, as they are already on the margins of society, only consuming as much as possible, or willing to, of the scraps society offers them. There is an inverse ratio of influence and consequence at play here, in that those who have invested heavily in the illusive entity called society, since it significantly reflects their ideology or ideology that has subsequently been taken on by successive dominant interests (a sense of tautology), as it is seen to work to maintain this dominance, risk the greater loss of cultural, societal, economic and self-integrity and identity, if society pushes them over. Those who have lesser or the least (or no) investment in societal trappings, would be conversely affected.

Society is the people in the sovereign space that political and economic historical processes have left them with up to the present. The people are reasonably equal in their initial embodied state, i.e. two arms, two legs and functioning senses and brainpower, but all are not born equal in terms of social capital. Paradoxically the 'sovereign' of space provides three adjectives and a noun when ascertaining its thesaurus implications. The three adjectives: one, independent (autonomous, self-governing, free, self-determining); two, supreme (dominant, ascendant, predominant, absolute, superior); three, outstanding (supreme, excellent, matchless, peerless). The noun: ruler (monarch, king, queen, potentate, emperor, empress, sultan, raja, rajah). Of all four the first adjective, independent, hints at equality and freedom of expression, movement and ideas, but can be regarded as the cruellest of the four thesaurus offerings. At least the other three are straightforward and direct with how it was, and is, in acknowledging a dominant to dominated societal system. Very little or no ambiguity is present within these monolinguistic imageries. Being independent hides the networks and flows of power moving along, back and forth, under the surface veneer of societal acceptance. For instance, what better way to manipulate and 'steer' the life pathways of the majority, than make them think they enjoy autonomy, self-government, free whatever, and self-determination. Perhaps, more accurately, it is a question of extent of having 'freedom' to enjoy these four admirable enjoyments, since the majority would have manoeuvrability to exercise autonomy, self-government, freedom of movement and expression and self-determination, but only within the rules and limits society grants.

It is safer to grant some movement for singulars and multiples, of whatever position in the social system. Doing so allows for spaces of emotion, embodiment, and sense of self-worth to flow, and identity to be maintained, be it subtly corrupted, than to have no movement. Lack of movement would create resentment and resistance that would threaten societal norms, values, and beliefs advocated by the second and third sovereign adjectives and accompanying noun. The advocacy of these latter three returns the narrative to 'society is the people in the sovereign space', but enhanced and adapted to 'society is the people in the reign space'. At least that is more honest in how the geography of human relationships develop and evolve through ongoing encounters, and how the geography of physical usage of land and sea reflect these wary encounters, for those that are enlightened. Or explaining the normalised encounters for the unaware who do not perceive the symbolic violence embedded in the practice and ongoing processes of power and resource imbalance.

So, the vagueness of the boundary between the inner and outer core societal metaphor that has been adopted to illustrate the haves, not so much haves, and have nots, is a deliberate investiture to disguise who runs society. However, the disguise is not a complete concealment to those affected by practices, decisions, and actions or inactions, since this is not a viable option. There is a requirement to advertise one's singular and/or multiple so the majority or general public (consumer market) are familiar with the brand name. Familiarity breeds degrees of acceptance and legitimacy, as doing so encourages a sense of trustworthiness. Whether the trustworthy process is a two-way movement of goodwill and quality of product is open to interpretation, ranging from a broad engagement with customers down to individual transactions and agreements, with both depending on the exchange context. For instance, there would be depths of concealment at the exchange moment, with only the surface agenda showing the least offence as possible. The hidden agenda remains hidden to protect those within the inner workings of the societal machine, to allow as free a reign as possible to practise the said hidden agenda. Thus, a two-faced system may be an apt descriptor to signify the workings of the inner core.

As free a reign as possible for the stakeholders of the inner core is a telling state of affairs, as each can be thought of as enjoying a slice or space of the overall sovereign territory of society, within each's 'mini' created sovereignties. An own places of self-expression working within the limits of the overall societal expression, and occasionally trying to extend it to their ways of seeing. Perhaps one or two singulars in the inner and outer societal cores aspire for their sovereignty to become or replace the societal sovereignty, so one becomes the other and perhaps beyond. Beyond depends upon the expansionist will of the singular who has come to represent society, similar to the medieval monarchs (the queen is England, the king is France, the singular is society), and the potential of that society to be strong enough to challenge another society and its sovereign territory. So, increasing one's space to produce extra societal empire building.

Mini sovereignty within societal sovereignty is not only for those in the inner core, as it is possible for all. It is just a question of scale. To illustrate, every singular aspires to produce their own sovereign space, a place of private reflection, action, and reaction. This place will partially be within the abstract power of the imagination and partially in the embodied concrete space, with the scale depending on one's own material resources. Therefore, societal sovereignty can be thought of as an assortment of diverse mini sovereignties, each competing for existence and identity at each's respected spatial scales of self-production. As an integral part of this process, the veneer of the public face of society masks, camouflages or masquerades the innumerable hidden drivers of society, which is just as well, as society could not function (at least in its familiar forms) without the covert spaces to power the overt spaces.

Large and Important Town

Within human settlements, the word society can produce the word city from parts of its letter combinations. When looking at the definition origins of 'city' from its noun, context is drawn from the Online Etymology Dictionary (2019):

> c. 1200, from Old French cite "town, city" (10c., Modern French cité), from earlier citet, from Latin civitatem (nominative civitas; in Late Latin sometimes citatem) originally "citizenship, condition or rights of a citizen, membership in the community," later "community of citizens, state, commonwealth", from civis "townsman,"

> Now "a large and important town," but originally in early Middle English a walled town, a capital or cathedral town. Distinction from town is early 14c. Between Latin and English the sense was transferred from the inhabitants to the place. The Latin word for "city" was urbs, but a resident was civis. Civitas seems to have replaced urbs as Rome (the ultimate urbs) lost its prestige (https://www. etymonline.com/word/city).

It is significant that the meaning of city involved a fluid movement from representing the people living there, to representing the lived place, but the 'developed' meaning does not really discount the former. For instance, the generations of people living in the 'city' would have formed the place in their images. These images would have been created from layered historical and cultural mini sovereignties to form and reform the physical geography, and hence human geography, of this place labelled city. Alternatively, the city in and of itself, without human intervention, would not be. It would be a dead place gradually reclaimed by nature removed from human interference. In fact, the city or settlement or 'large and important town' would not exist in the first place without human input, so the modern definition of city requires the extra of (citi)zen to provide a wholesome quality of meaning and functionality.

The city and large and important town can also be seen as mini sovereign spaces within the sovereign place that is society. It is these settlements that are the symbolic and actual place representations of societal intention. These places are society in its own evolving image, windows or mirrors, depending on usage, that are gazed upon and interacted through to help explain how society is. Although, focused place explanations may never fully achieve absolute interpretation, for no system of understanding can do that for whatever thing or practice is being investigated, but at least a meaningful level of appreciation and understanding can be achieved. Meaningful in terms of unwrapping some of the covertness of society, to produce a more wholesome appreciation of the overt societal surface that is familiar and easily recognised as 'that is just the way things are'. It is the comfortableness produced by the familiar, and practices, performance and perspective attributed to easy recognition, that encourage a realisation of 'false consciousness'; adopting a Marxist imagery of what appears real is an end product manufactured as real by those who wish to do this for self-advantage. Self-advantage does not necessarily imply the selfish self, although for some or many, this may be the case, but the self could also include the 'good' of society, so society maintains position in the world order of all societies. Of course, aiding society could also be regarded as aiding the aider, to maintain position of both. Namely, the position in that society, and the status of society measured against other societies. These positional movement are in the name of influence and power.

Within an Australian context, the 'large and important town' would arguably equate to the capital cities in the states and territories (Sydney, Melbourne, Brisbane, Perth, Darwin, Adelaide and the politically induced Canberra), realising the city definition of substantial and high-ranking. This realisation would be sourced and sub-consciously embedded from the socio-cultural values absorbed from birth, and through life, of what makes a thing or place distinct and authoritative. Such as, how place places importance on its size, economic clout and generation, centre of the 'action', charisma, influence, magnetic quality to draw in new people, and known beyond the societal spatial boundaries by those in other societies as a place to visit or live. Additionally, a place to do business in, a place for employment opportunities, and a self-sustaining economic entity. To continue, a place to attract the young, injecting further energy into the place, a self-perpetuating energy entity, and a busy, vibrant, inclusive, exclusive, repetitive, mundane system of performance and practice. Related to place is the business of being a city, and the business of being a citizen in a symbiotic relationship with the city. Since Australia is multicultural and experiences significant levels of immigration, it follows that multiple cultures living in the capital cities would bring influences from their previous societal ways of being. However, this does not necessarily imply that societal differences (from the 'old' to the 'new') would be too marked in relation to economic aspirations, as capitalist power runs across many cultural 'boundaries', so commonality of recognition would be present across cultural difference.

Service Considerations, Service Defines Society, Society Defines Service

A commonality of recognition in terms of making a living through the communal medium of monetary currency. It is currency that greases the wheels of systems within society. Systems can be thought of as business, government, religious, educational, welfare, unemployed, employed and touristic amongst others. What is common to all is the unavoidable use of money as a tool to allow these service systems to run. The term 'service' is intentionally used as it is the key term for the book's narrative, of which all theoretical and concrete imaginations and realisations engage with. A place of settlement (be that a city, town, or village) can be regarded as servicing human needs amongst a multi-layered usage and appreciation of what that term service may imply. A settlement is a service centre, servicing the requirements of those living there and those that fall under its spatial influence beyond the physical extremities of the urban sprawl, i.e. beyond the physical location of the settlement (city or town), but not beyond its economic and social reach, and experience some reliance upon it. When thinking about the term 'service' as the raison d'être for the book, the initial rationale assumed a simplistic definition of it as offering facility nodes within a network of places in the space of a settlement. Nodes in places may be office or shop locations or health provision (dentists, doctors' surgeries, eye specialists, foot specialists), non-government organisations and government organisations.

However, initially recognising and defining the term 'service' offerings as just nodes in places, was found to be only the surface façade of what service provision may really imply within societal maintenance and sustainability. The practices and performances of the agents (people who work for a service and those receiving that service) in these nodes and what the nodes look like in physical appearance, and the whys of why they are an integral part of society in its consumerist symbolic form, and the acceptance of the presence of these nodes by the general population as that is the way things are, and not questioning why that is the way things are, produces considerations of the 'service' question within layers of interpretation. The surface façade is only a beginning of the profound implications of service provision that services society, the city, citizen and civilian. *Services define society. Society defines services.* These two succinct phrases, if standing alone without any extra justification or explanation, deserve research attention. The curious and the imaginative, and those curious to be curious and imaginative would want to learn of a perspective that engages with how society is, and does, from its surface and hidden spaces that drive the process, and the connection of what has 'service' to do with it.

The potential of *Services define society. Society defines services,* can be appreciated when looking at what the term 'service' implies or represents in society.

Middle English, from Old French, from Latin servitium, *slavery,* from servus, *slave.*]

Usage Note: The verb *service* is used principally in the sense "to repair or maintain": *service the washing machine.* Exceptions to this usage include specialised senses in finance *(service a debt)* and animal breeding *(service a mare)*. *Serve* means "to supply goods or services to," as in *One radio network serves three states*. (American Heritage Dictionary of the English Language, 2016).

The following list of service association is drawn from The Free Dictionary (2019):

1. Work that is done for others as an occupation or business.
2. The performance of work or duties for a superior or as a servant.
3. An act or a variety of work done for others, especially for pay: offers a superior service to that of his competitors.
4. Assistance; help: was of great service to him during his illness.
5. An act of assistance or benefit; a favour.
6. Employment in duties or work for another, as for a government.
7. A government branch or department and its employees: the diplomatic service.
8. A department or branch of a hospital staff that provides specified patient care: the anaesthesiology service.
9 The armed forces of a nation.
10. A branch of the armed forces of a nation.
11. The installation, maintenance, or repairs provided or guaranteed by a dealer or manufacturer: a dealer with full parts and service.
12. The provision to the public of something, especially a utility: a town without sewer service.
13. The system or equipment used to provide something to the public.
14. A religious rite or formal ceremony.
15. To make fit for use; adjust, repair, or maintain: service a car.
16 To provide services to: That cable company services most households in the area.
17. To make interest payments on (a debt).
18. an organized system of labour and material aids used to supply the needs of the public: telephone service; bus service.
19. (Commerce) the supply, installation, or maintenance of goods carried out by a dealer.
20. the state of availability for use by the public (esp. in the phrases *into or out of service*).
21. a periodic overhaul made on a car, machine, etc.
22. the act or manner of serving guests, customers, etc, in a shop, hotel, restaurant, etc.
23. (Government, Politics & Diplomacy) a department of public employment and its employees: civil service. The work of a public servant.
24. (Industrial Relations & HR Terms) employment in or performance of work for another.
25. (Military) one of the branches of the armed forces.

26. the state, position, or duties of a domestic servant (esp. in the phrase *in service*).

27. the act or manner of serving food.

28. Services, the performance of any duties or work for another: medical services.

29. something made or done by a commercial organisation for the public benefit and without regard to direct profit.

30. Also called divine service. public religious worship according to prescribed form and order.

31. a ritual or form prescribed for public worship or for some particular occasion: the marriage service.

32. the serving of God by obedience, piety, etc.

More than 32 usages or interpretations of service were found, showing the saturated presence of its variety in society. The ones highlighted seem appropriate to include, as most, if not all of the 32 will be touched upon throughout the course of the narrative.

Society is made up of several constituent parts that interrelate and interweave with others in varying degrees of contact. A relationship of reciprocal necessity, as one constituent part services another, or others, to allow for all to maintain their service capacities. Thus, helping others to help oneself as a vibrant and viable service provider. It is this mutual arrangement of services servicing each other that is the lifeblood of society, for it and they would cease to be, if one or the other ceased to be. Or somewhere in between if certain services folded, causing ruptures in the societal framework, and knock on effects of other services beginning to buckle under the strain of weakened service support systems.

Societal health would be compromised if underpinned services were unwell. From the list of 32, familiar 'underpinned' service stakeholders in society are included: occupation, business, employer/employee, government, health, voluntary care, military, education, manufacturer, power utilities, religion, economics, and God. All these are valuable or invaluable to societal integrity. However, a significant one not included in the 32, but is in the American Heritage Dictionary definition, is animal breeding. The service of reproduction is vital to ensure the ongoing viability of society and to provide population to run the services. From this it can be speculated that immigration or cyber technology may offset somewhat a shortfall in 'replacement' members of society, to 'work' society. Perhaps this is part of the process that is society, in terms of adaptation to other forms of societal membership. Throughout human history, and the mass and minor movements of singulars and multiples, societies have absorbed and coped with these changes. The bottom line is society does what it can to survive and thrive along its shapeless shape continuum.

Alice Springs is in the Business of Servicing

To investigate how services define society/society define services through the inherent medium of settlement city and citizen, within a concrete context to 'service' the theoretical framework behind the process, the 'city' of Alice Springs is utilised as an exemplifier. The 'large and important town' of Alice Springs from initial estimates and appreciations of what 'large' and 'important' may imply, would not appear to qualify for such lofty accolades. However, this estimate depends upon the contextual considerations of what 'large' and 'important' may infer. Tim Baldwin the Minister for Lands, Planning and Environment, as a forward to the Alice Springs Land Use Structure Plan (1999), expressed the following observation of the Alice:

> As the N.T.'s major regional centre, Alice Springs is an important if not vital contributor to our growth and development. However, this does not adequately describe the importance of the town to the nation emotionally, as a tourist destination of world renown, as a service centre for a vast inland region, as a base nor for defence facilities nor to 25,000 people proud to call it home. (December 1999, p. 1)

Putting the politically embellished rhetoric aside, a key phrase is 'as a service centre for a vast inland region'. To emphasise the service centre's, almost exclusive, role Alice plays in terms of the comparative relationship between Alice Springs and 'neighbouring' settlements, it is worth looking along the Stuart Highway corridor between Port Augusta in South Australia (SA) to Darwin at the 'top end' of the Northern Territory (N.T.). Doing so shows the significant distances involved between the settlement of Alice Springs and its noteworthy other 'local' place settlements (population numbers are also included to offer an idea of settlement size). The demographic numbers are accessed from the 2016 Australian national five yearly census data (quick stats, Australian Bureau Statistics (ABS), 2016). All statistics were drawn from the Local Government Area (LGA) for equity of comparison, except for Yulara and Tennant Creek, in which LGA was not offered as an option. This does not discredit these latter statistics, since the offered population figures provide a fair reflection of dwelling numbers.

Port Augusta (SA): 13808 (1237 kms from Alice)
http://quickstats.censusdata.abs.gov.au/census_services/getproduct/census/2016/quickstat/LGA46090

Coober Pedy (SA): 1762 (668 kms from Alice)
http://quickstats.censusdata.abs.gov.au/census_services/getproduct/census/2016/quickstat/LGA41330

Yulara (Uluṟu) (SA): 1099 (440 kms from Alice)
http://quickstats.censusdata.abs.gov.au/census_services/getproduct/census/2016
/quickstat/SSC70302

Alice Springs (NT): 24,753
http://quickstats.censusdata.abs.gov.au/census_services/getproduct/census/2016
/quickstat/LGA70200

Tennant Creek (N.T.): 2991 (507 kms from Alice)
http://quickstats.censusdata.abs.gov.au/census_services/getproduct/census/2016
/quickstat/UCL715007

Katherine (N.T.): 9717 (1200 kms from Alice)
http://quickstats.censusdata.abs.gov.au/census_services/getproduct/census/2016
/quickstat/LGA72200

Palmerston (N.T.): 33786 (1472 kms from Alice)
http://quickstats.censusdata.abs.gov.au/census_services/getproduct/census/2016
/quickstat/LGA72800

Darwin (N.T.): 78804 (1497 kms from Alice)
http://quickstats.censusdata.abs.gov.au/census_services/getproduct/census/2016
/quickstat/LGA71000

Thus, due to the vast distances the Stuart corridor settlements are from the Alice, it can be established that Alice Springs is a 'large and important town' in terms of providing a service to those that live there and those that live in its surrounding environment (cattle and pastoral stations and Indigenous communities). Since other minor and major places along the north-south Stuart Highway corridor are of considerable distances from the Alice, lines of communication and connectivity are stretched. However, this does not imply that these other settlements are detached from the Alice in terms of common business interests, such as tourism. But the point is Alice Springs has been a traditional service provider for central Australia and continues to be so. Its remote human and physical geographical location and historical and contemporary economic character has created a place of 'pure' serviceability. 'Pure' in the sense that it has no traditional primary production to fall back on (mining, farmland, manufacturing, or sea port) to provide a sense of why it exists, as other large and important towns seem to generally possess to explain why they are there in the first place. Its existence can be put down to a question of service, which drives the local economy. These geographical factors provide a place rich in 'serviceable' research material, a valuable tool to gauge society.

Chapter Outlines

Chapter One: Provision and Package of the Alice, offers background to situate the place of Alice Springs as part of contemporary societal life. This contextual feel for what it is, provides 'fluid' and 'fix informative points' to the subsequent chapters, allowing for situatedness of these other chapters. To provide ammunition for dismantling or dislodging the surface veneer of society through the access portals of service nodes, a selection of theories from Pierre Bourdieu will be applied, adapted and extended upon. For a narrative of this size, 'a selection' is appropriate since utilising Bourdieu's entire immense armoury would be beyond the scope of the book's aim and may be counterproductive. Too much analysis can spoil the desired flavour of the broth's taste worthiness. Bourdieu's theoretical engagement is ***Chapter Two: Brainstorming Bourdieu***.

To bring the servicing of Alice to life, a solution was to communicate with an assortment of service providers who work and live in the town. So, an array of service agents was selected and accessed from a cross section of diverse occupations, providing in-depth representations that meaningfully epitomise how the Alice functions. The kindly volunteered information, time given, and insight, cover a range of perspectives of how the Alice is serviced, creating a comprehensive narrative that embraces what it is about, heading into the 2020s. Considerations of what is the 'correct' or 'reasonable' number of service agents to talk to is raised, with impractical logic dictating that all agents in town can conceivable be contacted, and asked for their input. Practicalities of time that can be spent in the 'Alice field', publisher limited narrative length, reader and author sanity in not including too much (in terms of writing and reading) and dulling the senses of all, hence blunting of what actually is engaged with, and the already acknowledged effectiveness of which agents have been engaged with and what they comprehensively provide, defends the decision to not having talked to more service sources. More would not necessarily be advantageous. Even though all who live in the Alice and its environs (roughly 25000 to 40000 individuals respectively), those that are ex 'Alice pats', and those that are passing through or have passed through (tourists, work related, visiting friends and relations, or have just 'lost their way') can be regarded as potential service agents, it is not feasible to talk to these 'all'.

Considering potential service agents, offers an opportunity to think about what a service agent is. Recalling the 32 indicators of what this thing called service implies, an agent can both offer a service and be a consumer of it, sometimes at the same time. She or he may be employed to act as a conduit to offer and pass on service paraphernalia to consumers, but at the same time this occupation or vocation (depending upon being paid or voluntary, or if the occupation and vocation have merged somewhat), offers a service to the agent as well. It may be a service sense of wellbeing, economic remuneration, a sense of identity, a sense of self-worth, whatever, but something is also gained by being a server...a sense of service. The consumer of the service or serviced is there to obtain something or seek support, but the action of being there creates service capacity for the service agent and represented organisation. Without input and representation by the serviced, the service itself would not survive. It simply would not be. Therefore, the serviced provides a service to the service. Finally, at different times the server becomes the serviced, just as the serviced becomes the server, as the former accesses other service providers as a pathway to current and future achieved means and ends, and the latter, if occasionally in a formal service role, plays that role for a time. Additionally, as a very necessary part of societal functionality, an 'informal' individual, who may form themselves into part of a loose, temporary network as circumstances dictate, also becomes a server. To clarify the 'formal' and 'informal' roles, a formal agent is regarded as working within a recognised organisation retaining economic capacity of some sort (public or private funding or a mixture of both). An informal agent may assist a family member, the family, relative(s), friends, and strangers without recourse to monetary payment.

It can be realised that all in society are servers and serviced. Every individual performs this role, with the proportion of time spent as one or the other difficult to measure, and perhaps just blur into one another. Whatever place an individual lives in as a 'dwelling place' (Heidegger, 1962) long-term (many years) or touched upon whilst passing through (short-term, i.e. perhaps a year or two), levels of server and serviced leaves a footprint of how that place is, however large, medium or small. Also, others of the dwelling's past (whose footprint may be fading, but still a vital contributor of that place's place) or temporary visitors whose footprint is light, but if enough visitors visit, as it would be millions over the years going through the Alice, would ensure that the combined footprint is heavy. Essentially the aggregate footprints of all, present and past and temporary, is what makes the settlement. Thus, the aggregate footprints of all the settlements in a sovereign place is what makes the space of society.

Therefore, the service providers communicated with, create 'theme' chapters (**Three to Nine**) involving a 'loose' connection of perspectives from service agents based upon commonality of service provision. These perspectives incorporate what the selected service providers do. Loose in the sense of constructed categorisation that makes it easier for the reader to read the narrative, and easier for the author to create a sense of order. Although, since the service providers, provide a service, it can be concluded that all enjoy connectivity with each other, so the remainder of the book could just be one immense chapter, but that would make the narrative difficult to digest. That is the way of Western scientific engagement. Looking at the 'whole' of something or a concept in its entirety in one go, is not the way of things. Selecting what are essential components in the system of the whole, to represent the whole, influenced from one's sociocultural heritage, is the way of Western things. This methodology results in the whole dissected into manageable chunks and reassembled to create a sense of wholeness of investigation. The author concedes to this 'partiality to produce wholeness' methodology as well, as having the capacity to see the whole in one go is left to the level of Deity. The irony here is that the place of Alice Springs, as with all settlement places, already possesses a sense of wholeness of being. Not in an absolute sense of no further progression is possible, but in a wholeness of an ongoing fluidity of change, in which the wholeness of the past and present creates possible movements into the future. Bordieuan theoretical engagement of practices and performance embellish the findings, and the author embellishes Bourdieu.

The service perspectives gathered for the theme chapters were produced from primary research carried out over a number of months during 2018. A list of prominent local Alice individuals and relevant persons in organisations were selected for requests to meet. The selection reflected a broad range of service offerings from differing spatial scales of consumer base, to create an 'ongoing snapshot' of the Alice from a broad perspective. 'Ongoing snapshot' suggest 'fixed/fluid' moments in time reflecting the meeting periods, since the service perspectives voiced are a product of accumulated practices, experiences and memories of the past to the present. But also taking into account 'ongoing' considerations, predictions and aspirations for the future. There was a conscious intention to not place assumptions, and hence restrictions, on the service agents being directly investigated. As there has to be a sense of freedom, fluidity and flexibility in what is being searched for, otherwise the findings and how they are found will not be allowed to '*naturally breathe*', i.e. striving for authenticity within its many guises and gazers.

Hence, when the meetings took place, only one question was asked to encourage freedom, fluidity and flexibility in responses. (Although, for some of the interactions with service agents in the Education service chapter, a series of supplementary questions were added to the main question. The rationale behind this was due to the comparatively similar service performance aspects of the three high schools, since these 'mini questions' demonstrated service results. This was not for competitive purposes, but for each of the schools to complement each other in promoting the holistic educational service provision of Alice Springs). The question was asked within the context of the profession and organisation the interviewees represented: essentially 'what do you do?' This allowed for the agents to be as expressive as they wished to be or felt comfortable doing so. The resultant responses for the vast majority, if not all, in their own characteristic way, showed passion, energy for what they were doing and sense of pride in the doing. All were generous with their time and not one talked for less than half an hour, in many cases one hour seemed the norm. This was very impressive from the catalytic point of one question. These performances, putting aside for the moment the content expressed, and just focusing on the ways the content were expressed, speaks volumes of how 'to serve'. The agents led the encounter after my general introduction, and I adapted my occasional responses depending upon the directions the conversation headed towards. Really, I became an involved passenger with the agents evolving into the driver of the engagement. In general, '*natural breathing*' saturated the encounters, producing fertile ground to authenticate service. I discovered that to serve is very much an alive (p)assion, (p)rocess, (p)erformance and (p)ractise. This should not be surprising, for how would society acquire its energy if its 'P' drivers were dull, lack lustre and showed low motivation.

Bourdieu speaks of and encourages reflexivity awareness when researching. Social science is, as Bourdieu states, "a social construction of a social construction" (Bourdieu, 2000, p. 172). Its reflexivity means gaining the possibility to check those factors that bias research (Bourdieu, 2001, p. 174). The first potential form of bias derives from the positioning of the researcher in the social space, the second from the doxa or orthodoxies of the field and the researcher's positioning within it, and thirdly from the fact that researchers actually have the time to do such research, outside of the necessity of other actions in the world (Grenfell, 2008, p. 226). My expectations of the book's service narrative derive from having lived in the Alice for two decades, so occupying a 'seasoned' position in the field, one that is subjectively objective, generated from my past, present and 'future' aspirations of doing a good a job as possible in completing the book. 'Future' is in quotes, for at the time of writing this paragraph, and actually until the last word and letter is written in the Conclusion, the book always remains incomplete. Let alone ignoring the processes that occur after 'finishing'; proof reading, re-draft(s), peer checks, publishing steps. Throughout the book's progression, the doxa and orthodoxies of my human geography/sociology fields influences greatly how the service narratives were interpreted and re-interpreted as a reflected book narrative. However, (limited) 'time is of the essence' is poignant for many researchers, including myself, and consequently one can only do so much!

The first of the theme chapters, ***Chapter Three: Religion***, is as the name suggests a 'Religious service', but not quite in the way of the act of public service following prescribed rules, i.e. a traditional going to church ritual. Although in a sense it is, as service providers in this area directly connect to particular religious belief systems, and do offer the public a service, following prescribed rules, to allow access to it. A feeling of ownership of the service process, on both sides of the relationship, is a necessary component for it to achieve positive affects and effects, and not just with a religious association, as all the theme services and the service relationship in general requires favourable mutual ownership. Religion traditionally has an intimate relationship with the 'upper' hierarchies of society, being a significant part of that exclusive echelon, and providing a 'legitimate' societal service role of the spiritual and mental wellbeing of the societal flock. Also, as a 'legitimate' powerful lever to influence the majority, encouraging the elitist minority to retain the 'right' to manipulate society. Although, perhaps not so much the second legitimacy these days, but still servicing the spiritual needs of those asking.

Providing a foundation to negotiate a pathway through life in society can be very necessary for the young (as in the age of primary and high school).

Servicing the youth of society with an educational background adapted to the needs and demands of society, equipping them with skills and knowledge to engage with this complex and competitive social entity, would seem an advisable matter of course. Being formally educated is one of the main normalising practices and is 'expected', which in itself is a telling indictment of how society operates. Not all youth completes the yearly ritual from pre-school to year 12 for various reasons, and the ATAR (Australian Tertiary Admission Rank) scores when finishing year 12 produce a range of percentage results. Both of these effects of the causes of societal education create a hierarchal system of possible choices of what to do next, which is probably what the 'grand' scheme of society wants, since it requires its agents to fill hierarchal practices and performances. Everyone doing the same thing, except in the context of everyone servicing society, is not advisable for society to function effectively. Thus, *Chapter Four: Education*, looks at these raised issues.

As a main regulator and 'guiding hand' of society is the government organisation, and its organising of the vast majority of services offered, through regulation and funding, it would be amiss to not include it as a theme, as it is a main player or 'big agent' in how society is and continues to be...hence *Chapter Five: Government/NGOs* (non-government organisations). All of the service agents in the theme chapters are connected to government in some form or another, who legally suggest what is permissible and what is not, with the 'suggestion' generally backed up by monetary leverage. For instance, many service agents working in the same or similar fields would be in competition to receive government funding. A main concern with government is economics and how to encourage investment, profit and employability, i.e. the 'business' of being a government and the agent tasked with ensuring that society sustains, and the other service agents sustain as well. If to be so bold, government is the 'hand' of society as its agent of serviceable construction and destruction.

Welfare provision can operate under several agents, with some not recognised from initial assumptions as being part of the welfare umbrella. For example, welfare may equate to unemployment benefits for many people...

> Welfare is a type of government support for the citizens of that society. Welfare may be provided to people of any income level, as with social security, but it is usually intended to ensure that the poor can meet their basic human needs such as food and shelter. Welfare attempts to provide poor people with a minimal level of well-being, usually either a free or a subsidised supply of certain goods and social services, such as healthcare, education, and vocational training. (Bullock and Trombley, 1999, p. 919)

But there are also service agents that act in supporting roles for the welfare agent, and are valuable in their own right, ways, and means, to assist the wellbeing of people. All, both service and welfare agents, are tasked with being a set of welfare services that keep people within the societal system, if it looks like the latter are 'falling through it' or have fallen through. This is because the efficiency of society can be compromised if too many of its members become 'dysfunctional' members, or 'former' members who have no inclination, will, interest or capacity to return to the 'fold'. Consequently, all are encouraged to conform, and demonised, marginalised or 'looked down' upon (by some or many, but it is incorrect to say by all), if not conforming, which again is another telling indictment of societal expectations, norms and values. Thus, *Chapter Six: Welfare*, which is supported by many agents in the Alice.

This entity called Australian society, as well as absorbing influence from many multicultural sources and other societal global players, has an historical legacy that goes back to its colonial inception. This legacy is a volatile and conciliatory relationship with the Indigenous language groups of Australia. The general trend from the beginning of contact was one of marginalisation and dispossession, which ended up, and continues to end up, with reliance on the services of society to keep going, within various levels of social life quality or inequality. Since a sizable proportion of the Alice demographic is Indigenous, and a place of one of the highest ratios of Indigenous to non-Indigenous peoples in Australia, and one of the main economic drivers for the town, it is appropriate to include it as one of the themes. So, *Chapter Seven: Indigenous*. An ironic point in the book's context of servicing, is the colonial action of the last two centuries has created a service industry devoted to Indigenous issues and concerns, one that the Federal government has to be seen to address. Therefore, Alice Springs has many Indigenous organisations and support service agents responsible for Aboriginal issues in the town and surrounding environs.

Contemporary society has created an excess or surplus demographic beyond the working environment that is affluent enough to travel to places and spaces beyond their regular, everyday dwelling place. This surplus may be retirees who travel for months at a time, or those of various ages that take a couple of weeks off work, international travellers, and 'potential' students (both abroad and at 'home') utilising a 'gap year' to work and play around the country of Australia. Also, technological advancements in terms of ease and cost of travel, and the mass market of travel, developed over half a century or more, has made it possible for these travel aspirations to be realised. Consequently, services are not only restricted to those processes that provide essential assistance to negotiate the pitfalls and perils of social life, there are other services that propagate wants and desires beyond the basic necessities of life. Performing and practicing these services are not essential to live, but can offer a sense of well-being and respite from the everyday 'sameness' that many people face. This does not imply that the 'sameness' is necessarily a negative thing, but an occasional change is as good as a welcoming rest. However, for many, these surplus services beyond the basic may be regarded as essential, to create a sense of self-freedom of movement and decision making beyond the capitalist subordinate model of subjugation encountered over most, if not all, of the life cycle. A paradox is the propagated propaganda of these surplus services still operate under the societal rationale of making a profit, so the sense of freedom of moving and deciding is still bound within societal rules, values and norms. One of the key surplus services in the Alice driving the local economy is tourism, thus, *Chapter Eight: Tourism*.

Since human society is made up of...humans! a key implication is that politics is rife amongst all levels of communication and interaction. Regardless as if it is firstly the 'formal' practices and procedures of elected politicians and the general two party machine, with occasional independents adding to the mix, to secondly, the political negotiations between two parties (businesses or individuals for example) who are required to talk to each other to get things done or grease the wheels of close contact (regular or not). The latter definition is comprehensively covered in the other theme chapters, as close quarters politics intimately runs through their spaces of service production; 'close quarters' within the context of many one-to-one interactions of the server to the serviced. Since the latter is dealt with elsewhere, the former or first definition is the theme of *Chapter Nine: Politics*, and engages with the 'formal' of politics in the Alice and environs. The environs are not only the immediate surroundings of the Alice, the central region, but also involving connectivity to the government in Darwin. So, also providing a service at the Territory level. Of course, 'close quarter' politics is still very much a part of the life of formal politicians, but they are simultaneously working at a 'distance quarters' of the needs, wants and desires of their assigned electorate and beyond. In the case of Alice Springs, elected Territory government representatives of the people would not only be concerned with their own electorate, but also the concerns of the whole of Alice Springs and its 'beyond', just as the mayor of the town and associated councillors would consider Alice as a whole within their constituent parts. Essentially, politics is communication reflecting the power plays of the involved agents, each striving to manipulate the finite resources of society in the space tasked as their legal sphere of responsibility towards the public...a political servicing.

The effects and affects of service causes in the Alice flagged by these theme chapters, and other services not directly engaged with beyond the scope of the book's narrative, is *Chapter Ten: Dwelling Reactions to Alice Springs*. Essentially a chapter that considers what Alice Springs as a place to live means to those that dwell there, i.e. reacting/performing to the service provisions on offer...a method to gauge the relationship effectiveness of service as society and society as service, and perhaps strengthen the connection with service/societal production as something worth having.

The last chapter *Conclusion: Concluding the Service* finalises the process of servicing. Drawing from the key findings of what has gone on before in the narrative, both from its concrete and theoretical contemplations, filtered through Bourdieu's select theories, the chapter offers a discussion on the intimacy of servicing processes that is the template of society and how it operates. A realisation is formed that the human species, just like all other fauna and flora existing on planet Earth, is trained and constantly trains itself to maintain the colony of society. Hence a tension arises between the members of society and society itself. To illustrate:

...*Who is Serving Who*!!...the individual self, or the self of society or perhaps an amalgamation of mutual serviceable benefit.

Chapter One

Provision and Package of the Alice

Pumping the Heart of Society

Alice Springs is a settlement located close to the physical geographic centre of Australia. Although it is not central in terms of population numbers celebrated by the state and territory capital cities, it enjoys a sense of metaphoric centrality. This symbolism is constructed by Australian society, and encouraged by local service agents, to paint a red picture of the central area being the red heart of Australia. A symbolic or abstract image of the life blood of society coursing through the veins of its settlements and their accompanying services, with the heart or motor that pumps the life giving fluid being Alice Springs. This poignant image is an apt way to begin this chapter, since the major argument of the book is the concentrated and absorbed association of services and society. What better analogy to highlight this than picturing the settlement of Alice and its blood vessels of services being pumped around the place of the Alice, but also Alice and its central environs as the engine or heart pumping the energy that drives the rest of Australia. Obviously in 'reality' it is not like that, as each settlement has their own hearts, ...or is it!, as symbolism can be powerful enough to represent society in its own image(s), and the red heart 'hook' can implant itself within the nation's consciousness and unconsciousness.

A paradox with the red heart imagery is considering the physical geographic isolation of the Alice. How can the heart pump societal blood through to the other live places in the societal system, if the isolation compromises network communication integrity? Perhaps the strength of communication resides within the myth, rather than the harsh reality of the almost quarantined place of the Alice with places beyond its localised centralised reach. Lack of societal inclusion of close physical quarters perspective ensures a societal exclusivity, which produces a sense of societal service uniqueness in the context, or more appropriately lack of context, of having another or other significantly sized settlements in close adjacent. This allows for a 'purer' service flow to take place, as the local services exist for the localised demographic, whereas settlements close to each other may be 'contaminated' by some service reciprocity. Although there is nothing fundamentally flawed or inadequate in these latter places, of service performance, and would create their own service particularities of research approach, the 'pure' former allows opportunity for an authentic serviced 'oneness' of place not corrupted by outside influence.

Of course, the very nature of settlement in society implies that there is a commonality of purpose and connectivity of all, so the Alice and no other place in Australia can be purely removed. If this were possible, the Alice would cease to be a part of society and be 'apart', hence making the book's purpose pointless. The point is that society is made up of a settlement continuum of 'pure' to 'corrupt' service levels of provision, which in practice may be only slightly diverse from one other. This is a good thing, showing that these settlements do indeed belong to the same societal networked system, but also showing that there are subtle differences in the system, making the system stronger. The only reason that Alice is 'pure' in this context is due to its isolation, but that makes it a stronger service settlement as it must rely on servicing itself for much of its time and space, but within this same time and space, society is also stronger. Alice is unique, but not so unique as to make it an invalid choice for the service focus and service place representative of the book to society.

Colonial/Postcolonial Serviced Historical Background of the Alice (1870s-1990s)

After having established credentials for the Alice as suitable material for service analysis, the remainder of the chapter situates the Alice in terms of its colonial/postcolonial serviced historical background, to supply context to the serviced Alice of the Twenty First Century. Colonial and its post, are intentional parameters to work the space of Alice from, for two reasons. The first is the lack of information of the Alice from its pre-Alice Springs nee Stuart (the name of the Alice Springs place before it officially became Alice Springs in 1933) days of a pure (this time within its purest sense) Indigenous place that became the Alice. It was an Indigenous service centre that worked within the central Australian Aboriginal language groups and accompanying cultures and age-old customs. The second is since Australia is a colonial/postcolonial society, and the point of the book is to look at a settlement which has experienced and continues to experience these colonial cousins, the colonial correlation of the Alice to Australia is absolute. The amalgamation of colonial and postcolonial in the 'progressive development' of Australia is intentional, as both are present within its characteristic. The colonial may have been the sole component of country and cultural acquisition over two centuries ago, but with ongoing Indigenous resistance and dominant cultural attitudes changing over those two hundred odd years, postcolonial attitudes were born and rose to the surface of society. But the rub lies within the depth of society, as the colonial origin remains in those depths. Hence, there is a duality of colonial and post.

The origin of Alice Springs was due to a service reason, the service being communication of a national and global disposition, in the form of a telegraph line running from the south of Australia to England. The Australian part of the line was built between 1870 and 1872, with the telegraph line passing through what is now Alice Springs, reinforced by the building of a telegraph repeater station, the original colonial building and simultaneously original colonial symbol of 'Australia' first reaching the space that became Alice. The initial message flowing along the completed line was sent by Charles Todd, the man accountable for its construction, 'We have this day, within two years, completed a line of communications two thousand miles long through the very centre of Australia' (Exploring the Stuart Highway, 1997, p. 27). So, the servicing of the Alice began. The telegraph repeater station was the 'on the ground' service seed of an abstract idea, turned concrete, of the southern, western and eastern Australian major economic settlements being serviced by global markets and in turn servicing them, notably the British global market and its Victorian Empire. This 'on the ground' service seed acted as a catalyst for the fledging settlement to slowly, but surely expand, and eventually the Alice grew into a service centre for the localised encircling environments, a service status that continues to this day.

In the beginnings of a 'new' settlement overlying the old, in the case of the Alice this implies colonial British culture overlying the local Indigenous cultures, producing the serviceability parameters depends upon the physical geography of the location and how the 'new' culture 'reads' this geography. The 'reading' would be reliant on the 'old world' geography of the northern hemisphere drawn from Britain and northern Europe land and space appreciation, and how land is exploited for farming, mining, and settlement purposes. These 'fixed' positional perspectives would appraise the place and space in and around the Alice, speculating how much of the physical location would bend to the will of this speculation. From colonial eyes the land would have appeared harsh and challenging, which is arrived at by setting up aspirations and aims that overlaid the realities of the situation, by abstract hopes of making a living. So, judging the harsh and challenging conclusions were wholly dependent upon pre-conceived perceptions. Looking at the Alice and surrounds at that time from Indigenous perspectives, would have produced different implications of what harsh and challenging may mean in practice. The 'looking' and 'utilisation' of whatever is the focus, is governed by what one wants and what one is used to, and how the natural physical limitations of the focus, in this case the place and space of land within the Alice sphere of influence, allows how much one can obtain of that want.

For example, during the 1880s there was a slow progress of pastoral farming leases, as the mean Sun annual temperature was high in conjunction with low rainfall, and arid and semi-arid soil to work with. Hatwig (1965) offered a significant observation when commenting on the state of pastoralism in the last third of the Nineteenth Century:

> the Centre became a small man's frontier...The Alice Springs District...was too marginal, fickle and isolated a pastoral country for large scale pastoral enterprise to succeed in it. (pp. 150-151)

This is a poignant example of how service aspiration is dictated by available resources, both human and natural, unless or until technological invention and intervention alters resource capacity. Or another service is made available, adding to the mix of the first, allowing alternate means to expand a fledging settlement. For instance, there would have been significant correlation of the 1888 conception of Stuart and the strong attraction of gold discovered in 1887 at Altunga. The goldfields of Altunga were located approximately 100 kilometres east of north east of Alice, but not too far away for the Alice to serve it by providing mining equipment, general supplies and foodstuff, and as a communications hub (telegraph repeater station) to the world outside. Also, the Alice was served by the essential demands of living from the miners, a mutual serving environment until 1903, when Altunga closed. Nonetheless the serving capacity of the Alice was growing, and one thing that can ensure further service growth of any settlement is exposure to communication networks in the form of transport.

During January 1927, the commencement of a railway line from Oodnadatta headed northwards for Stuart. Consequently, by the middle of 1929, Stuart became the northern most railhead connecting to the populous southern settlements. An instant 'game changer' in terms of access, that ensured the proximity of the southern settlements became a lot closer in terms of 'time/space compression' (see Harvey, 1989), producing higher levels of existing and newer service possibilities, as transport costs would fall and population would rise. Darwin would also be looking on with heightened interest by considering its own service needs, when assessing transport costs and time to transport by sea or overland. Being a railhead has distinct economic and political advantages, which would have not been overlooked and been an asset during further goldfield finds in the 1930s. Examples include the Granites (approximately 600km north west of Alice (Wilford, 2003)) gold find in 1932, and the 1933 gold discovery at Tennant Creek (500km to the north). Supplies and goods would have fed these fields via the rail head.

One of the—if not the most—draining servicer in human society is the service of war. During the Second World War in the 1940s, the Alice became the vital defence and offence service link of the north and south of the country. As well as its traditional role as a communications hub, it became a military hub to store and process weapons, transport, and military personnel servicing Darwin and offshore further north. As services ensure the survivability and sustainability of their associated society, Alice had a vital service role to ensure the survivability of Australia as a colonial society at that time. Servicing the military service machine, an essential servicer of society, came in the form of the Darwin Overland Maintenance Force, of which numbers reached a peak of 3000 vehicles and 8000 personnel (Central Australia the war years 1939-45). It was tasked with moving men and material, via the Alice, up to Darwin, and from 1940 to the beginning of November 1944, 194,852 troops passed through the Alice (Blunt, 1982). The immense number of war materials present and passing through, both human and machine, compared to what existed in the Alice pre-war, would have altered its service capacity beyond recognition, both in level and complexity. The original pre-war civilian numbers were about 400, with military presence almost nonexistent, but by January 1943, there were 956 civilians as opposed to 4600 military personnel (Smith, 1991).

Continuing the observation of transport significantly contributing to service increase and complexation, and directly associated with servicing war, was the Seven Mile Aerodrome, built (as hinted) seven miles south of Alice. The Department of Defence acquired it from Hayes Undoolya pastoral lease in 1939 (Domenico Pecorari, 2005). An original colonial service (pastoral) servicing a defence server. It was utilised by the Australian and United States air forces. After the war it became the Alice Springs airport, which it still is today. Also, the wartime constructed sealed road from Alice to Darwin, continuing and supplementing the 'sealed' railway line from the south to Alice, was a necessary addition to cope with the flow of military movement. After the war it remained, encouraging further service activity for the Alice.

Creating and increasing service capacity for a settlement does not just rely upon the efforts of those who live there, for that may just achieve certain plateau levels which would be difficult to break through to higher service provision. Being an isolated settlement can only achieve so much. To actually progress, in terms of service capacity, a place/settlement has to offer something that the society sees benefits in. This may be an ongoing arrangement, or particular to the necessities of a time period. Physical geographic location can be key to this, especially if the location is strategically significant to the networked shape of society at that particular moment, or set of common moments that are projected to last for a time. The shape of society, or shaping society, just as with the individual settlement, can only move, hence change, adapt, and develop, if not operating in isolation in relation to other societies. It reacts to the actions of the intentions of these 'other' societies, and in turn they react to that society. For instance, Australia at war during the 1940s was driven by other societal influences beyond its borders of domestic influence, and was changed by these global encounters. Similarly, the Alice during the war years and the legacy of that time was altered, with new layers of service functionality overlaying the older ones, and adding to or superseding them.

Legacy and related experiences and memories of a settlement encountered and temporarily visited from those who do not permanently live there, increases the service capacity of it. Thus, not just relying upon the efforts of those who do live there, to feed and nourish the service animal. For example, the legacy of military personnel being based at the Alice for a few moments during their lives and having a direct and profound encounter with it. Since, due to their sheer numbers, the general Australian awareness of pre-war Alice as just that extreme remote location depicting the general centre of the country, assuming that anyone in the southern settlements even gave the Alice a first or second thought, became more than that. Now a significant number of 'non-Alice'

Australians and Americans had direct experience of it, and consequently could relate that knowledge to families, friends, and those beyond close emotional attachments. The Alice had now become real and substantial well beyond its localised capacities. Word of mouth or the modern version, word of social media, can be more powerful than organised advertising, to make or break a product. Consequently, the 'product' of Alice Springs was heading upwards within its service complexity, as the economic potential of tourism and encouraging more people to come and live in this 'not so' remote location became possible. So, the added considerable attribute of first-hand memory to the telegraph, rail, road, and air communication access ways, minimised the isolation of the place, producing fertile ground for service growth.

To illustrate this service growth, from 1947 onwards, which happened to be the time of regular civilian flights, greater than 95% of the town's growth in population happened (Parkes, Burnley and Walker, 1985). Migration was the most significant contributor. For example, in 1947 there was 2078 people living in the Alice (Census of the Commonwealth of Australia, 1954), increasing to 3017 by 1954, an expansion of about 33%. Business offerings grew in the form of that bastion of capitalism, banks, via the 1946 reopening of the English, Scottish and Australian Bank due to temporarily closer because of the war, closely pursued by the Bank of New South Wales, and Commonwealth Bank. Also in 1946 the opening of a store by the station and stock agents of Goldsborough Mort (present day Elders Ltd) (Smith, 2005), followed in 1947 by Dalgety, indicated that the pastoral industry was still going and servicing. The year of 1947 saw the Centralian Advocate's (the Alice's current twice weekly newspaper) initial printing. Noel Loutit's agency and general merchandising business opened in 1948. The first pharmacy opened in 1950 and a jeweller shop in 1953. The point is that population numbers that contact a settlement are key to its wellbeing, and the greater the contact, i.e. the greater the numbers, the wellbeing will be sustained and improved upon.

Contact can be direct (those that live in a settlement) and indirect (those that pass through perhaps in the form of tourists). It is due to the potential opportunity to service the tourist industry that Len Tuit appeared in the mid-1950s. He initiated tourism to Ayers Rock (Uluṟu) by coach from the Alice, which is still ongoing today by other service providers (for instance AAT Kings) on a greater scale of operation. This is an example of how a fledging service industry can grow into something much bigger, but still retaining the original idea as the rationale for the project, and draw in other service providers to expand their operation or produce new service operations to cater for the influx of a mass tourism market. For example, accommodation provision, in direct reaction to tourist pressure, in the form of the first motel built in the Alice, the Oasis, was constructed in 1958. There were also, supermarkets. A Woolworth's opened in November of 1960, and other services such as cafes, restaurants, and in-town tourism appeared. All these reacted to the service demands of tourists. This service 'knock on' effect is typical of how a settlement operates and flourishes, of how one service can affect other services and change their character in terms of scale and efficiency, also of how services in one place can create service provision in others. For instance, during the early 1960s, neighbouring tourist destinations used Alice as a serviced base, such as Glen Helen and Palm Valley.

With a significant increase in the population of a settlement, a natural and expected effect is more children, and consequent expanding demand for education in both the primary and high school sectors. In 1951 the Bath Street Catholic Primary School opened, with Ross Park Primary following ten years later. In the high school area, a new school was built in 1953, with a second (Anzac Hill) in 1960. Education service provision would not be the only consequence of a younger demographic, as demand and opportunities for leisure and recreation emerged for adults and children alike. In the Alice these came in the forms of, initially horse racing, to Australian Rules football, basketball, tennis, and for those more mentally minded, drama and opening of the town library in 1953. These 'extra work' provisions would depend upon the wealth creation realisation of a society and which settlements benefit, as a result of the related economic benefits, or are in an environmentally advantageous space economically geared, to the macro wants of the leaders of society (both politically and economically), and excess time and monetary profit producing opportunities and demands for 'play time'. 'Frontier' settlements, due to their nature of being 'on the edge' of society, can offer wages and entrepreneurial openings of a higher return on investment than more centralised and 'normalised' established settlements. This may be due to supply and demand of available and willing people to go and live in these periphery places is not great, so the incentive cost is driven up.

There may be an irony working in the background of society of how places within it are diversely regulated, which influence competition levels. Those places which are more exposed to the 'centrality' of societal mores, needs, wants, and requirements, generally the ones 'closer' to what is regarded as 'comfortable civilisation' with access to a wide variety of service provision, much of which is not necessary for direct survival, but necessary for a 'quick and easy gratified consumer fix', suffer much greater competition with each other to gain employment. Also, the lure of a wide range of service provision offering, attracts in other individuals beyond that place and space who carry qualifications and experience that challenge further the local capacity to gain employment. In addition, like minded services will be in competition with each other to attract would be consumers to devour their offered products, so costs and wages will be regulated, i.e. driven down to optimum levels to still make a reasonable profit for the owners and shareholders, and still ensure their sustainable survivability. This is not to say that those places and spaces on the periphery do not experience regulative tendencies just as much as the more central ones do, but perhaps the level of meaningful regulation comes down to the in-built competitive capacity of each settlement. Less competition means less effective regulation, more competition means more effective regulation.

The implication is that societal rules, norms, and expectations in terms of legalities developed and adapted over generations, or in the case of Australia 'piggy backing' the British legal system and adapting it to the localised contexts, are only a surface veneer hiding the basic characteristics of animal tensions and conflict over spatial control of a territory. Thus, territory of a society at a macro level, and its micro settlement places with their own particular characteristics in their 'place' in society, express symbolic violent tendencies to control, dominate, and subordinate. 'Hiding' in this context may actually be a tautology, as the legalities offered on the 'surface' of society to guide the people to appropriate ways of behaving and performing in their roles as societal agents, encourage behaviours that reflect animal tendencies to try and establish terrains of superiority and attendant inferiority. There is, in-built, into the legally contracted societal behavioural system, perhaps unconsciously so from the human 'uncivilised' state, a creation of energy to survive, which grants 'freedom' of movement to exploit, thus creating societal hierarches. This performance parallels societal systems in nature, both fauna and flora. Essentially it is natural to be uncivilised within civilised society, and humans do well to keep a lid on their 'wild' tendencies, or at least keep a sense of controlled control over the wildness of society and its attendant settlements.

So, the one and a half decades from 1945 to 1960 saw Alice grow in relation to numbers of people and consequently raised economic and construction levels. These gains and attendant services needed to be sustained to keep the momentum of the Alice going over the next decade and hopefully improved upon, which is what happened. Since during the 1960s the gains were strengthened and given an enhanced state of durability. For instance, in relation to population gains, there was an increase of 37.7% between the mid-1966 and mid-1969 (Shrapnel, 1970). A significant demographic increase of over one third, places pressure to produce more settlement infrastructure, so upgraded or new facilities and services had to be realised. The implication was more construction and building work. Since access to and from the Alice was relatively easy at this time, and continues to be, in terms of travel time (via road, rail and air) and these in turn being cost effective, the services of tourism were having a greater impression. Hence increases in infrastructure construction were a direct correlation of the substantial rise in tourism, which meant new visitor accommodation was built. For example, the amount of rooms in guesthouses, motels, and hotels in November of 1964 were 300. Just over four years later, in January of 1969, the availability was 423. Within this time frame, tourist number demand went from 26,600 in 1966 to 38,000 by 1969 (Shrapnel, 1970).

Any societal settlement cannot get very far without government intervention. It is government and its state system that 'governs' to maintain the glue that holds society together in a loose to rigid form, depending upon which societal system is scrutinised. Nevertheless, without a governmental framework to run whatever is the societal system engaged with, the whole (society) would fragment. For instance, its administrative powers and retention of public purse strings substantially determines the performance levels of a settlement, and without this support, many, if not all settlements would struggle to survive. The place of the Alice is no exception. For in the 1960s, and ongoing to this very day, the service levels of tourism, and indeed any other service industry in the Alice, was eclipsed by government supported workers. These workers, such as those in the Northern Territory Science, Education, Health, and Administration sectors, were the central catalysts for the growth of the Alice by a noteworthy margin.

Regardless of what governmental body is in charge, the reliance upon it is paramount to the lived place and space around, and in, whatever settlement, to keep them going. For instance, in the Northern Territory during the 1970s, the administration of Alice's political economy had been partly 'transferred' from the Federal government based in Canberra (Australian Capital Territory), to the Northern Territory government based in Darwin. The transfer occurred due to the process of the Northern Territory political system moving to a fully elected legislative Assembly in 1974, and by 1978 self-government. The 'transfer' from one Territory to another was partially symbolic, since the Federal government kept hold of substantial powers involving the Northern Territory, including Aboriginal land rights legislation. So, the Northern Territory government is still reliant upon the Federal government.

The population of the Alice in 1975 was 13,300 (Alice Springs Urban Development Study, 1975), and the place was evolving into a modern service hub. To illustrate:

> Compared to the 1930s, it was no longer "a Town like Alice", but a town like any other small city anywhere in the English speaking world. Traffic lights, four lane roads and traffic police. A visitor could take his choice of motels, caravan parks or hotels of international standard. Alice had become a town of supermarkets, starting with Woolworths, Coles and K. Mart. Suburbs had developed; the east side, the Gillen area, Sadadeen, Mt. Nancy, Undoolya Road...all with their supermarkets. (Bowman, 1993, pp. 76-78)

In 1965, supermarkets in their basic format arrived on the streets in many major settlements in Britain. Basic in the sense of combining or centralising all the then known food products offered, that previously would have been traded through individual small service outlets. In terms of consumer convenience, economic pressure to 'out bid' the small service providers by trading at a lower rate than they could possibly sustain over varied time periods without experiencing 'service dying', and willingness for consumer choice to pay less for goods, encouraged a partial re-structuring of the societal framework. It was not that the sum of the whole service capacity, in the context of supermarkets compared to their former smaller service competitors, rose or fell, it just became concentrated into fewer stakeholders' hands and control. Smaller food provision servicers dissolved into a larger, more concentrated servicer, which paradoxically drew the acquired 'mini' services into a smaller, more densely populated place and space, as contrasted to the physically utilised 'spread out' spaces formally offered for the same products. This partial restructuring of society, as the 'partial' suggests, would not effect and affect the remainder of societal workings too much, at least the observer may like to think so. For the very presence of (super)markets: (Super...superior, better, enhanced, improved, high-quality, high-class, topnotch) would cause a knock on reaction in the rest of society, and profoundly alter people's perceptions of how things are done, and what to expect from services.

For example, other service providers would look at the supermarket model of concentrated, mass presence offering many services under the one umbrella of services, and may begin to feel insecure. This insecurity would be based upon competition within their own service space and place, as if the competition began building up their own service capacity, creating space to progress and take over, then oneself should try and do the same. Also, service providers who formally supplied the mini food servicers with products from their farms, with perhaps favourable monetary returns, would now have to trade with the supermarkets within the resultant harsher economic environment, at least from their perspective. For instance, those who enjoy a bigger slice of the service pie of society, enjoy greater freedom to dictate terms of how services operate. So, power in an overt, but still covert, way was being concentrated by this symbolic shift of emphasis of consumer behaviour. Overt, by the obvious presence of these new imposing structures of mass food provision, and covert by the unseen agenda put in place to channel all available resources to produce a sustained, profit machine. The result was that the population and effected service providers were encouraged or trained to practice and perform particular movements, to maximise profit and influence for the concentrated few holding the service power.

Thus, the service capacity of the Alice by the 1970s was enveloped within the supermarket service enigma that pervades all of modern society. Within this context of concentrated service provision, the Alice Springs Urban Development Study (1975) adopted and adapted these filters of perception to project what the service space of the Alice should look like by the Millennium:

> Provides for "low profile" future building which will be modern but un-obstructive of the landscape which so distinguishes "the Alice" from anyway else. At the same time, the central business district has been replanned to provide for more efficient and intensive commercial, retail and tourist development to accommodate the growth that is

forecast for the town. (Alice Springs Urban Development Study, 1975, p. 7)

A key phrase 'to provide for more efficient and intensive commercial, retail and tourist development', is highlighted for two reasons. Firstly, the performance words of 'efficient' and 'intensive', setting the scene of how services should operate and indeed 'perform. Secondly, incorporating significant service industries as the chosen ones for the quote: commercial, retail and tourism; bastions of societal capitalism. The subsequent quote draws in Alice's physical geographical spaces to bolster the bastions, providing a sense of authentic normality.

> The larger Alice Springs envisaged for the year 2001 should therefore be comfortable and efficient but just as much in harmony as it is today with the outback vastness of the Centre, its colours, The Todd River and its fringing gums, the encircling MacDonnell Ranges, the town's weathered hills and rock outcrops. Indeed "The Alice" should then be even more attractive to the tourism which is the largest contributor to its economic life. Also take into account that urban planning should provide optimum employment, leisure and quality of life opportunities for residents and visitors. (Alice Springs Urban Development Study, 1975, p. 7)

The above quote paints a romantic and alluring notion and imagery, creating an atmosphere of welcome-ness and well-being to attract visitors, both temporarily ('be even more attractive to the tourism which is the largest contributor to its economic life') and on a more permanent basis ('urban planning should provide optimum employment, leisure and quality of life'). Both the temporarily and the permanent are pushed from behind by the even present undercurrent of economic performance. The adhesive that holds society and services together. Human services are strengthened and encouraged, and similarly weakened and discouraged, by the natural topographic setting they operate within. If the topographic landscape is perceived to be harsh and challenging, offering extreme temperature ranges, human numbers tend to be smaller of those settling there. This perception has direct correlation with service levels and tends to limit them somewhat, as compared to the perceived more 'moderate' climate and 'easier' living environments that the majority in Australia migrate to.

The point is that there is intense intimacy between the physical and human of geographic interpretation, when it comes to settlement choice. Out of necessity, people have to find employment, whether it be legal or illegal, and given the choice, the majority would prefer working in a living environment regarded as 'nice' and 'comfortable'. These will depend upon personal preference, as they do not imply the same thing for all. This is just as well, as settlements in society would be bland in terms of their sameness of function and design, and other settlements that currently exist perhaps would not, if the population was monophonic. Fortunately, the population is not, and although settlements within a society do 'enjoy' a sense of sameness, they also simultaneously enjoy a sense of difference.

The sense of sameness and difference a settlement retains, i.e. its personal identity, reflects characteristics of quantity and quality. A small settlement such as the Alice, has not, and probably into the foreseeable future, the potential for a sizable quantity of people to live there. Its relative remoteness and perception of being on societal 'frontiers' would make many people shy away, assuming that they would ever consider it as a 'dwelling place' (Heidegger, 1962). However, those that do live in the Alice and those that move there to work or as tourists, tend to retain a certain quality. This quality involves a sense of adventure and challenge, and for some an 'escape' from societal limits. There is no claim suggesting people who do frequent the 'outback' of central Australia stands apart from those who prefer a more established and 'seasoned' urban existence, for each retains their own sense of adventure and challenge. Also, for the majority who dwell in the Alice and its environs, would have experienced 'both' living spaces anyway, and drawn from each to enhance their quality of life. Sometimes it is quality that can out manoeuvre quantity in what a settlement is and evolves into, and the quality levels of services on offer can also rise above the capacity of services offered in larger settlements.

Although, in terms of demand levels, it may be the quantity of people that dwell in or are passing through a place, that influence service provision more than quality measurements. It is easier to count at an embodied level and understand an absolute, unambiguous total of individuals, than to investigate their abstract, non-fixed desires, needs, and wants. However, the paradox arises when individuals are 'counted' through the doors of service providers, as the quantity indicators osmosis into quality interactions between servicer and serviced. It is here where the 'quality' of the service offered is put to the test, and cannot hide behind product advertising rhetoric, since the quality indicators of the served or consumer comes to the fore and the servicer has to react to that. This is where the in-built bureaucratic nature of servicers can be found wanting, as the rigid structure may only partially, or in certain cases, totally block what the consumer is seeking. However, for some service providers this is not an issue, as the 'transaction' between themselves and the serviced, is straightforward. For example, in Western supermarkets prices are fixed in advanced, and customers pay that price. If not paid, the service offered does not take place. There is no or little room for negotiation within these multinational corporate entities. Perhaps it is a question of scale, for when purchasing goods in individually owned shops or markets in Middle Eastern countries and South American, for instance Mexico, flexibility in arriving at a mutually acceptable price through verbal sparring is a normal process.

It is significant that the consumer is directly interacting with the service owner in these latter cases, and not employees or agents working on behalf of the owner in the former example, i.e. Western supermarkets. The level of access of the consumer to whoever owns the service, creates power differentials of whose agenda is the most dominant and influential before, during, and after the encounter. The level of power differential also allows for particular environments to dictate behaviour, which can override cultural conduct learnt in one's society. For instance, practicing the 'submissive' non-negotiation of prices when being submersed in the supermarket experience, quickly and almost instantaneously goes out the window when given opportunity to voice what price you are willing to pay, when travelling through the lives of a different society or indeed private, one-to-one transactions with others within your 'own' society. For example, when purchasing or selling goods (cars or furniture) owned by one or other of the two parties involved. The key concept is ownership, i.e. retaining control of the service being offered. It is this ownership that dictates the extent of responsibility attached to the service.

This is perhaps why services offered by government and government funded service providers have a degree of the impersonal about them. For in the case of government, it is the collective whole that 'owns' the service, embedded in the portfolio of selected ministers. It is the authoritative position awarded to the minister on a temporary basis, rather than the minister as his or her own person, that supplies the 'ownership', so ownership in this context has an in-built flaw. The flaw is of not feeling complete ownership over the service, therefore not feeling total responsibility, thus creating an impersonal environment. This is not to indicate that those who work in these government related services do not retain a conscientious work ethic, but the impersonal environment would be a living factor taken into account when offering quality of service provision to the consumer.

In Alice Springs by the middle of 1984, the permanent population was 22,000 (Alice Springs Regional Outline Structure Plan, 1985). During this period, the Alice had one of the fastest population growth rates in Australia of 5%. To further encourage the increase, the road south of the Alice, the Stuart Highway, was sealed in 1987 all the way to Adelaide. Thus, enhancing the quality of one of the key communication access ways. So, when attempting the daunting journey, it would not be so daunting, creating greater numbers of service consumers to visit and perhaps stay.

The early 1990s and to the present, has seen the emergence of neoliberal economics on a global scale. The rise and potency of international neoliberal Anglo thought processes and associated economic rationality was difficult to resist, assuming there was will to do so, and Australia as a minor player and interdependent and dependent on global financial flows, went along with this to survive and compete. As Lloyd (2008, p. 49) observed, Australia was easily enmeshed into the global Anglo ideological and policy constellation. The neoliberal turn marked a decrease and distancing from a social democratic welfare state model of capitalism, within general Australian societal economics.

However, within the Alice, due to its periphery societal status in terms of location and demographic makeup, welfare presence at the time remained much alive, and still is. Alice's location ensures that prospects to gain employment are favourable as compared to the majority settlements in the rest of Australia, not insignificantly assisted by many working people only staying for short time periods. Hence, employment vacancies come up on a regular basis. Considering the demographic makeup, a sizable minority of the town and environs are Indigenous, so the Indigenous welfare industry of Alice has developed into a vital economic interest, both for non-Indigenous and Indigenous people alike. To illustrate, government and private expenditures, partially due to tourism prospects and partially to addressing Aboriginal social challenges, stimulate local Indigenous effects on the Alice economy. However, a major legacy of colonialism is the psychological and emotional affect it can have on the colonised. One irony of colonisation is that, if the colonial system becomes affluent enough and accepts some responsibility for culturally violent performances against minority groups, a set of welfare service provisions emerge and adapt to the contemporary political and economic climate of society to deal with the resultant colonial legacies. The Alice is a prime Australian settlement example of this.

The Millennium and Towards the 2020s

By the beginning of the new millennium, Street Ryan and Associates (1999) created a report reflecting the Alice Springs economic profile. The findings hold currency twenty years later. To illustrate, the local market conditions are sturdy with a 5% unemployment level and workforce involvement reaching 73%. The comparison is favourable to the national figures of 9 and 60% respectively within the rest of Australia. It should be noted that the numbers of high percentage employed represents far more non-Indigenous locals than Indigenous. The town's infrastructure is well placed, as the amount of recreation and community services are higher than what is considered 'normal' for a settlement not quite reaching 30,000 people. Health service provision is wide ranging, helped by the fact that the Alice Springs hospital is a training establishment. That, combined with significant Indigenous usage, ensures that all in the Alice enjoy a high health service delivery. There is also an Indigenous health establishment, Congress, supporting Indigenous health service in the Alice. The other bastion of settlement service that people consider as important as health, education, is also well preserved, with student/teacher ratio rated as one of the lowest in Australia. The foremost service industry sector in terms of numbers employed and businesses involved, is retail.

As in common with most established settlements, construction, business and property are prominent in the Alice. An example of property recently constructed is the new Law Courts, completed in 2017. An imposing building, purposefully designed to be imposing, set up behind the town's post office in the central business district. As Western settlements generally have their main post office as the fixed point when measuring distances between settlements, it may be a significant location selection for the Courts, to be the centre of 'legitimate' societal processes. The most prominent service in the town is Government, continuing the trend that became noticeable in the 1960s. Approximately one third of the local workforce 'enjoys' direct correlation with Government work or are affected by Government legislation. Within the multi-layered government structure of Australia; Federal, State/Territory and local (council), political influence in the Alice can mainly be thought of as originating from the Northern Territory government, based in Darwin, and to a lesser extent from the Alice Springs Town Council. Although, as the purse strings are controlled by Canberra (Federal government), ultimate influence permeates from there. Ultimately, all who dwell in the Alice are subjected to governmental persuasion, i.e. well beyond the one third employment effected figure, so government is the single most distinctive and dominant service provision in the Alice; as it is within society and within settlements.

However, Government processes and performance is itself subjugated to economic processes and performance within powerful intensities of engagement. Government economic policy and intervention has to strike a balance between settlement welfare provision and what sensibly can be afforded to service public needs, and what the economic market is performing at, both currently and predicted longer term, to determine the level of provision of these public needs. Continuing with the Street Ryan and Associates (1999) economic summary of the Alice, service and consumer behaviours dictate the employment structure of the town. Tourism and manufacturing are weakly signified or operate at levels lower than the national average. Also lower than the national average are micro businesses. This is despite most town businesses being small, of which 62% have five or less individuals employed. Essentially, the most instrumental economic service providers in the Alice are governmental (as indicated), which include the Joint Defence Facility at Pine Gap, Indigenous, mining, construction, and tourism. Pine Gap is a military establishment patronised by Australian and United States personnel and is located a few kilometres from the town. It generates yearly running costs of around $70 million (Australian dollars).

The central business district is the most important commercial and retail hub in the Alice, consequently important to the town's service levels. It also services the minor settlements in central Australia. So, the Alice can be regarded as a service centre or a centre of services. Accordingly , its vitality and prosperity is imperative to the economic performance and subsequent quality of life of the wider region (Cornell Wagner, 2002, p. 8). Concisely, the main services of the Alice are... numerous civic services and government departments run from the central area, as well as other administration and business services. Additionally, privately owned shopping complexes (Alice Plaza and Yeperenye Centre) as well as private suburban supermarkets (IGAs;

Flynn Drive, North Side, East Side and Larapinta) , Piggly Wigglies (Gap Road) and the Alice Food Market. Plus, a pedestrian mall (Todd Mall) which encourages access to the central area, and finally some major retail chains (Coles, Woolworths and K Mart). The trend for Alice Springs, as with the majority of settlements, is to improve the quantity and quality of services. This improvement was suggested by then Chief Minister of the Northern Territory in 2015.

> This budget sets the foundation for Central Australia to grow and prosper with significant investment in economic and community infrastructure projects that create jobs and makes Central Australia an even better place to live. (Giles, 2015, front page)

Alice Springs Demographic Services 2016

The Australian national census count occurs every five years. The latest was in 2016. Alice Springs and its surrounding environment is part of that human geographic counting. It would be sensible to supply some of the Alice's number crunching of people and related services to support the service theories presented in the book, and to contextualise the situated conversations presented in Chapter Three onwards. Essentially, the number and characteristics of the people in and around a settlement place influence what services are, or should be in place, subsequently operating those services and/or engage with them as users. The following census statistics have been selected as worthwhile inclusions contributing to the service capacity of the Alice. They have been drawn from the statistical categories of Local Government Areas, Statistical Area Level 3, and to individualise Indigenous Australian Alice residents, Indigenous Regions. The Australian Bureau of Statistics (ABS) (Australian Statistical Geography Standard (ASGS) (2016) defines these three categories.

A Local Government Area (LGA) is an ABS approximation of officially gazetted LGAs as defined by each State and Territory Local Government Department. The boundaries produced for LGAs are constructed from allocations of whole Mesh Blocks (MBs). The ABS reviews LGAs on an annual basis with changes implemented by inclusion or exclusion of whole MBs.

LGAs cover incorporated areas of Australia. Incorporated areas are legally designated parts of States and Territories over which incorporated local governing bodies have responsibility.

Statistical Area Level 3 (SA3) provides a standardised regional breakup of Australia. SA3s are built from whole Statistical Area Level 2s (SA2)) and aggregate directly to Statistical Area Level 4 (SA4) in the Main Structure (which incorporates all levels). SA3s do not cross State and Territory borders. These boundaries generally reflect a combination of widely recognised informal regions as well as existing administrative regions such as State Government

Regions in rural areas and local Government Areas in urban areas. Note that SA2s are medium sized general-purpose areas built up from whole Statistical Areas Level 1 (SA1). Their purpose is to represent a community that interacts together socially and economically. As for SA1s, they are generally designed as the smallest unit for the release of census data. Finally, SA4s regions are the largest sub-State regions in the Main Structure of the ASGS.

Indigenous Regions (IREGs) are large geographical units loosely based on the former Aboriginal and Torres Strait Islander Commission boundaries. IREGs are designed to cover the whole of Geographic Australia and do not cross State/Territory borders

Within the settlement of Alice, the LGA and IREGs can be thought of as the space of Alice Springs within its 'urban' consideration, whereas SA3 includes not only the Alice urban but the immediate surrounding 'rural' environments as well. Immediate can be a misleading term, since some of the rural settlements (Indigenous and Stations) may be hundreds of kilometres out from the Alice. This last one is included, as the people there utilise the Alice services. The ABS designation for Alice Springs are: Code LGA70200 (LGA); Code 70201 (SA3); Indigenous Regions (IREG).

Table 1: Alice Springs and Environment Community Profile.

Community Profile			
TYPE	LGA	SA3	IREG
People	24,753	36,077	4,591 (Aboriginal and/or Torres Strait Islander)
Male	49%	49.6%	46.5%
Female	51%	50.4%	53.5%
Median Age	35	33	28
Families	5,640	7,753	
Average children per families with children	1.9	1.9	
Average children for all families	0.7	0.8	
All private dwellings	11,162	15,333	1,477 (households)
Average people per household	2.6	2.8	3.1
Median weekly household income	$1,937	$1,715	$1,265
Median monthly mortgage repayments	$1,950	$1,950	$1,950
Median weekly rent	£350	$180	$185
Average motor vehicles per dwelling	1.8	1.6	

Source: QuickStats 2016 Census Australia Northern Territory. Alice Springs: Local Government Areas/Statistical Area Level 3/Indigenous Regions.

The number of people in the LGA as compared to SA3 shows a difference of 11,324 more people frequenting the latter geographical space. This number is significant when compared to the LGA total of 24,753, showing that nearly half again of the serviced population of Alice live beyond its immediate boundary. This substantial number would influence particular logistic challenges to access the town's services and within a sense of delayed gratification, since the immediacy of services would be limited. There are more females than males, although barely, except slightly greater difference in the IREG. If services are gender bias, depends upon the context of the service offered, and if a service offers more than one service within its repertory, perhaps targeting males or females when requiring separation between the two.

Table 2: Age range.

Age (years)	LGA	SA3	IREG
Median age	35	33	28
0-4	1,808	2,639	427
5-9	1,808	2,713	929
10-14	1,567	2,373	
15-19	1,423	2,334	721
20-24	1,377	2,676	
25-29	2,091	3,248	622
30-34	2,176	3,207	
35-39	1,829	2,623	611
40-44	1,773	2,576	
45-49	1,907	2,612	597
50-54	1,868	2,482	
55-59	1,723	2,279	375
60-64	1,357	1,755	
65-69	860	1,079	319
70-74	514	651	
75-79	307	383	
80-84	187	256	
85 +	164	195	

Source: QuickStats 2016 Census Australia Northern Territory. Alice Springs: Local Government Areas/Statistical Area Level 3/Indigenous Regions.

This separateness may be institutional or culturally driven, influenced also by local situatedness. Australian society encourages family as its basic unit, and from the 'Families' numbers of LGA and SA3, this unit is substantially established in the Alice and environments. Part of this encouragement comes in the form of practical and tangible services to produce family sustainability. For instance, many of the Alice's services would have a family connection inbuilt into their portfolio. Since food, water, and shelter are reputed to be the basic necessities of life, the shelter aspect features heavily in society and in the Alice, and with that, its accompanying support commitments. The commitments of retaining ownership of the shelter (private dwelling) and the costs involved to do so (balancing income, mortgage and/or rent repayments) ...such are the costs to maintain one's services. Also, the costs to access one's services via transport, for example motor vehicles.

The classic pyramid shape of lifelong demographic distribution is roughly in existence in the LGA and SA3. Although the 0-4 and 5-9 range numbers for both are higher than the older age ranges, until finally being surpassed in the 25-29 and 20-24 LGA and SA3 figures respectively. It is significant that the IREG top figure resides within the 5-14 age range, reflecting a downward trend of numbers throughout the remaining years of life. Social exclusion and marginalisation can seriously affect a sense of wellbeing and health perception (both within cultural myth and cultural reality). The 'lesser' life span of Indigenous people in general is also illustrated in the median ages of the LGA, SA3, and IREG (35, 33 and 28 years respectively). Many service providers in the Alice cater to Indigenous needs, solely or partially, as part of their portfolios. This situation is not coincidental, due to the significant number of Indigenous people living in the Alice and environs, and the legacy of colonialism carried within them, and the legacy of the colonisers feeling a sense of responsibility to 'service' them. The numbers across the age ranges are roughly constant up to the mid-sixties, with an understandable drop after that, but still remaining constant within the natural context of attrition (leaving town to retire and/or completing 'life's contract'). As the age range span is constant, the service provision must reflect that consistency.

Table 3: Achieved Education Level.

Education Level (people 15 years and over)			
Level	LGA	SA3	IREG
Bachelor Degree level and above	4,248	4,811	158
Advanced Diploma and Diploma level	1,638	1,898	124
Certificate level IV	751	876	88
Certificate level III	2,456	2,966	247
Year 12	2,346	3,009	348
Year 11	1,160	1,547	279
Year 10	1,677	2,560	490
Certificate level II	16	47	8
Certificate level I	10	32	5
Year 9 or below	1,403	3,533	722
No educational attainment	171	566	132
Not stated	3,211	5,870	575

Source: QuickStats 2016 Census Australia Northern Territory. Alice Springs: Local Government Areas/Statistical Area Level 3/Indigenous Regions.

The attained education achieved, show strong numbers qualifying at the peak of their respective levels, i.e. High School Year 12 and Graduate status at university. These achievements, as with all levels included in Tale 3, do not necessarily imply that they were achieved within the Alice Springs education system. There would be a mixture of local and extra-local education experiences, since the nature of the Alice has been one of permanent and temporary presence of people. For instance, over its history, the Alice has been a transitory place for many non-Indigenous people. This is not to say that the quality of people who do dwell in the Alice is questioned as being of an insubstantial form, far from it, as it is the constant rejuvenating nature of fresh energies from new people that helps to maintain the attributes of the service environment carried on by the 'long stayers'. The combination of old and new people, although always carrying a degree of transition as service users and service providers in the same and adjacent service fields must adjust to new personalities, is valuable for service health and well-being. The levels of education achieved by all living there can, 'roughly', determine quality of services and quality of those who choose to utilise them in a settlement. 'Roughly', since the level of 'formal' education cannot solely judge one's ability, as other personal characteristics and opportunities for development/advancement come into play. However, in societal terms and restrictions, one's level of educational attainment is generally used to 'label' where one is in society, which in turn can make one act as if this label is fixed.

Table 4: Country of Birth.

Birth Country (top responses)			
Ancestry	LGA	SA3	IREG
Australia	15,930	25,862	2309
New Zealand	872	992	
United States of America	678	683	
England	665	731	
India	657	689	
Philippines	484	511	
Australian Aboriginal			1,631
English			657
Irish			239
Scottish			138

Source: *QuickStats 2016 Census Australia Northern Territory. Alice Springs: Local Government Areas/Statistical Area Level 3/Indigenous Regions.*

The Alice enjoys a rich multicultural presence far more than indicated in Table 4. Note that the ABS parameters in this case highlight 'top responses' of ten countries. In the ABS (2011) Census of Population and Housing, the Alice Springs part lists 40 counties of origin, which do not even include the Central Australian Indigenous language groups, who in a sense are 'micro' countries of origin. The point is the Alice deals with a multicultural heritage of differing exposure to the 'Australian' way(s) of life. Each country's people retain cultural and societal values that conflict and compromise with the benchmarked

Australian version. Benchmarked in the context of the reality of living in the designated space labelled Australian, and its attendant norms, values, customs, and expectations. Hence, services provided in the Alice are constructed within the Australian way of life, and the margins of adjustment of people from whatever origin background, Australia origin included, to be absorbed within some or all these service provisions, vary in intensity. Even though services offer a reasonably constant level of service framework, within necessary adjustments over time and employee variable characteristics, it is the cultural baggage of the service users that influence quality and acceptance levels of services. As indicated, one's country of origin would be a factor in this quality and acceptance, or countries of origin, as for example in the IREG, some Indigenous Australians retail a legacy of their own language group and English or Irish or Scottish.

Table 5: Labour Force.

Labour Force (15 years and over)			
Employment	LGA	SA3	IREG
Worked full-time	9,302	11,193	821
Worked part-time	2,537	3,177	239
Away from work	766	979	96
Unemployed	430	1,639	164
Not in the labour force			1,641

Source: QuickStats 2016 Census Australia Northern Territory. Alice Springs: Local Government Areas/Statistical Area Level 3/Indigenous Regions.

There is an expectation in society to be part of the labour force, to go along with the capitalist system of production. This 'forced' labour is partly to do with societal survival and maintaining profit for those owning businesses, and for non-owning business individuals to survive by raising money for food and shelter. Any individual 'profit' beyond the basics can be invested for the future or spent in pursuit of leisure and recreation, and other material assets beyond the shelter. If a settlement has a healthy economic environment with ample work opportunities, and people willing to take up these opportunities, only a certain range of service provision would be required, i.e. service types of the more welfare driven persuasion would be rare. However, the 'rare' scenario is not the case in Alice Springs, as to cope with the welfare difficulties faced by a sizable number within the Indigenous community, for example amongst the 1,641 people indicated in the IREG, there are many welfare related service providers. Some of these are not necessarily targeting just Indigenous support needs, as all cultural groupings can access these, but nonetheless a sizable demand for welfare services is present, so correspondingly there are a sizable number of welfare services. Fundamentally, the working and non-working levels of a settlement reflect and are reflected by service levels and their particular characteristics.

Table 6: Occupation.

Occupation (15 years and over)			
Occupation	LGA	SA3	IREG
Professionals	3,054	3.508	207
Community and Personal Service Workers	2,037	2,736	217
Clerical and Administrative Workers	1,778	2,000	213
Technicians and Trades Workers	1,548	1,791	118
Managers	1,520	1,856	105
Labourers	982	1,437	128
Sales Workers	880	1,010	71
Machinery Operators and Drivers	522	633	58

Source. *QuickStats 2016 Census Australia Northern Territory. Alice Springs: Local Government Areas/Statistical Area Level 3/Indigenous Regions.*

One's labelled occupation, source of revenue or means of support offers greater individual detail than to the blanket term of working full time or working part time. These latter are generalised overall figures of involvement in work, but do not state the type of work. Although all work involves partial commonality of regular hours, some repetitiveness, communication with others, deadlines to meet, and accountability, difference occurs from the original rational of why the type of occupation was created in the first instance. It is this rational that individualises the service on offer, and allows potential service users to recognise the existence of services they wish to engage with. Each of the occupations listed in Table 6, retain a quality of service provider. An interesting occupation to consider as a slight standout amongst the rest is Community and Personal Service Workers. This category includes the macro level of the Alice community as a whole, and also the micro of the individual. Experiencing services as a user and as a servicer can span across a general bureaucratic framework, right down to the intimacy of a one-to-one encounter. So, in a sense, all the other categories constructed by the ABS as 'occupation', can be thought to reside within the whole of community service provision right down to the individual person.

Ranges of occupations generally exist because of 'parent company' requirements. 'Parent' in this context is Industry and its paternal and maternal ABS categories. ABS categories in and of themselves are echoes and representations of the makeup of society, and a reductive quantifying process of classification. Reductive implies that the quality and context of what is being counted is discounted, probably due to lack of time the demographic may have available in answering ABS census questions, and policy makers afterwards processing them. Many policy makers have an influential accountant, i.e. limited economic budgets and pressures, hovering in their decision-making background, who may only wish to process 'simplistic' numbers, rather than investigate too deeply the detailed circumstances of what these numbers 'represent'. Nonetheless, within the context of these decisions, concerning Industry, is practical decisions regarding the level of settlement service provision within government policy considerations of a targeted settlement. Hopefully, a holistic consideration of the health and wellbeing of that settlement. Since government is heavily involved in creating service provision, an ironic side effect is the not insignificant presence of government administration. It is the largest employer in the Alice, and if taking into account that government funding supports health and education, and these employees are government workers, government employee numbers are even higher, probably to the point in which the survival of the Alice would be in jeopardy without government support. Perhaps the service of Government represents the servicing of society or is it vice versa!

Table 7: Industry of Employment.

Employment Industry (top responses; 15 years and over)			
Industry	LGA	SA3	IREG
State Government Administration	844	901	120
Hospitals (except Psychiatric Hospitals)	813	829	
Other Social Assistance Services	386		40
Accommodation	344	785	38
Primary Education	343	486	
Local Government Administration		563	48
General Practice Medical Services			61

Source. *QuickStats 2016 Census Australia Northern Territory. Alice Springs: Local Government Areas/Statistical Area Level 3/Indigenous Regions.*

The historical colonial to postcolonial contemporary legacies and number crunching of the LGA, SA3 and IREG in Alice Springs and environs, create a platform or reference point that its societal services work from, sustain, evolve, and dissolve. These contextualise the theme chapters within their service offerings. To help bind the society/service glue of mutual survivability/ functionality/necessity of purpose to this contextualisation, Bourdieuan considerations of how society is, is added to the mix.

.

Chapter Two

Brainstorming Bourdieu

Pierre Felix Bourdieu (1930-2002) was a distinguished French philosopher, anthropologist, sociologist, and public intellectual (Johnson, 2002). He engaged with several theoretical/practical concepts underscored within societal power undercurrents, highlighting particularly elusive and sundry performances, in which power has been sustained and passed on through generation after generation. This power sustainability is be a combination of conscious intention to maintain superior kinship status in society, as a long-term project, and everyday practice that becomes normalised and 'conventional' to maintain one's power position. As a result, one becomes part of the power hierarchy and acts accordingly, with the act naturalised and becoming unconscious within its consciousness. Hinting at consciousness and unconsciousness, Bourdieu draws upon both states of existence to accentuate the corporeal, bodily, physical, earthy nature of social life, emphasising the social dynamics of embodiment, soul, personification and practice.

Since Bourdieu's array of work is 'powered' by underlying forces of power which creates and recreates society in its own image, his main concepts (flagged in this chapter) are deemed appropriate to theorise how society is serviced. This is because the service industry that powers society and is an integral aspect and practice of society, is created in the image of societal power brokers, or the underlying forces of power. The structured and structuring system of society is sustained by long-term projects and day-to-day interaction and performance, depending upon who is/are 'running the show' and has the best 'feel for the game' of playing society. These structured/structuring and 'feel for the game' imageries are part of the Bordieuan space of concepts, indicating what will be looked at in this chapter, which incorporate the following concepts: Linguistic Inquiry, Field, Political Field, Powering the Symbolic, Culturing the Capital, and Habitus. Since these concepts are not mutually exclusive, theories, beliefs, and arguments may be repeated in more than one concept, but the 'difference', perhaps subtly, is in the particular concept context.

When utilising the works of eminent truth seekers, it would not be possible to incorporate the whole of the author's narrative within this book, as book word limits, and sanity of the readers have to be considered. For instance, there can be too much information offered, resulting in an information overload that can undervalue the focus of the book. Consequently, its purpose and meaning can be subsumed under a mass of detail and analyst, thus producing a self-defeating process and performance. Besides, narrative space must be made available for other authors to question and enhance the Bordieuan view, as well as myself extending these raised concepts beyond their currency, in the name of servicing society.

Linguistic Inquiry

For any society to function at a coherent 'uniform' level to sustain a 'like-minded' way of thinking, doing, and being, the agents or individuals, or agents as groups or institutions, within it, must speak the 'same' language. It is this language of similarity that grease the communication networks and flows of society allowing people to talk to each other to negotiate their everyday and long-term aspirations of business and leisure. Language and its inherent communication are how society moves, for silence would produce a society of static, and its eventual dislocation and demise. Although, silence can be used as a weapon of control and influence, for what is not said is often the heart of the matter, or truth of the matter, and its concealment ensures the least path of resistance to the aims of the unspoken agents representing power, or those agents who are the power. There is language and language in society, for some have linguistic prowess and ability for a clear and loud voice, but others do not, so language would have diverse volumes and status depending on who is speaking. It is a language of difference.

Bourdieu saw this difference partially concealed behind the surface veneer of apparent neutrality of communication exchange of mechanistic language. This 'neutral' language machine was theorised by de Saussure (1974) who ironically advocated that 'speech (is) the product of the language' (Bourdieu, 1990a, pp. 30-31). The irony is there in the pronouncement, i.e. of the position of speech in language. Regardless of if this position is questionable, the speech process retains an assumption of non-neutrality. For instance, if speech is the product of the language, which in a mechanical sense it is, language is formed as a static object of analysis. This results in a fragmentation between language (langue...self-sufficient system of signs) and its recognition in practice (parole/speech...situated realisation of the system by particular speakers). Thus, language is perceived as a logos (symbols, signs, emblems, insignia, designs), instead of a praxis (process by which a theory, lesson, or skill is enacted, embodied, or realised). As Bourdieu and Wacquant (1992, p. 142) note, the implication is that the speech act is lessened to the mere performance of a fixed model. Chomsky (1965) produced a similar division between 'competence' (knowledge of a 'possessed' language by an ideal speaker/hearer in a completely homogeneous speech community), and 'performance' (actual language use in concrete situations). Within this transaction environment, language does possess the speaker and listener in its limited tentacles of how to express situations and how to express the positionality of orator and receiver. Limited in terms of words cannot fully express of what is meant, and the receiver cannot comprehend fully what the speaker is saying, as they possess their own interpretive characteristics, and what is not said...kept silent.

Saussure states "in language, there are only differences" (1916, p. 118). However, since there are differences in how differences are perceived and practised, Saussure's differences in the context of language differs from those of Bourdieu. Saussure views an arbitrary connection between the signifier (*signifiant*) and signified (*signifié*). Thus, *langue* as opposed to *parole*, consists of a regulated set of differences in which each sign gains meaning first of all by virtue of a "negativity," that is, through its difference vis-à-vis all other signs within the system (Schinkela and Noordegraaf, 2011, p. 75). The difference is within the words used and their meanings, rather than why these particular selected words in the communication performance. Bourdieu (2001) regards langue and parole as part of the speech performance, and hence characterised by power. Bourdieu's apprehension to this type of distinction is that the linguist does not question this performance, which actually is the 'product of a complex set of social, historical, and political conditions of formation...the completely homogeneous language or speech community does not exist in reality: it is an idealisation of a particular set of linguistic practices which have emerged historically and have certain social conditions of existence' (Thompson (ed.), in Bourdieu, 1991, p. 5). Bourdieu (1991, p. 5) labels this, 'the illusion of linguistic communism'.

So, a key difference is that Saussure saw language as logos, instead of practice, whereas Bourdieu inverted that position. Thus, language is understood as a *praxis*, instead of a *logos* (Moraru (2016, p. 34), in which language use is replaced by linguistic practices. The former (logos) represents a stagnant, unanimous and uncritical appreciation of how language works. The latter (praxis) represents a sometimes biting/bitter, disputed, fluidity of word appreciation and depreciation. By comprehending language as a powerful instrument, Bourdieu (1991) voiced a diachronic (concerned with the way in which something, especially language, has developed and evolved through time) approach in preference to a synchronic (the simultaneous occurrence of events which appear significantly related but have no discernible causal connection) version. Power can take time to become established, perhaps over a number of generations, and social environments will heed or advance the process. Favourable environments for power advancement would be the preferred option for those seeking it, and since acquiring more power is proportional to acquiring more influence of how the social game is played, complete with writing the rules, the social environment would purposely become more favourable. Therefore, since 'power can hardly be seen as a purely local/synchronic concept' (Blommaert, 1999, p. 7), the production and dissemination of linguistic resources are connected to favourable historical time and social space generated power performances (see Moraru, 2016, p. 35). So, Bourdieu (1991) emphasises 'intrinsic historicity' (Blommaert, 1999, pp. 6-7).

The connectivity of practicing linguistics, their context production, and the power of history, is pulled together in Bourdieuan thought via the relational nature of things (relationism):

> against all forms of methodological monism that purport to assert the ontological priority of structure *or* agent, system *or* actor, the collective *or* the individual, Bourdieu affirms *the primacy of relations.* (Wacquant, 2014, p. 15)

Considering the process of creating power throughout history, and the re-ordering of society into social layers of privilege and not so privileged, the purification of language via the purification of thought would provide the upper classes a *de facto* monopoly of political power. When analysing this, Bourdieu draws upon Condillac's theory of the purification of thought, in the sense of 'purity' of thought determined by those wielding the power to influence society to their face of society. Promoting the 'official' language of this face to the eminence of the national language, an important component with forming the entity known as the nation-state, would advantage those already possessing this knowledge speak, further increasing their advantage. It would not be coincidental that linguistic unification be unified within this limited language form, as those obliged to learn it would become 'part of a political and linguistic unit in which their traditional competence was subordinated and devalued' (Bourdieu, 1991, p. 6). Limited in terms of those who become the 'students' of this language have restricted knowledge of why they are learning it. A restricted knowledge of the hidden agenda of why these chosen particular words and phrases, and restricting the knowledge of their own language by applying understanding and input to this dominant one.

The national official language, once learned though social and cultural normalisation processes, maintained and strengthened over time to achieve a level of acceptance without question, would permeate the communication systems of society. This would be at all levels, assuming society is regarded as a stratified system, as language construction would purport it to be, and through all types of interaction. Interactions such as, through the 'front line' service providers present in many of the significant settlements in society, interactions on a one-to-one or one-to-small group basis, and interactions through the main domains of society (government, industry, defence, education, and religion), talking to each other as well as to the general public or 'lay people'. Lay people is in the context of not possessing the professional 'expertise' of the agents of these domains to varying degrees of learning and experience. The legal profession is a classic example of language expertise differentiation. The distinction and status of those performing within the space of that specialised oratory is marked from those who are not, with ignorance of the law as no defence, an ironic limitation. An irony of expectation of learning law language without the luxury of years spent doing so, and being penalised for the impracticability of little or no time to do so. Although, one can pay for a law agent or law advocate to speak for them, if one can afford it, those in most need of law advocacy, due to legal illiteracy, often cannot afford to.

In terms of service provision, each service provider would have their own language system, though still based upon the dominant one, that the service users or layperson would have to negotiate through. An effective interaction for both parties would depend upon the aims of each in the encounter. For example, the user realising a sought for return that is favourable, and the provider 'servicing' the user from within the parameters of the service system in place. To achieve these aims, the system may retain degrees of flexibility and inflexibility in terms of its prepared performance of service. However, it would be the official language of the service provider, as a sub-language of the official language of society, but still very much attached to it, that would determine levels of flexibility. Sub-languages of the main dominant language, owe their existence to a long-term plan. As Bourdieu (1991) offers:

> The subsequent normalisation and inculcation of the official language and its legitimation as the official language of the nation-state was not just a matter of political policy: it was a gradual process that depended on a vanity of other factors, such as the development of the educational system and the formation of a unified labour market. (p. 6)

A capitalist economic system requires a compliant educational and employment system, the former *hopefully* leads onto the latter, hopefully in connection to economic survival and necessity caused by the system(s). It is a tautology of systems.

Within the levels of interaction, services included, language is the key to control and influence. If language is already controlled before interaction takes place, advantage is heavily skewed to the creators of the language and their paid agents. Also the user, in accepting this control, consciously and/or unconsciously, adds to that advantage. Thus:

> actual speakers are able to embed sentences or expressions in practical strategies which have numerous functions and which are tacitly adjusted to the relations of power between speakers and hearers. Their practical competence involves not only the capacity to produce grammatical utterances, but *also* the capacity to make oneself heard, believed, obeyed, and so on. Those who speak must ensure that they are entitled to speak in the circumstances, and those who listen must reckon that those who speak are worthy of attention. (Bourdieu, 1991, pp. 7-8)

Individuals within services who act as spokespersons, would not have authority to speak by themselves, unless they are of a rare type that commands attention and respect. It is the service institution that supplies them with authority to speak. This 'endows the speaker with the authority to carry out the act which his or her utterance claims to perform' (Bourdieu, 1991, p. 8). A Weberian 'legitimate order' (Bendix, 1977, p. 294) of acceptance to make services work.

Field

Language requires spaces to perform in: spaces of scale from the nation sovereign territory and beyond to interact with other nations' territories, through the spaces of services, right down to the 'basic' unit of one-to-one communication. This is not to say that all do not offer a sense of service, as part of the interaction. In a Bordieuan sagacity, these service places can be thought of as fields, or at least acting out their required actions within different fields of influence. For instance, fields, according to Bourdieu, are charted by configurations of relations of power between actors sharing commonality of interest or aim, but also involving competition between them over resources or in defining supply and need (Martin, 2003). Also, fields as a "terrain of contestation between occupants of positions differentially endowed with the resources necessary for gaining and safeguarding an ascendant position within that terrain" (Mustafa and Johnson 2008, p. 6). These positions and associated forces compose a "structure or a temporary state of power relations" (Mustafa and Johnson 2008, p. 6).

Field is a network, structure or set of relationships which may be intellectual, religious, educational, cultural, etc. (Navarro 2006, p. 18). People often experience power differently depending upon which field they are in at a given moment (Gaventa 2003, p. 6).

Spaces of scale can also be thought of as spaces of fields within the one field. For instance:

> Society as a whole forms a field, which is structured according to relations of domination. But society also contains a range of fields; it should be seen as the paramount field, from which other fields are never fully separated. The first task in the analysis of any field is to understand its location within the social formation. Fields will vary according to how much autonomy they acquire from the entirety of the social field. (Peillon, 1998, p. 215)

A service as with a field (which could be one and the same), retains varying degrees of independence from dominant forces in society (i.e. government and big business amongst others). It would have its own history, legacy, meticulous traditional/modern ways of performing and associated norms, beliefs and values, and 'groomed' agents to represent it who struggle to obtain a stake in it. Depending upon the extent of separation from the dominant overall societal field, will influence if the service or related field has influence beyond its place and space of production. To illustrate, if a service or field does achieve an autonomous level which is highly differentiated, characterised by acute boundaries, it will cease to have any impact on practice beyond that intensely controlled space (Peillon, 1998, p. 215). Bourdieu theoretically saw fields incorporating most attributes of social life and its competitive nature. Competitive characteristics and attendant rigid conditions of these 'social fields' are suggested by Rawolle (2005, p. 708), adopting a number of properties highlighted by Bourdieu (1993):

- are structured spaces of positions;

- have general laws or logics that guide interactions and the stakes towards which practices are oriented;

- contain social struggles for the stakes and the forms of capital valued and conversion rates between different forms of capital;

- require a socialised body endowed with a habitus [analogous to Searle's (1997) concept of Background] that orients the dispositions of agents to the stakes, and so to the continuation of that social field;

- are structured by a state of power relations at a given point in time;

- produce distinctive patterns of strategies adopted by different agents relative to their own position and trajectory;

- function analogous to a game.

Within the social world itself, including symbolic systems such as language or myths, exists objective structures independent of the consciousness and will of agents, capable of guiding and constraining their practices or their representations (Bourdieu, 1989, p. 14), who adds that social structures are what is called fields. This Bordieuan version of structuralism is correct in so far that agents are limited in terms of performance within that 'objectively' designed structure, but the owners of that structure or field subjectively constructed the designed structure. Hence, a type of post-structural objective independence, purposely perceived as objective by the agent users, but actually subjectively created to produce unseen or unrealised purposeful results. Also, perhaps unseen by the owners of the creation, as it is passed down through generations continuing this structuralism and becoming so accepted and normalised, that very few notice it had a starting point. This process is an ongoing constructivism, as Bourdieu also knew, constantly generating and regenerating itself:

> By con-structivism, I mean that there is a twofold social genesis, on the one hand of the schemes of perception, thought, and action which are constitutive of what I call habitus, and on the other hand of social structures, and particularly of what I call fields and of groups, notably those we ordinarily call social classes. (Bourdieu, 1989, p. 14)

Bourdieu's habitus and social classes will be engaged with later. Continuing with fields as a site of struggles/contestation, individuals seek to sustain or change the spread of capital forms particular to it. Bourdieu (1986) refers to four generic types of capital: economic capital, cultural capital, social capital, and symbolic capital. Within the resultant encounters performed and fought over at the site of struggles, these particular types of capital or resources are perceived to be valuable and differentially distributed within a field at a specific time (McDonough and Polzer (2012, p. 361). According to Bourdieu, people maximise their standings by accumulating and using these four different types of capital. When doing so, the value of capital is specific to the *field* within which individuals (or more precisely, individuals of the same class conditions) compete and manoeuvre (Cheng, 2012, p. 11). These said individuals retain commonality of essential assumptions:

> All participants must believe in the game they are playing, and in the value of what is at stake in the struggles they are waging. The very existence and persistence of the game or field presupposes a total and unconditional 'investment'. A practical and unquestioning belief, in the game and its stakes. (Bourdieu, 1991, p. 14)

The process and performance of this 'unconditional investment' has already been adhered to by those 'playing the game' of social life, reinforcing that Field is the termed used by Bourdieu to capture the rules of the game and to symbolise struggle and competition within different social spheres (Bourdieu & Wacquant, 1992, p. 18). Fields can be conceived of structured spaces that are organised around specific types of capital or combinations of capital (Swartz, 1997, p. 117). The agent unconditionality of the social environment, is an almost inevitability of how society has evolved, as an inbuilt unquestioning part of that evolvement. Bourdieu assumes a primary connectivity between interests and actions of agents, which is a sensible assumption, but also advocates that interests are not solely based upon economic incentive. There is more to it than that, as the social field can be described as:

> a multi-dimensional space of positions such that every actual position can be defined in terms of a multi-dimensional system of co-ordinates

whose values correspond to the values of the different pertinent variables. (Bourdieu, 1985, p. 724)

and the form taken, at every instance, in each social field, by the distribution sets of the different capitals (embodied or materialised) as instruments for the commandeering of the objectified product of accumulated social labour, defines:

> the state of the power relations, institutionalised in long-lasting social statuses, socially recognised or legally guaranteed, between social agents objectively defined by their position in these relations; it determines the actual or potential powers within the different fields and the chances of access to the specific profits that they offer. (Bourdieu, 1985, p. 725)

So, within the 'fixed' structure of the designed 'objective' field or service, resides an intense fluidity, of those scheming, hoping for, going along with, and innocently subjecting themselves to the game of service field agents. Knowledge of the position occupied in this space contains information as to the agents' intrinsic properties (their condition) and their relational properties (their position) (Bourdieu, 1985, p. 725).

Bourdieu (1990, p. 50) shows that relations between the players or agents utilises many functions to create this thing called economy. Economy being the only one normally recognised, or at least to the fore of rationality, for economism is how much monetary profit can be achieved. Economism acknowledges no other interests not produced by capitalism, via an abstracted real operation (Bourdieu, 1990, p. 113). An operation tuned to 'Callous cash payments' (Marx, 1848/1996) and biasing the construction of relatively autonomous fields who retain capacity of maintaining their own axiomatics (i.e. self-evident; goes without saying) through the fundamental tautology that 'business is business':

> It is as if economic calculation had been able to appropriate the territory objectively assigned to the remorseless logic of what Marx calls 'naked self-interest', only by relinquishing an island of the 'sacred', miraculously spared by the 'icy waters of egoistic calculation', the refuge of what has no price because it has too much or too little. (Bourdieu, 1990, p. 113)

However, Bourdieu maintains that practices retain other principles than conscious ends or mechanical causes, and follow an economic logic without following narrowly economic interests:

There is an economy of practices, a reason immanent in practices, whose 'origin' lies neither in the 'decisions' of reason understood as rational calculation nor in the determinations of mechanisms external to and superior to the agents. (Bourdieu, 1990, p. 50)

The practice in question tunes itself to the particular field or service logic it is immersed within, refining it to the lowest cost.

Therefore, a field is a 'particular social universe' defined by the 'stakes' ['*enjeux*'] for which social actors compete (Jackson, 2008, p. 166), who tasks Bourdieu's field composition by saying that it is a problematic theoretical construct, since there is lack of lucidity in nearly all of his many explanations of the concept. Perhaps the reason being resides within the character of fields and their lack of exactness, since the lack of lucidity maybe what fields are all about. If that is the case, Bourdieu's engagement with them is possibly a 'best fit' analysis, for it may not be feasible to achieve 'completeness' of field meanings and implications. Jackson (2008, p. 167) does concur, by admitting that there is evidently a certain amorphousness to the concept of the field, an imprecision worth accepting. This is hardly surprising, since a field is a network of objective relations between agent positions, but also defined by 'distribution of different currencies of power' and by a 'logic' that is a 'specific necessity' to the field and is 'irreducible to [the logics] that govern other fields' (Jackson, 2008, p. 166). Bourdieu (1987, p. 86) also view fields as a 'social world' that is 'constantly in the process of progressive differentiation' and also 'the sum of the structural constraints on the action of its members'. While fields are relatively autonomous, they are also constantly being shaped and re-shaped by internal struggles and by external developments in related fields.

Summing up and situating the field, the fluidity of Western European societies beyond the Middle Ages is regarded from a Bourdieuan perspective as differentiation of distinct fields, each retaining certain formations and blends of value and capital and specific institutions and institutional mechanisms (Bourdieu, 1991, p. 25). This diversity produced a distinct market economy of production and exchange, and a centralised state and legal system distancing from religious dogma and developing artistic and intellectual fields. These enjoy some connectivity with each other, being interwoven in multifaceted circumstances, and Bourdieu wishes to discover how they are connected and structured, but all the while not reducing one field to another, or regarding everything as if it were just a secondary effect or by-product of the economy (Bourdieu, 1991, p. 25). The connectivity and structure of the field:

i.e., the unequal distribution of capital is the source of the specific effects of capital, i.e., the appropriation of profits and the power to impose the laws of functioning of the field most favourable to capital and its reproduction. (Richardson, 1986, p. 19)

Political Field

Behind how fields work are agendas of power, seen and unseen, the latter perhaps more powerful than the former. These agendas of power are political in nature, and not just drawn from the definition of the party-political or state governmental. Politics is also belief based, in which principles, views, theories, and opinions are present and ensure fluidity and/or a sense of permanency in field craft. Field craft is the process and performance to sustain and work the field to particular means and ongoing ends. Categories of perception, the schemata of classification, bolster these means and ends. Essentially, the words and the names which construct social reality to achieve the pinnacle of political struggle, a struggle to enforce the legitimate principle of vision and division (i.e. 'theory effect') (Bourdieu, 1989, pp. 20-21). The effect and effectiveness of theory then becomes realised in practise, creating a hierarchy of agents immersed in the field service. Agents are both classified and classifiers, but they classify according to (or depending upon) their position within classifications (Bourdieu, 1987b, p. 2). To classify produces classes, producing differentiation of outlook, status and access to wealth, privilege, and power. To classify produces acceptance of those being classified for the classifiers. To classify, ensures the rules of the game in fields are set. To classify implies intentionality to artificially create societal fascination and acceptance of class and positional advantage, rather than question does class actually exist.

Bourdieu (1987b, p. 2) asks this question of 'do classes exist or do they not', which is a political question involving the very objectivity of the social world and the resultant social struggles, and speculates that:

> it is possible to deny the existence of classes as homogeneous sets of economically and socially differentiated individuals objectively constituted into groups, and to assert at the same time the existence of a space of differences (which is) based on a principle of economic and social differentiation. (Bourdieu, 1987b, p. 2) (Culturing the Capital section goes into detailed consideration of class 'existence')

It is advantageous for service providers within their fields of production, and also the state and government within society's field of production, to assume and reinforce the notion of class stratification and thus create a customer base of compliant users:

> an adequate theory of theoretical classes (and of their boundaries) leads one to pose that the political work aimed at producing classes in the form of objective institutions, at once expressed and constituted by permanent organs of representation, by symbols, acronyms and constituents, has its own specific logic, that of all symbolic production. Groups are not found ready-made in reality. And even when they

present themselves with this air of eternity that is the hallmark of naturalised history, they are always the product of a complex historical work of construction. (Bourdieu, 1987b, p. 8)

The political field is the space in which agents create their version of what the world is and through the process, recreate what the world is. Through this continuous game of field representation of world representation, agents also muster support of those who supply them with power (Thompson, editor's Introduction in Bourdieu, 1991, p. 26).

Accepting things, processes, individuals, groups, fields, and services at face value, does not allow for a critical engagement of why these are as they are. This is not to say that engaging critically provides all the answers, but one's awareness levels would be raised for whom or what one is interacting with, providing greater insight as to where they are coming from. An inference of Bourdieu's methodology is that an adequate analysis of political discourse should be underscored by a systematic reconstruction of the field where it is constructed and received, including its particular organisations, production, and perception, and how it relates to the wider space of the social (Thompson, editor's Introduction in Bourdieu, 1991, p. 28). Although acquiring an awareness may be helpful in one respect of providing an informed choice of whether to enter the field or not, and what to expect from it, in another respect there is an hierarchal structure in place which limits decision making and courses of action. Only those who can mobilise the relevant resources retain capacity to partake in the struggles defining a field (Peillon, 1998, p. 216). Bourdieu conceptualises these resources as capital, and the position an agent retains in a field is influenced by the brand and capacity of capital he and she operate within. The four types of capital introduced in the Field section are succinctly defined (Peillon, 1998, p. 216):

- economic capital, which corresponds to material wealth.

- cultural capital, which covers educational credentials and cultural goods.

- symbolic capital, the form taken by all types of capital when their possession is perceived as legitimate.

- social capital, which refers to the mobilisation of people through connections, social networks, and group membership.

In Bourdieuan understanding, social capital is 'the sum of the actual and potential resources that can be mobilized through membership in social networks of actors and organizations' (Anheier, Gerhards & Romo, 1995, p. 862).

From Bourdieu's interconvertibility theory, capital types interact and can be exchanged for one another and every type retains elements of the others (Casey, 2005, p. 1). Extending these 'capitals' to the political realm, Casey (2005, p. 1) continues, political capital is an amalgamation of capital types, combined for specific political markets. However, defining political capital can be problematic, since people are left to figure out their own meaning of it influenced by politician or journalistic usage (Suellentrop, 2004; Kennicott, 2004). Perhaps that is the hidden purpose behind the fluid definition, so the general public do not perceive too much realisation of political manipulation of their thoughts. Bourdieu sees political capital as a variation of social capital and "the source for observable differences in patterns of consumption and lifestyles" (Bourdieu, 2002, p. 16). Political capital is arguably the most imposing type of capital, and the markets of political capital are repeatedly connected with control over and among actors, especially coercive power of any institution (Casey, 2005, pp. 6-7). It is the politics of 'market demand that shapes capital formation' (Casey, 2005, p. 1). Conversely, political capital may not be the most imposing type of capital, since many capital types are associated with economic capital, which is why economic capital dominates capital studies, demoting all other forms to "disinterested" states (Bourdieu, 1986, p. 242).

The brand or brands and capacity an agent holds, provides tools of political action since agents, who retain membership of the social world, as we all do within varying degrees of influence and power, retain knowledge of this world and consequently can act on the social world. The action creates and imposes mental, verbal, visual or theatrical representations of the social world, to make or unmake groups by producing, reproducing or destroying the representations that make groups visible for others and themselves (Bourdieu, 1991, p. 127). The 'Culturing the Capital' section engages in further detail of Bourdieu's capital. Agents in the field environment, who advocate on behalf of the field's raison d'être, can be regarded as working within a professional role, as the concept of field is utilised as a replacement for the concept of professional (Schinkel and Noordegraaf, 2011, p. 72). The concept of profession is 'dangerous' as it creates an 'appearance of neutrality' (Bourdieu and Wacquant 1992, p. 242):

> Profession" is a folk concept which has been uncritically smuggled into scientific language and which imports into it a whole social unconscious. It is the *social product* of a historical work of construction of a group and of a *representation* of groups that has surreptitiously slipped into the science of this group. (Bourdieu and Wacquant 1992, pp. 242–243)

Within the rhetoric of the professional political agent, the political field offers a universe of political possibilities, but is limited in practice. Limited, as

Bourdieu (1979, p. 460) points out, by those agents expressing their political views as working from an established political environment, an environment already possessed with an inbuilt agenda of how things are or should be. This causes a silent, closure effect of what can be politically engaged with, and what politically cannot be engaged with, as the latter has already been 'dealt' with behind public persona. Political wheels within political wheels, leading to:

> suspicion of the political 'stage', a 'theatre' whose rules are not understood and which leaves ordinary taste with a sense of helplessness, is often the source of 'apathy' and of a generalized distrust of all forms of speech and spokesmen. (Bourdieu, 1979, pp. 464-465)

Eventually, what is invested in a social field, political field included, is styled by Bourdieu as doxa (Schinkel and Noordegraaf, 2011, p. 78). The presuppositions of a field are stipulated by doxa (Bourdieu, 1990a, p. 66), which defines a field (Bourdieu, 1997a, p. 22). Fields require a 'quasi-bodily' lived experience, and field doxa delivers this taken-for-grantedness of a shared common-sense world (Bourdieu, 1990a, p. 68). Fields also have to be taken seriously, in terms of the illusion of a social game is important (Bourdieu, 1994, p. 151). The functionality of a social field gains credibility through doxa and illusion, nurturing belief in the fundamental classifications of this field, and the belief of struggle over these basic classifications (Schinkel and Noordegraaf, 2011 p. 79).

Politics begins with the condemnation of the silent, hence unspoken contract of adherence to the established order that defines the original doxa, therefore, political subversion presupposes cognitive subversion, a conversion of the vision of the world (Bourdieu, 1991, pp. 127-128). Within the process of political subversion, the struggles and tensions between orthodoxy (convention, custom, accepted views, prevailing attitudes) and heterodoxy (dissent, deviation, sacrilege) occurring within the political field, hides oppositions between the set of political propositions taken as a whole (including both orthodox or heterodox) (Bourdieu, 1991, p. 132). The hidden aspect is:

> beyond the reach of discourse and which, relegated to the state of doxa, is accepted tacitly without discussion or examination by the very people who confront one another at the level of declared political choices. (Bourdieu, 1991, p. 132)

Essentially, Bourdieu's political field is ordered around access to capital which is expressly political. Occasionally this field is shown as a market offering diverse political products (Peillon, 1998, p. 217):

> the political field is the site where political products, issues, programmes, analyses, commentaries, concepts, events, are generated in the competition between the agents who are engaged in it, and between which ordinary citizens, now reduced to the status of "consumers", must choose'. (Bourdieu in Accardo and Corcuff, 1986, p. 123)

and the proper political power of *government* which, however dependent it may be on economic and social forces, can have a real impact on these forces via its control over the instruments of the administration of things and persons (Bourdieu, 1991, p. 182).

Services retain capacity for 'proper political power' within their own governance political field structures, and it is these structures that dictate the shape, form and progression and or intentional static-ness of fields. When entering these service fields, political activity occurs among three societal actors or agents: individuals, groups, and institutions (Casey, 2005, p. 8).Though :

> what prompts, engenders or negates political action among actors however, can differ greatly among actors. This alternately affects the creation and content of political capital, as well as potentially determining its purpose. (Casey, 2005, p. 8)

so it is important to be aware of the political field in the workings of services, for the rationality of the service lies within that 'worked' process.

Powering the Symbolic

> In the reality of the social world, there are no more clear-cut boundaries, no more absolute breaks, than there are in the physical world. (Bourdieu, 1987b, p. 13)

If there are no clear-cut boundaries in the social of the world, in relation to its 'natural' state, the implication is of fanciful, artificial boundary creation: boundary or boundaries that create difference. It is a purposeful endeavour to produce ownership over the workings of society, i.e. the power to control and have the power to control. It would be in the interest of those who regard themselves as having the means and ways to 'run the societal show' to separate themselves from the rest, be that in a way not too noticeable in practice. The goal is to manipulate their revelation of the social world, and the disunion that drives the process, into the official revelation, into *nomos*, the official principle of vision and division (Bourdieu, 1987b, p. 13). Who holds the power to nominate how society is, originates from the state, although it is not as clear cut as that. For example, post-state corporations and powerful states can influence how other state societies should function, i.e. a state's 'expected' behavioural patterns, pressured by money, military, and resources. Fields also within the state can enjoy some autonomy from the state, but ultimately depends upon it to legitimate themselves. The implication is that the state is also 'legitimate', resulting in the monopoly over legitimate symbolic violence:

> Symbolic violence is, fundamentally, the imposition of categories of thought and perception on the prevailing social agents. This is the incorporation of unconscious structures that tend to perpetuate the action structures of dominators. Symbolic violence is in some ways, more powerful than physical violence, since it is incorporated even in modes of action and knowledge structures of individuals, and imposes the legitimacy spectrum of social order. (Nicolaescu, 2010, p. 6)

What is fundamental about symbolic violence and the struggle for control is the legitimacy of the process and of its divisions, e.g. symbolic power as 'worldmaking power' (Goodman, 1978). This is the power to impose and to inculcate principles of construction of reality, and particularly to preserve or transform established principles of union and separation (Bourdieu, 1987b, p. 13). Preserving and transforming within political symbolic systems, act as structured and structuring instruments of communication (Bourdieu, 1991, p. 167), implying that this process is already structured to particular means and ends and has ability of structuring others to its structure. Bourdieu (1991, p. 167) adds that the instruments of construction or destruction (depending upon the ability of individuals to recognise these as one and/or the other), safeguards that one class dominates another (symbolic violence) by drawing from their own distinctive power to pressure power relations that underscore them, and adding to the 'domestication of the dominated' (Weber, 1985). Symbolic systems owe their distinctive power to the fact that the relations of power expressed through them are manifested only in the misrecognised form of relations of meaning (displacement) (Bourdieu, 1991, p. 168). Although, some agents can see through the misrecognition, both as service providers and users. This may make some of the providers advocate more for their 'masters' and may make some service users smarter in how they negotiate with required services.

Symbolic systems enjoy a layered representation. Layered in terms of below the surface and as the surface. In the context of fields/services, the surface is the overt persona, visible to all and utilised and appropriated by the group as a whole. It enjoys a sense of respectability and acceptance as a familiar and normalised aspect and member of societal everydayness. Everydayness defined as perceived unquestionable nature, as how things are and 'should' be. Below the surface of the surface mechanics of the field/services is where the reality of the process resides. Namely the process produced by a body of specialists and rigorously run by a relatively autonomous field of circulation and production (Bourdieu, 1991, p. 168). Symbolic power does not:

> reside in 'symbolic systems' in the form of an 'illocutionary force' but that it is defined in and through a given relation between those who exercise power and those who submit to it, i.e. in the very structure of the field in which *belief* is produced and reproduced. (Bourdieu, 1991, p. 170)

Bourdieu (1991, p. 170) continues, belief allows transformation to take place, in which the laws of transformation administer the metamorphosis of the diverse capitals into symbolic capital, specially the work of euphemisation (dissimulation and transfiguration). This process retains a real:

> transubstantiation of the relations of power by rendering recognisable and misrecognisable the violence they objectively contain and thus by transforming them into symbolic power, capable of producing real effects without any apparent expenditure of energy. (Gramsci, 1978, p. 197)

If people do not know they are being manipulated, they are manipulated without resistance, and unwittingly and wittingly assist the process.

'In Hobbes' view', writes Durkheim (1960, p. 136), 'the social order is generated by an act of will and sustained by an act of will that must be constantly renewed'. The overt/covert aspect of the social order is through symbolic violence, which is the 'strong arm' of the sustainable will, the paradoxical 'strong arm' within its subtle application. However, if it is correct that symbolic violence is the gentle, disguised form which violence takes when overt violence is impractical, it can start to lose its potency and euphemistic effectiveness, when misrecognition dissolves into recognition (Bourdieu, 1990a, p. 133). Regardless of the stage of misrecognition to recognition experienced by society or a field/service, constructed difference or distinction is imbedded within the field or the very structure of the social space, when perceived through categories adapted to that structure (Bourdieu, 1985, p. 731).

Culturing the Capital

Bourdieu's broad focus centres on 'how individuals' routine practices are influenced by the external structure of their social world and how these practices, in turn, contribute to the maintenance of that structure (Cockerham, Rutten & Abel, 1997; Jenkins, 2002). Utilising culture as underwriting Bordieuan theory within this context, advocates a thorough perspective that integrates cultural processes of social differentiation into the broader systems of unequal distribution of life chances (Abel, 2007, p. 43). Life chances in capital is unconditionally crucial 'to account for the structure and functioning of the social world..., capital in all its forms and not solely in the one form recognised by economic theory' (Bourdieu, 1986b, p. 242). From this theory, capital incorporates both material and non-material resources that determine an actor's freedom of action and his or her chances for profit in a particular social field (Schwingel, 2003, p. 83). The actor or agent works within a relational space and calculated against three axes or dimensions (Atkinson, 2010, p. 2):

> the overall amount of capital that the individual holds—including *economic* capital (wealth and property), *cultural* capital (signifiers of cultural competencies such as owned artworks or educational qualifications), and finally *social* capital (resources based on personal networks and associations with certain names or titles); the composition of their capital (i.e., whether it is predominantly economic or cultural); and the individual's trajectory through social space over time as his or her volume and composition of capital evolves. (Bourdieu 1984, p. 114)

Orthodox economists generally stress economic and monetary forms of capital, but they also include human capital relating to the skill and educational traits of labour (Bauder, 2008, p. 317). Some other capitals are estate capital, associated with landholdings (Marx and Engels, 1953, p. 51) and variable capital, referring to labour (Marx and Engels, 1867, pp. 223-224). Bourdieu (1984; 1986) and Bourdieu and Passeron (1977) sanctioned capital's multidimensional disposition by recognising various 'species of capital', such as political, military, scientific, technical, symbolic (Bourdieu, 1977) and cultural capital. Cultural capital is further subdivided into objectified, embodied, and institutionalised (Bourdieu, 1986, note 14). The objectified focusses on the form of cultural goods (pictures, books, dictionaries, instruments, machines...), the embodied in the form of long-lasting dispositions of the mind and body, and institutionalised, conferring original properties on the cultural capital it presumably guarantees (Bourdieu, 1986). With institutional, cultural capital includes adaptive cultural and social competences that enjoy familiarity with the institution, its processes and expectations, possession of relevant intellectual and social skills (e.g. 'cultural knowledge and 'vocabulary'), and greater 'strategic conception of agency' (Lareau and Weininger, 2003, cited in Edgerton and Roberts (2014, p. 4). Lareau and Weininger (2003) regard technical and social behavioural skills as synergistical elements of cultural capital, influencing individual capability to conform with prevailing evaluative requirements. Developing the capital meaning and implications from its purely monetary form to incorporate the social and the cultural, allows for an integrated perspective of society and production processes (Gibson-Graham, 1996). Marx viewed capital primarily as a 'means of exploitation and domination' (Marx, 1867b, note 13, p. 794). Bourdieu instead emphasised the role of capital in the reproduction of society (1984, note 14, p. 2).

Reproducing society is a constantly rejuvenating generational process, to maintain the so-called class distinctions in society. So-called, because Bourdieu's comprehension of class involved aspects diverse from the traditional Marxist marked and structural boundaries that distinguished different groups and individuals. Bourdieu's interpretation of class is not the rigid Marxist boundary between social groups, but more about those in neighbouring positions within social space enjoying comparable 'conditions of existence' reflected by capital assets, thus generating analogous habitus (Atkinson, 2010, p. 3) (Habitus is the next section). 'Conditions of existence' is implied by Bourdieu as agents' relative space from material necessity and the consequences this causes, with those in the lower levels of society holding less capital and exposed more to social demands and urgencies (Atkinson, 2010, p. 3). Each class condition is defined, simultaneously, by its intrinsic properties and by the relational properties which it derives from its position in the system of class conditions, which is also a system of differences, e.g. differential positions, i.e., by everything which distinguishes it from what it is not and especially from everything it is opposed to (Bourdieu, 1979, pp. 171-172). The 'individual' habitus of 'same' class members amalgamate in an association of homology, meaning differentiation within homogeneity characteristic of their social conditions of production (Atkinson, 2010, p. 6):

> No two members of the same class will have had the same experiences in the same order, but it is certain that each member of the same class is more likely than any member of another class to have been confronted with the situations most frequent for members of that class, and so while the habitus brings about a unique integration of experience it remains an integration of the experiences statistically common to members of the same class. (Bourdieu 1990a, p. 60)

and are conveniently imagined (constructed) to maintain certain means and ends.

This comprehension includes class structure as a multidimensional social space, accentuating consumption, seen as an environment of social life in which economic and cultural capital possession can be 'theatrically' shown, and its persistent emphasis on the symbolic dimension of practices, identified as the vital conduit between structural proximity, on the one side, and co-membership in a social class (or fraction), on the other (Weininger, 2002, p. 151). For instance, the 'Traditional Working-Class Milieu' is marked by unskilled and skilled labour, physical work and scarcity, perception of distancing from those in power, and simultaneously valuing close relationships with friends, neighbours, and colleagues (Vester, 2005, p. 84). When regarding Bourdieu's social space, this milieu is bestowed with low levels of economic and cultural capital, contrasting this is the 'Liberal-Intellectual Milieu', which has high levels of economic and cultural capital (Ambrasat, von Scheve, Schauenburg, Conrad and Schreoder, 2016, p. 4). This latter milieu enjoys cultural distinct practices, high intellectual standards, and self-appraises as an enlightened vanguard, responsible for the universalistic values of justice, peace, and democracy (Vester 2005, p. 81).

Universal values depend upon whose values of justice, peace, and democracy. In a given social universe, where these universal values perform, the powers or forms of capital compete to appropriate sparse goods, and the structure of this space is provided by the distribution of the various capitals, capitals capable of conferring strength, power, and consequently profit on their holder (Bourdieu, 1987b, p. 4). It is this holder and those like him/her who retain similar levels of strength, power, and profitable gain, that advocate the values of justice, peace, and democracy. The ways these values are understood, maintains the power characteristic in the hands of these holders, or elite 'class'. However, there is disagreement that cultural capital does provide full influence in the processes through which relationships of class inequality are organised and reproduced (Bennett and Silva, 2006, p. 88). There has been:

> considerable modification in the context of debates centred on, first, the different forms that cultural capital takes, and, second, on the need for its analysis to take into account how it operates in the context of relations of race and ethnicity, which Bourdieu paid little attention to, as well as the intersections of class and gender which, although never entirely neglected by Bourdieu (see Bourdieu, 2001; Adkins and Skeggs, 2004; Silva, 2005) were never adequately theorised either. (Bennett and Silva, 2006, p. 89)

No social theory by one person can cover 'all the bases', indeed it is difficult for a whole cohort of social theorists to construct social completion within its ever evolving incomplete form. So, Bourdieu is fallible, like the rest of us!

The majority of properties of cultural capital, in its elemental form, connects to the body and presumes embodiment (Bourdieu, 1986). Bourdieu indicates that members of an elite social group may signify their status through embodied cultural capital by understated 'gestures or the apparently most insignificant techniques of the body—ways of walking or blowing one's nose, ways of eating or talking' (1984, p. 466). Consequently, those who do not possess the code to read or enact these cultural performances, lack access to important symbols of status (Bauder, 2008, p. 318). The social practice and social reproduction of such symbols and meanings, allows the upper classes to execute their dominant culture through cyclical reproduction (Lin, 2001, p. 14). Symbolic capital closely relates to cultural capital and is a product of domination. According to Bourdieu, it legitimises domination through social ranking or distinction, allowing symbolic systems to "fulfil a political function"

(Swartz 1997, p. 83). Within the political/social, the embodied cultivation of cultural capital can be attained by, fluctuating magnitudes, influenced by the period, the society, and the social class, in the lack of any deliberate inculcation, and hence unconsciously (Bourdieu, 1986). It is the unconscious that makes cultural capital so effective, so potent, and 'blind's the 'illiterate' masses to its purpose of power and control. It is illiterate in the sense of an uneducated unawareness of how culture differentiates and brings 'together', or at least appears to bring together. For how can there be dissent, if people think they are together. The unconscious consequence is:

> any given cultural competence (e.g., being able to read in a world of illiterates) derives a scarcity value from its position in the distribution of cultural capital and yields profits of distinction for its owner…the transmission of cultural capital is no doubt the best hidden form of hereditary transmission of capital, and it therefore receives proportionately greater weight in the system of reproduction strategies, as the direct, visible forms of transmission tend to be more strongly censored and controlled. (Bourdieu, 1986b, pp. 18-19)

The symbolic wealth of the scarcity value appears to be the undivided property of the whole society, assessible to all on the basis of individual ability and effort, but social origins shape its appropriation (Bourdieu, 1973, p. 73).

So cultural capital from an objectified perspective, bestows itself as an autonomous, coherent universe, an historical product having its own laws, rising above individual wills and remaining irreducible to that which agents, or even the aggregate of agents, can acquire (Bourdieu, 1986b, p. 20). However, it is important to acknowledge that cultural capital:

> exists as symbolically and materially active, effective capital only insofar as it is appropriated by agents and implemented and invested as a weapon and a stake. (Bourdieu, 1986b, p. 20)

Symbolic capital is nothing other than economic or cultural capital when it is known and recognised. Since, when it is known through the categories of perception that it imposes, symbolic relations of power tend to reproduce and to reinforce the power relations that constitute the structure of social space (Bourdieu, 1989, p. 21). Also, it is important to acknowledge that social world legitimation results from agents applying to the objective structures of the social world, structures of perception and appreciation, which are issued out of these very structures and which tend to picture the world as evident (Bourdieu, 1989, p. 21). The world as evident reduces the social space to one dimension, but paradoxically creating a two-dimension space of those that 'set the pace and those who follow' in cultural appropriation. From this:

it is clear that the exchange rate of the different kinds of capital is one of the fundamental stakes in the struggles between class fractions whose power and privileges are linked to one or the other of these types. In particular, this exchange rate is a stake in the struggle over the dominant principle of domination (economic capital, cultural capital or social capital), which goes on at all times between the different fractions of the dominant class. (Bourdieu, 1979, p. 125)

So, it is not only a two-dimensional space of class distinction, but also two or more-dimensional spaces of the dominant class. Service providers and service users operate within this capital environment. Their performance is influenced and monitored (self-monitoring and social monitoring by the wider service community (individuals, groups and institutions)), by how capital works within its many forms and its very presence.

Habitus

Bourdieu's notions of field, capital, *and* habitus arguably is the eminent noteworthy and fruitful observation to comprehend relations between objective social structures (institutions, discourses, fields, ideologies) and everyday practices (what people do, and why they do it) (Webb, Schirato and Allen, 2002, p. 1). Habitus is defined as:

> systems of durable, transposable dispositions, structures predisposed to operate as structuring structures, that is, as principles which generate and organise practices and representations that can be objectively adapted to their outcomes without presupposing a conscious aiming at ends or an express mastery of the operations necessary in order to attain them. (Bourdieu and Passeron, 1990, p. 52)

Objective social conditions are connected by habitus to people's behaviours and is often expressed in particular lifestyles, including health lifestyles (Cockerham, Rutten & Abel, 1997). Habitus is central to the interface between the individual and its socially structured environment, and thus is key to explaining social inequality, its dynamics, and reproductive arrangements (Abel, 2007, p. 49).

Habitus can be intimately associated to the psychological structuralism offered by Piaget (1970), in which cognitive structures and the assimilation and accommodation of knowledge from the social environment play a crucial role (Lizardo, 2004). Piaget's action schemes and logical schemas can reflect habitus as a 'structured' and 'structuring' (i.e. generative) structure (Lizardo, 2004, p. 386f). Habitus is more than cognitive, extending to the biopsychosocial, since the operational principles of the habitus is present at assorted tiers of the individual, from brains (e.g., neurophysiological processes, patterns of feeling and thinking) to minds (e.g., cultural scripts, individual strategies) as well as in social and symbolic systems (e.g., social institutions and representations) (Pickel 2005, p. 442). Habitus is mutually a system of schemes of production of practices and a system of perception and appreciation of practices, implying a sense of one's place, but also a sense of the place of others (Bourdieu, 1989, p. 19). To maintain dual systems of practice production and perception and appreciation of practice, the habitus does not operate at the level of the conscious (Atkinson, 2010, p. 4), but instead functions 'below the level of consciousness and language, beyond the reach of introspective scrutiny or control by the will (Bourdieu, 1984, p. 466). This 'unchosen principle of all choices' (Bourdieu, 1990a, p. 61), accommodating action and practices is based:

> not on consciousness or intentional aims but on the dispositions and inclinations built out of a practical, prereflective, corporeal sense of limits and realistic possibilities, leading agents, as captured in the phrase "that's not for the likes of us," to refuse what they are refused in reality anyway. (Bourdieu 1977:77)

So, habitus is not an automatic and unfeeling conversion of objective structures into action, but a generative and innovative capacity for thought and action within boundaries (Bourdieu and Wacquant, 1992, p. 122). The inclination of habitus is to realise intuitive 'lines of action' or strategies inciting the utmost profit of agents, both economic and symbolic (Bourdieu, 1990a, p. 16; 2000a, p. 55; Bourdieu and Wacquant, 1992, p. 25). By virtue of the habitus, individuals are already predisposed to act in certain ways, pursue certain goals, avow certain tastes (Bourdieu, 1991, p. 17). Individuals carry with them cultural baggage or histories that are present in the habitus, which implies their performance can never be fully measured as the result of conscious calculation. Instead, practices are the product of encounters between a habitus and a field enjoying a sense of harmony with each other (Bourdieu, 1991, p. 17), who continues by noting that if the harmony is not present, an individual may not know how to act, and be literally lost for words. The habitus, a product of history:

> produces individual and collective practices, more history, in accordance with the schemes generated by history. It ensures the active presence of past experiences, which, deposited in each organism in the form of schemes of perception, thought and action, tend to guarantee the 'correctness' of practices and their constancy over time, more reliably than all formal rules and explicit norms. (Bourdieu, 1990a, p. 54)

The subconsciousness of the habitus is formed through bodily learning process, in which the limits and regularities of the world are engraved into the habitus as a practical, nonconscious appraisal of what goods, practices, and assumptions are reachable (the 'feel for the game') (Atkinson, 2010, p. 3). 'Learn bodily' (Bourdieu, 2000a, p. 141), through the necessities of family and domestic performance (Bourdieu, 1977, p. 78), acquired mostly in childhood, contributes to the habitus through 'silent censures' (Bourdieu, 2000a, p. 167) and explicit and implicit training/instruction/teaching, which frequently indoctrinate their efforts via corporeal suffering and primitive/intuitive emotion (Bourdieu, 2000a, p. 141). Also, through subconscious types of mimesis (imitative representation of the real world in art and literature), and 'sheer familiarisation, in which the learner insensibly and unconsciously acquires the principles of an art and an art of living' (Bourdieu, 1990a, p. 74). As the habitus 'habit' is generally absorbed in childhood, this does not imply inflexibility concerning its evolving potential within the individual, since habitus is an open system of dispositions continually exposed to fresh environments beyond the 'childhood' phase (Atkinson, 2010, p. 3). It is:

> endlessly transformed through a dialectic with its environment. (Bourdieu 1990b, p. 116)

Conversely:

> agents are statistically bound to encounter similar, reinforcing situations as a result of their objective social conditions of existence. (Bourdieu and Wacquant 1992, p. 133)

however, since the habitus and childhood enjoy intimacy, and the habitus is the filtered prism allowing through new experiences, it is extremely robust (Atkinson, 2010, p. 4).

Attacking the unconsciousness of habitus as a 'non-voluntary voluntary' way of visualising performance and producing the resultant practice, as not considering alternative ways of arriving at a decision and acting accordingly, Alexander (1995, p. 144) sees Bourdieu as offering an unfinished 'sociologised biologism'. This overlooks the subjectivities and complexities that the 'self' infers, removing the connotation of motive (Alexander, 1995, p. 139), removing intentionality and reflexivity from social life (p. 146) and eliminating a 'thinking, feeling self' (McLennan, 1998, p. 139). Also, pinpointing the superiority of the bodily, limits conscious activity to an 'epiphenomenon, almost an *effect*, of the body' (Jenkins, 2002, p. 93), which denies the 'life of the mind' (Reay, 2004, p. 437; Sayer, 2005, p. 29). Questioning the habitus concept because of its seeming 'vagueness' (DiMaggio, 1979; Jenkins, 1992), encourages the implausibility of its role in the reproduction of culture and social structure (Goldthrorpe, 2007). Therefore, habitus, considered from Bourdieu's original comprehension and perhaps beyond, appears exceedingly difficult to operationalise when adopting standard measurements, not least because of its tight coupling to social practices (Ambrasat et al, 2016, p. 2).

Perhaps that is the point with habitus, in that it is not confined to standardised measurement schematics. To look, to really look, at the practiced interactions and relationships between an actor and their encountered field:

> one has to escape from the realism of the structure, to which objectivism, a necessary stage in breaking with primary experience and constructing the objective relationships, necessarily leads when it hypostatises these relations by treating them as realities already constituted outside of the history of the group without falling back into subjectivism, which is quite incapable of giving an account of the necessity of the social world. To do this, one has to return to practice, the site of the dialectic of the opus operatum and the modus operandi; of the objectified products and the incorporated products of historical practice; of structures and habitus. (Bourdieu, 1990a, p. 52)

Crossley (2001) acknowledges that Bourdieu does accept that there is conscious or 'rational' action, but questions that he views it as an exception, separate from the habitus, only appearing in times of crisis when the habitus is ineffective (see, e.g., Bourdieu 1990b, p. 108; 2000a, p. 64). However, Bourdieu's entire blueprint is a position of ontological or causal realism, believing that objective structures exist, but also our comprehension of these structures and orientation toward them is filtered through our habitus (Jackson, 2008, p. 164). The concept of the habitus enables a 'matching of the subjective and the objective, what we feel spontaneously disposed to do and what our social conditions demand of us' (Eagleton, 1990, p. 157). Thus, there is a fundamental mechanism to reproduce political, social, and economic structures in society (Jackson, 2008, p. 165).

In searching for ground between the subjective and objective filtered impression of the social world, and indeed the world, and beyond, as is and of itself, Bourdieu denies the mystical/divine ego of phenomenology. Agents do retain an energetic concern of the world, constructing their vision of the world, but this construction is carried out under structural constrictions (Bourdieu, 1989, p. 18). When carrying out the constricting construction, the familiar world tends to be 'taken for granted', as natural, and as a 'natural' perception:

> If the social world tends to be perceived as evident and to be grasped, to use Husserl's (1983) expression, in a doxic modality, this is because the dispositions of agents, their habitus, that is, the mental structures through which they apprehend the social world, are essentially the product of the internalisation of the structures of that world. (Bourdieu, 1989, p. 18)

Agents see the world as natural, and 'naturalise' it without too much critical questioning more easily than one may assume, especially when filtered through the agenda of a dominant.

Realising one's individuality and practicing it, implies that identity theory shares various assumptions with recent cognitive reinterpretations of the habitus, and assist with connecting stratification and lifestyles (Ambrasat, 2016, p. 7). With identity theory, making meaning is pivotal to identity and behaviour with things and identity carrying specific meanings, while habitus incorporates the bodily, affective, and cognitive spaces that produce meaning generally non-reflectively (i.e. aesthetics and taste) (Ambrasat, 2016, p. 7).

Bourdieu (1984) views habitus creating/reflecting social differentiation, i.e. social class. Differences between individual habitus resides in the singularity of their social trajectories, to which there correspond series of chronologically ordered determinations (resolve, willpower, grit) that are mutually irreducible to one another (Bourdieu (1990a, p. 60). Hence, '[j]ust as no two individual histories are identical so no two individual habituses are identical' (Bourdieu, 1990c, p. 46). From this 'individual' habitus difference or division, evolves group mentalities of loose and tight dispositions, so creating habitus as 'the product of internalisation of the division into social classes' (Gieseking, 2014, p. 139). So, the habitus, echoing the introduced class concept within the Culturing the Capital section:

> animates the action of collective social actors as well as individuals. Actors who share a similar position within a given field are likely to develop similar dispositions and thus similar practices. Bourdieu stresses that institutions inevitably develop a collective habitus in their function as social actors. This is reflected not only in internal debates on specific issues, but also in the rhythms and in the social practices that give shape to everyday working practices and social relations. (Jackson, 2008, p. 65)

Bordieuan Service Summary: Relevance to the Performance of the Service Interaction

Linguistic Inquiry; the performance of language is central and essential to the workings of service provision in society. Language is the medium of direct communication between the servicer and the serviced. This will be permeated with power differentials that ebb and flow as the communication process, progresses, normally skewed towards the servicer in terms of what agenda has been set as the ground rules. In many cases, the serviced reacts to these rules and negotiates a pathway along them. This does not imply that the ground rules are purposely 'unfair', as pragmatics of the service encounter may dictate how the process has been designed, to 'process' in as an efficient manner as possible. Although 'efficient' may be a loaded term, depending upon perspective, that inadvertently skews the service encounter or advertently designed to do so. It would depend upon the service context. Essentially, language application is not neutral, whatever 'neutral' implies, and service performance operates within that non-neutrality of experience. Associated with language as the medium of direct communication between the servicer and services, is indirect communication. This is in the form of servicer infrastructure (buildings, offices, locations), which may be imposing to make a statement of positionality and power. This infrastructure creates a precursor to how the language performance will happen, a disarming of the serviced and arming of the servicer, and a symbolic statement of agenda setting. Essentially, a loaded service.

Field; can be thought of as the space of interaction between the servicer and the serviced, and is a space of complexity. Complex in terms of what drives and influences within that space in terms of economics and base line costs, monetary profit, and culturally. Culturally implies the culture of the serviced place and accompanying modus operandi, the self-culture of the service agent working within that culture, with possible resultant tensions, and the culture of the serviced who enter the field of the service culture, with again possible resultant tensions. Interaction in the field space produces symbolism, and just like language interpretation, the symbolism construction and appreciation depend upon perspective, i.e. how the symbolism of the service field has been created to set the environment of the field space for the users, and the symbolism brought to the field space by the users. This 'symbolic' clash would encourage a fluidity of field service performance, in which a field of service would operate within society's field or Field (capital F is deliberately included for emphasis of society being the dominant entity that services all the fields under its umbrella of spatial influence). So, within the 'field' of service performance, field is where the service happens, both 'physically' (the actual physical location and Online space) and 'abstractly', influenced by cultural and symbolic appreciation, application, and understanding. Both the physical and abstract are situated within the maternal/paternal social field, which undeniably produces a complex performing service space.

Political Field; the field by which the four fields of social, capital, symbolic, and cultural make up the product of. The amalgamation of the four, as they are interdependent, creates a performative serviced product that is political in nature. As political processes are essentially power processes, the political field flags power processes that occur during the service encounter. These processes may be overt and covert. The covert, and indeed the overt, may not be evidenced or realised by both the service agent or the serviced during the interactive performance, because of the 'normalisation' of how the service is presented, and the agenda of the service 'owners' of how they run their service, again both within its overt and covert form. Consequently, since power of the political field is involved, the service performance is markedly affected.

Powering the Symbolic; symbolic capital – another name for distinction – is nothing other than capital, in whatever form, when distinguished by an agent internalised within the structure of its distribution (Bourdieu, 1985, p. 731). The limit of an agent's power is proportional to their symbolic capital, i.e. to the recognition they receive from a group (Bourdieu, 1985, p. 731). Regardless of if the agent is a service provider or a service user, the recognition they draw from others, i.e. group, dictates the level of movement and decision making whilst in the service environment. Concerning the level of recognition, it is the symbolic violent capacity of the field and where it resides along the misrecognition to recognition continuum that influences the relational ability, capability, and aptitude of the agent with her or his service/field; although, individual character traits should not be underestimated as a causal factor in the relationship. It is these traits that generate recognition and an ability to use that knowledge at a practical level, when negotiating with other agents.

Culturing the Capital; to be 'cultured' is to possess knowledge of how the intricate workings of processes that power society, work, i.e. having a 'feel for the game' and knowing when and how to play a 'winning hand'. Within the performance of the service interaction, an ability to draw upon one's cultural capital will offer an informed experience. Those lacking this capital or retaining it in a limited form, can be manoeuvred and manipulated towards a service resolution dictated by the service provider. Since a 'full' knowledge of cultural capital may be lacking by the serviced agent, he or she might not receive the optimum negotiated solution perhaps being entitled to. On the other hand, those that hold a generous amount of cultural capital, can negotiate effectively. Indeed, the service interaction process is defined by those who create and sustain cultural capital, i.e. service owners and service agents working for the owners. It is that defined cultural service environment and attendant symbolism that service users perform within, and perhaps 'without', e.g. being marginalised or excluded from the environment and symbolism.

Habitus; when there is an encounter between a service user and service agent, and consequently the service organisation the service agent represents, a communication flow between them is set in motion. This communication flow is not one that is based on a sense and practice of 'nothingness' of the two participants, i.e. a blank slate, it is based on 'loaded' assumptions and presumptions brought to the 'table' when conversing. These premises, beliefs, opinions are powered by prior learning, experience, and feeling acquired over a lifetime up to the present moment. Also, at the moments of the now during the service performance interaction, as learning, experience and feeling adapt to the context of the encounter. These three preparatory and applicable tools of service communication, according to Bourdieu, can be sourced from the unconscious of the individual, to produce/construct behavioural patterns that maximise advantage in negotiating a favourable outcome in whatever life throws at her or him. The service encounter is part of this 'throwing', perhaps a significant part, of life's combat to survive, and moreover to thrive. This unconscious process is drawn from the habitus, namely a sense of unconscious service to service the service encounter.

Link to Interview Chapters

Bridging the Gap!

The engagement with Alice Springs as a living place, a lived-in place, a dwelling place, and the selected concepts offered by Bourdieu on how society operates, and contextualising them within service filters of appreciation, create bridges to the following theme chapters (Three to Nine). These bridges serve as metaphors of connectivity to the information imparted within these themes, assisting that information, as service performances, to be appreciated through the filters of Bourdieuan societal communication processes, and the particularities of the place of Alice and accompanying space in central Australia. Thus, producing a society as service/service as society interpretation and explanation.

The themes 'voice' many of the service performances and provisions on offer in Alice Springs and its environs. The voices involve both first-hand sources of information (*italicised*) of locals' kind enough to impart what their services involve, and author interpretation of observing, hearing, being made aware of, and doing some of the services offered in the Alice (non-italicised). The strength of these voices (myself included), in terms of authenticity of service information/offerings in the Alice, lies within the actuality that all dwell in the Alice. The dwelling time in this space may vary from a few months to many years, but the disparity of duration is powerful enough to achieve authentication.

Powerful in the sense that quality of service levels are enhanced by sourcing experiences of societal life beyond the place of the Alice, providing energy and fuel to optimise the service performance within the Alice's and environs space…but also drawing on the place of Alice itself, as living there, to inform best service practice. Hence there is a local to regional to beyond service capability. To enhance the authentic voices further, limited or no interference on the way the voices express themselves was implemented, or 'non-implemented', by myself. Also, there was a recognition that the 'rawness' of expression, devoid of much of the 'polished' finish that characterises many mass media interviews, added to the passion and emotion of service provision, i.e. the words on the paper coming alive…are worth much more than the sum of their parts.

Understanding the spatial scales (local, regional and beyond) of service provision is important and vital, as effectively offering services, and using them, would necessitate a broad geographical space of appreciation, since all places, Alice Springs included, would experience considerable influence from 'outside'. For example, focusing on the Alice Springs context, 'outside' would imply government involvement, both at the Territory and Federal levels, across the vast majority of service provision offered. There would be governmental expectations to follow particular policy guidelines, leveraged by economic/monetary provision. 'Outside' would also involve 'parent' companies who may be national or globalised in form, of which a service provider in the Alice is but one node within a network. Thus, the one in Alice would have to be mindful of policies advocated by 'head office'.

As a proviso when reading these voices, I wish to state that all the content within the theme chapters have been selected and interpreted with the view that it is my opinion and understanding of how Alice Springs and environs are serviced. This is to protect the kindness shown by the other voiced contributors to the book, so all will remain anonymous, as will the organisations they represent (unless consent has been given). Any intentional or unintentional inference is mine, not theirs, and they and their organisations should hold no responsibility for any of the content in this book.

It is apt that the 'bridge' metaphor has been introduced, since the first voice of the themed part of the book acts as a bridge to conduit and focus the reader's mind on linking, associating, and bonding the place of the Alice and Bourdieu's select concepts to what lies ahead amongst the serviced themed voices. This bridged voice is of a central Australian Indigenous person, highlighting that miscommunication can occur between those who provide the service and the serviced, especially in the context of cultural difference, without a translator to mediate the process:

> *Illiterate out in the bush, remote community. The urban Aboriginal people, they come to schools, they live long enough with the people who speak the language, the non-Indigenous. We got these urban people who just ask questions, sort of broken English. Made it hard for people to understand. Newcomers. Anthropologists...they think they know everything. The recording would be the best thing. You can understand after going through it. Rewriting. You get the person you are talking to, can you explain this to me more. You get a better understanding of what the story is all about.*

> *It's to do with Indigenous people and the non-Indigenous. I work between them. Interpret. Interact. In-between the two. It's a bridge. Get them to understand what they mean to each other, and in-between you've got this person who can talk both languages, understand both sides...interpreter. Getting the meanings across to each other. A person in-between. It's an interaction. Say you've got an Aboriginal person from a remote community, out in the bush and they come straight from the bush, and don't understand city life. Being with non-Indigenous is new to him or her. You want to try and get yourself*

known to him or her, but you got to understand you can't talk to each other. You got to know the language. So you get this one other person. Someone else to be in-between. That way you talk to him and tell him your name is ...my name is...introductions...you got someone in the middle that knows you, and knows someone else, and you're getting to know both people, and you know the language from the both sides.

It's like a bridge that you walk across to the other side...you've got Harbour Bridge, Manly and Circle Quay...you got someone there you want to meet, you've got this bridge to take you there. You get to know the place. That's Manly, it's got a bridge, some people, a little island that you can walk around. So is Circular Quay. So you know both sides. But you have this bridge that can get you across to both sides. Make connections. That's what relations are all about when I talk to my people and non-Indigenous.

It's a long-term thing. You need someone to be in-between. All the time. If you want to know someone from out bush...let's say there's someone in New Guinea that don't know anyone here in Australia, who don't speak the language from here, and you have someone from there who can talk the language and was here before, and he has been travelling towards Papa New Guinea and Australia, and he'd be the best person to talk to. The person he knows and the person he knows from here. Then he'll be the best person to get in contact. Like government...government don't know the languages of Australia. Australia doesn't know New Guinea language, so there has got to be someone in there. It is like an embassy.

People should understand that there are people in-between that you can talk to, to get to the other end of the line. Connecting your people. We got this media that connects us from one end of the line to another. Telephone and satellite. Motor cars...it can take you from here to Adelaide and back, and you're still talking to someone who's never been here, but in Adelaide, have connections and then come back here and get another connection, and then you've got another connection with someone else in Brisbane, so travelling, transports...they connect you. Liaisons and connections are all about. That's what interpretation is all about. People can understand each other. Knowing each other. Talking to each other...and connect. It's a major role that can be played and practiced here in Australia. Even wider.

The service performance is about making connections, creating communication processes between the servicer and the serviced...constructing the bridge! As within the majority of service encounters, the luxury and presence of an interpreter is not feasible, so the strength of understanding between the service parties (servicer/serviced) and what each brings to the table and the resultant outcomes (or not), is determined by the 'interpreted bridge' created in the communication process. The communication may resemble the 'Harbour Bridge' or be rickety and liable to come crashing down—or somewhere in between. The following themed chapters are concerned with attempting to make their particular service encounter resemble a Harbour Bridge...strong, resilient...consequently, the service experience and duration is also aimed at being strong and resilient.

Chapter Three

Religion

Religion—in whatever form it has been constructed, from historical up to present socio-cultural evolvement—has a history of providing support for those who struggle to meet societal demands. Society, or the agents that construct the expectations that become, and are, the 'norms', 'values' and 'expectations' of what it is to be a fully-fledged, compliant and useful member of society, set out the parameters and hence limitations to be a 'child' of society. If one happens to be or becomes, in the course of their life, a 'limited' character, religious services can offer a societal safety net to 'capture' the fallen and set them back on the path to reintegrate with societal mainstream. These services can be thought of as societal corrective surgery, treating the 'afflicted' within this umbrella of service provision, guiding and supporting them through this spatial half-way house until they can service themselves. The half-way house is an in-between space, for instance, the serviced are not on the societal scrap heap (excluded, excommunicated) and not, at the moment, of being quite a fully functional societal child, instead they are a serviced work in progress to be gathered back into the folds of society. However, a balancing act of how societal agents want people to be, and what people actually are, which may be different, plays in the background of the process. For example, one NGO in the Alice offers social teaching targeting the most 'vulnerable' people, but at the same time considering cultural sensibilities. There have been some religious phrases utilised here, intentionally so, emphasising how religion serves the case of society in its quest to ensure survivability and sustainability. Part of that role is to gather in the 'lost'. The following voices try to do just that:

> *A large non-government organisation (NGO) in Alice does a whole range of things, largest component is transitional housing, services for homeless people and tenancy support. We have flats in the Gillen suburb, that's all what they call transitional housing for families experiencing homelessness. It provides a house, home, and support to help address the issues of why people become homeless, whole myriad of reasons of course, and the idea that they can stay in there up to two or three years, move into public housing or private rental. At the moment we are in the throes of, and have been for quite a while, the next two blocks, set aside to what we call community housing, low costs social housing. So lower rents, but people have to be working, and it's fixed to about 70% of the market rate. They might be in low*

paid employment and can't quite meet the threshold of private rental in terms of bonds and rents that they want per week, so community housing is set up to go through it with them. They can sign up as long as they are paying rent and they can stay there as long as they need. So, with transitional housing, some will go into community housing. With transitional housing, might be some with four kids, so we may have a range of one, two, three, four-bedroom flats, whereas community housing is all two-bedroom units, so it is limited to how many people can be fitted into one house. Also, with two bedrooms, might be a single mum with a child, or couple of children, might be a young fellow just breaking into work, young couple, that sort of stuff. So that's the housing. Along with housing, we do living skills, introduction with looking after a house as far as people need, going through how you set up your power and water, pay rent, pay bills, tax file number, all those sorts of things.

Then we have disability and aged care. Aged care services support for the elderly who are still in their own home; this has a variety of activities including pick them up, run into town to do their shopping or to pay their bills, or just go round and spend time with them. There is social support, practical support. There is the aged care social support group, run once a week, a morning. They get picked up for whatever it is they nominate what they want to do for that day, may have someone come and talk to them about something they are interested in. Then we also have Meals on Wheels. So, those who are stuck at home on their own, not able to cook for themselves. The hospital provides meals and they are delivered out to them on a daily basis. Then there is the disability service, which is now the NDIS (National Disability Insurance Scheme). It kicked in on the 1st July (2018). So, at the moment, the NGO does co-ordination of support. We don't do direct service delivery, but co-ordinators of support and are involved in that transition of the disability services from what it used to be, to the NDIS. So, their role is if you've got a client, there is a suite of services that they need, ongoing in their life, and to ensure that services remain in place, there is money there to pay for them. Maybe working out what their package needs to be over a period of a year or five years, negotiating that and ensuring those services are there for that person.

Then we have in the adult space the Outcare program, which is the Prisoner Release program. Men exiting prison who are put on parole or at the end of a sentence, a lot of them are on parole, but are working already so when they come out, we provide accommodation and support. Just to allow that transition between prison to whether they are going back out to community, whether they are moving into their own place in town. Again community housing, when we have it operational, will probably become an exit point for some of those whose occurrence is with the Outcare program.

We had the financial services, which does finance some counselling and NILS (No interest loans scheme) loans, which has had a few changes now, administered by Good Shepherd out of South Australia, but up here our staff do the assessments and link people into that so they can get their NILS loan. NILS loan is up to $1500, for white goods, tv, they need a bit of assistance to get, and then they are set up, with deductions, until the loans are paid out. Once the loans are paid out, they can do it again. We used to have problem gambling as part of the financial services team, but that is now run by Lutheran Services.

We have the prison Chaplain whose whole time is out at the prison, and provides chaplain services to prisoners. They call him the co-ordinating Chaplain and he'll arrange for other church denominations to come in and provide Church services each week. He organises Sorry Business if prisoners are unable to go to a funeral with family. Fairly broad range of services he does, general catch up with people. Prisoners will request to go and talk to him about whatever is on their mind at the time.

Then we have Communities for Children and our aspect is as a facilitating partner and to work with other partners in the community to provide a range of children's programs and services. Akeyulerre, Lutheran Parenting Program, Baby FAST, MCSCA (Multicultural Services) Playgroup, Relationships Australia (Children's Counselling).

Then we have youth programs. We do Out of Home Care for young people who have been removed from home for whatever reason, we provide funded residential services, staffed 24/7. There are up to four young people at any one time. The ones that you read in the paper, heavily involved in much of the anti-social behaviour. We have the (IYSS) Intensive Youth Support Services for young people who are on the cusp of entering the juvenile justice system or the Territory Families (TF) protective system, because there are issues at home, or they are struggling, so the idea is we provide that support to them early for anything upwards to two years or so. Usually involves working with the family as well. Might be about just getting back into school, family relationships and a range of other problems as a result of intergenerational and complex developmental trauma. And helping them to find alternative ways of dealing with life that doesn't embroil them in the Justice or Protective systems.

We also have a Leaving Care program, Moving On, which is for young people who have been in Out of Home Care and after TF who no longer have any involvement with them. Between the ages of 16-25 years, they are able to come back in and access support. Having a period which they can go through up to 25, adding things up...I need a hand with this and this. The extended care model is not happening here. In Victoria the NGO is what they call the Home Runner program, extending young people who have been in foster care. So when they hit 18, and it goes all awry or the Department (government) stops paying for them being in foster care, so they're looking at extending that Care Act until 21. Purely that recognition that at 18 you are not quite ready, some are ready, some aren't, but there's bound to be something that goes wrong. Just that extra support around. So that's the sum of what we do.

So, in terms of adult education, we may try to link adults with education. Whether they take it up is another thing. For some prisoners exiting prison they may have had access in prison, so coming out, if they are still studying, certainly seems to be coming more of a focus. Adult education for people in transitional accommodation, the life skills program that they do is a form of adult education. With the Out of Home Care when they're still young people, access to education is difficult, sustaining them in education is even more difficult, because often they come with a suite of issues that impact on how well they manage themselves. Often, they are quick to anger, poorly developed social skills, lashing out whether verbally or physically. A whole range of different behaviours. Then you have a range of those young people all in the one school, and the school can't balance that, and the school has fairly tight rules of engagement in terms of behaviour. So that's difficult for young people, which continues to hamstring them in later life with their lack of education. We have lots of young people over the years regulated to one hour a week, or one hour a day at school because of their behaviour. For some indiscretion, physically attacked another student or teacher, or just been so disruptive in the class, they get a brief suspension and a re-negotiation back to school. They might have an hour a day and build on that, but they are behind the eight ball because everyone is looking at them already. I (the student) gets frustrated because I can only go to school for an hour or two, I want to be there the whole day and know I can cope with it. It frustrates me that I can't, so behaviour escalates, and they get a longer delay in terms of their capacity to do be at school for more hours. An overwhelming gap. So, education, and the education department or the education system is the majority 60% who cope with the curriculum reasonably well, then of course you have that 20% who struggle and kind of do it, then have another 10% who are really struggling, getting through bits of it. Added support here and there and we tend to operate in that last 10%. Literacy and numeracy skills are often very poor, if at all, and behaviour says they will be unable to sit at school for a day, let alone a week, let alone a month, let alone a term and manage everything and get a good education out of it.

Even alternative education, Alice Outcomes, St Jo's, they're overloaded with young people. Again, we're a small town. There is not a huge choice in terms of educational institutions. Certainly, when they shut ANZAC Hill (high school), it had provided between it and Centralian Middle school (used to be Alice Springs High School) a good balance. Like the old hire tech system used to be...ANZAC Hill was more geared for that vocational education.

Non-government organisations do very little without government funding, unless they have a good relationship with philanthropic organisations. A mix of Commonwealth and NT Government funding. Homeless funding is a mixture of Commonwealth and State. Those agreements have been around since the late 1980s, around funding and homeless services. It's changed a little bit, but that has always been a dual provision. It depends on what the program is, so the young people stuff is Territory Families, not Territory Government funding, and yet there will be some aspects of the youth justice system that will have Federal funding attached to it. So, it's a range of Federal, State or Territory funding.

What this NGO offers spreads across a number of service provisions; housing, education, health, prison, covering the young to the old. They area cross section of what makes up many of society's components and those that dwell within it. Other NGO's that maintain a religious flavour also offer social services. These incorporate the space of the Alice and some of its surroundings, for example areas to the south and east of the Alice such as Titjikala and Finke. Age and youth assistance are practiced, and for the more 'mature', aged care advocates are accessible for remote locations as well as in–town. For the young, regulated visits are offered for removed children in a safe environment. In connection to this, counsellors are tasked with engaging human relationships with parent and child, and extending this to relationships and family. Family protection is important, so services are in place in communities and over the Territory that thinks about daily strategies covering the life duration of people, from the young to the old, incorporating youth programs at one end of the life spectrum to elder abuse at the other.

Other services that some NGOs advocate include the Community Development Program (CDP). This is a separate employment service that runs in remote Australian regions, Alice Springs environment included, which relates to Work for the Dole. Indigenous communities are the target cohort; for example, in the APY (Anangu, Pitjantjatjara, Yankunytjatjara) lands. CDP is one of those service provisions that come from beyond the Alice local in the form of the Department of Prime Minister and Cabinet, at the Federal government level. The Alice Indigenous town camps are not left out as NGO contacts are made in these places. Additional service support echoing somewhat the transcribed NGO offerings, include economic capability and wellbeing, alcohol and other types of drugs, tenancy, and targeting agencies, schools, children groups, couples, families and individuals. Finally, since the transcribed NGO mentioned support for prisoners exiting prison in terms of education provision and access to a prison chaplain, other support is offered to crime victims as part of the counselling delivery. The next transcription voices an emergency relief organisation:

> We provide emergency relief. People come in during emergency situations or crisis situations. We can give them food vouchers to spend at Woollies (Woolworths)...they've run out of money. Also give them crisis accommodation in town. We also give blankets out to homeless people. Jackets to keep warm. We also help out with energy bills, people don't get cut off. Help out with power and water cards...meter cards that they sell around Alice Springs. Telstra (telephone) bill as well. Help out with buying clothing in second hand shops. Helping people link up with different services...a lot will come in here and escape from domestic violence...link up with the women's legal aid service or women's shelter, things like that. We target anyone. There's lots of places in town that do Indigenous, St Vincent de Paul Society and the Salvation Army are the only places that do non-Indigenous. We do everyone.
>
> We're funded through charity donations through our shops. Also get funding through DSS (Department of Social Security), Federal funded. We also do travel a bit, we advertise that, because everyone wants to travel in Alice Springs...We do travel contacts to get people out of town if there's violence...payback and stuff like that, someone will get killed or hurt and then their family members will get attacked. So, we get that family member(s) out of town for the next few months or so. The problem is...payback used to be organised. It's not really organised anymore. It's a free for all. (Old way payback) They all get

together in one spot and carry it out, and then that will be the finish of it. Nowadays, it's just payback to anyone and everyone.

Labelling this theme chapter 'Religion' may indicate a reductive idea that service provision for those on the margins of society, or have 'fallen off' it, is only offered by religious affiliated organisations. That may set up artificial limits on the character of the service agents within these organisations, and others who offer informal similar services beyond/outside these organisations. Those within religious organisations are subjected to the regulations and procedures advocated by the said organisation in relation to what they are expected to offer as service provision, but what also should be taken into account is the driver of habitus. This would act as an unconscious influence on the character of the agents, putting an individual flavour on the quality and depth of what the service is translated into in practice. Similarly, the trait of helping others beyond the scope of religious organisations, draws upon one's own habitus.

It is imagined that the majority of people in society, if not all, to greater and lesser and very subtle extents, provide a service to help other. This may range from helping out a family member, relative, friend, not so close acquaintance, to a stranger. The assistance may be fleeting or more comprehensive and long term. The point being, a formal and informal (which aggregating the amount of help, may be the larger of the two by a significant amount) service 'industry' to 'gather in the lost, assists the overall wellbeing of society (including Alice Springs and environs) in seen and unseen ways and means. Wellbeing can be a loaded term, as measuring the mental, spiritual, and emotional health of someone is challenging…nonetheless society would not be able to function as well as it does, without this special service to help being well.

Chapter Four

Education

Considering the case of schooling, in the methodological supplement to *The Weight of the World,* Bourdieu stresses that to:

> grasp the essential of each [person's] *idiosyncrasy* and all the singular complexity of [his or her] actions and reactions, sociologists must uncover the objective structures past and present expressed in the actual academic establishments through which they traverse, and which are themselves organized with other academic institutions in a relational field. (Bourdieu et al., 1999, p. 618)

The objective structures of academic establishments in the context of Australian society can be subjectively structured to both follow the agenda of said establishments and the engendered agenda of the paymaster of the Australian Federal and State and Territory governments. Educating people, particularly the young and perhaps more malleable members of society, to the mainstream sociocultural of society, can be seen to service society in a number of ways and intended means. For instance, sustaining and acceptance of fields, political fields, and assorted capitalisms to maintain societal structure. Education retains its own habitus as well as the conscious levels of learning. Habitus in this context implies the unconscious absorption or acquisition of societal norms, values, and expectations as part of the behavioural and experiential patterns and routines of being a student, i.e. a student of society. The conscious level of learning is associated with gaining the knowledge and critical thinking skills to be competitive in accessing the myriad of employment options that power the economics of society.

The following voices are integral to the educational service of the Alice. This is what they express:

> *The title of the role is Course, Career and Transition Advisor which describes what I do. I provide enrolment interviews for our prospective students and their families. They come along with some of their legal documents, most recent reports and also a story about why they are enrolling with the high school. We are the only government provider in Alice. There are two other independent schools. The other part of the role is to get an idea what the young person likes, is interested in, so that while they are studying with us, we can research*

more about what they want to do. They can choose subjects for university entrance or if they're keen to get to work, or VET (Vocation, Education, Training).

Meet Year Nine students and their families...feeder schools, Middle school visits start in Term Two...just becoming a familiar face, so that it is easier for them to ask questions about what's going to happen. We invite them over to our campus, and they spend some time getting to know the building, the location, the daily routine, because it is different to other schools they have been to. A point of difference between us and the Independent schools is our flexible timetable that allows students to combine VET, work and school. We don't have compulsory uniforms, sirens, or diaries reflecting the workplace or university.

Students are practising time management, getting to a place on time with all the equipment they need. Just being able to manage themselves so that once they do go to work, that's just a given. They understand what that looks like. Once at uni, they are a much more independent learner.

Year Ten is quite structured, especially the first semester. So that they understand what being a senior student looks like, but once they have cottoned on to that, then they can progress a bit more quickly...they can enrol in Stage One subjects in semester Two of Year Ten. All of our Year Ten's do VET, so they are already contributing towards their pattern for the Year Twelve certificate, the NTCET (Northern Territory Certificate of Education and Training). Some students structure their learning, whether its subjects and courses, or a combination, and can finish Year Twelve at the end Year Eleven. Just because of the way they combine what they are interested in doing.

Student/Parent/Teacher nights are held at the beginning of every term. We provide Parents Career Transition Support workshops, so that we are updating families on learning and working in a changing world, and what the NTCET requirements are. About 30% of Australian students go to uni using an ATAR. It's less here as Alice Springs has more job opportunities and some students aren't prepared to go interstate, haven't got the finance, or the drive or support to go interstate. A lot of our students' families haven't finished Year 12, let alone been to uni. There are students planning further education, but they often have a sibling or it's their parents' expectation. So, a big variation between students and their expectation.

Often students reflect later on the information they have learned, and make decisions based on that, but generally the age group we are dealing with are more into their sport and social life, than they are into studies. Year Tens have an annual trip to Darwin and take in the CDU (Charles Darwin University) Open Day. So, they're exposed to campus life. The one here (CDU campus in Alice) is very much fit focused. Provides great facilities for adults who are working, so they can access courses at night to upskill or prepare for a job change. But we are really fortunate to have it and located so close to our campus (School campus). All of our Year Tens do a VET course and it's a great experience for them.

There are things we'd like to improve, and one of them is student relationships with lecturers who are more used to working with apprentices or adults. If they don't get along with a teacher or lecturer, then they don't often persevere. There is a lot of resilience that still needs to be learned. It would be great if education really approached learning from a student's perspective, rather than what we know as education. There are examples from overseas where students are offered subjects they're interested in...yes of course you need literacy and numeracy, but for our cohort to redesign what they are learning or how they are learning it...because we hear all the time, especially about fellas being more hands on, and learning more through active, doing...so it would be good to have the space to have a different approach.

Education is about the whole person. We've got a student well-being team that meets weekly. We have referrals of students with issues, whether it's family or school related or something that's interrupting their daily life. There are massive issues in the community. Having been here for a long time, the community has really changed, but the same challenges are everywhere. We're just a small part of a bigger community, but things like different cultures...so when we arrived forty years ago, there were basically Indigenous and non-Indigenous people living in Alice Springs, and now on campus we've got 12 different cultures represented. A VET prep course, Reading, Writing and Mathematics skills for VET for ESL (English as a Second Language) students, as offered in Darwin would be valuable. Because our Year Tens do a compulsory VET, it would be fantastic to offer a pre-VOC (Vocational) program as far as introducing them to the language of VET, because it is different, and they learn differently.

Students who have grown up listening to another language or speaking another language, don't speak or interpret English the way first language speakers do. It would be a really great thing if CDU Alice Springs could introduce VET prep. The other thing that advantages our students applying for university is Research Project B, an elective offered to our Year 11 and 12's. It's a pathway for admission to the majority of SA/NT tertiary courses as it's giving them the planning, research, synthesis, evaluation, and project management skills they need as uni students. Flinders (university) are looking at 60% of their offer coming from an ATAR (Australian Tertiary Admissions Rank) and the other 40% coming from research projects. So, there is a big impact if you want to get ahead, you can start while you are in Year 12...learn the skills you need to be an independent tertiary student that's now considered when you are applying to uni.

There are lots of opportunities, and we do recognise that Alice is VET focused. For instance, for teachers and senior students taking part in Research Project B...if our students are choosing to do this in Year 12, or some of our students are doing it in Year 11 even, to have someone from the uni come and run workshops to show them the connection between what they are doing in Year 11 or 12, and how that relates to their First Year at uni...it's an ideal opportunity. Makes it seem more achievable, because they are already doing it really, what's expected of them. It takes out that confusion in the First Year...they know how to approach writing and referencing and research. Good to get some of those things that are offered at Casuarina (CDU Darwin campus). It is not always necessary that someone is based here...even if they visit and do an annual workshop or something. It's one of those things when you're thinking about the recruitment process...what's going to encourage students to apply...it's relationships, being more familiar and being confident in knowing that once they start, they're actually a step ahead, because they've already had an introduction of how to approach the learning part of it.

(Year 12 intense) It is a shorter amount of time, and it's much more academic. Some people say it's harder than uni. Although, they've got more support, because you've got that face-to-face and small groups, so you can get feedback pretty instantly. Whereas you're not sitting in a lecture theatre...You can go online and get repeats of the lectures, things like that, and then you have your tutes (tutorials), so you've access to somebody and other students to talk it through with, but it's a different way of learning. One they are not used to.

(online) It's navigating who...how to get a response or who to contact, that sort of thing, because you obviously get lecturers e-mails and things like that, but a very isolating experience. If you know you are

going at least once a week, there is a commitment. Do something by the next time. Whereas an online learning environment, oh well, tomorrow, or the weekend. I think, young people, familiar as they are with that space, like face-to-face too. Although, experience of Alice, that's one of the things working with teenagers, I've noticed a huge change in the way they do connect, or not. One example of that, we had a guest speaker coming...it was a group of Eleven's and Twelve's...probably about 40 or 50 students, so quite a good number, but in the theatrette, they sort of spaced themselves all over the place. I said to them, he was running a bit late, can you all come and sit together to form a group. It took me three times to get them to move, and because we had time to chat, I just said to them, is this a product of the way you socialise, because you are not sitting with each other. You don't feel the need to be a group. From the presenter's perspective, you look much friendlier and interested if you are sitting together. Whereas if you are sitting apart and there is space everywhere, it just looks disconnected. The way that people do communicate is very different. The instant. Say what you think. Not really given it time for yourself to process, with young people is a real issue. Interpreting what somebody said, messaged, e-mailed or whatever.

Our school is 50/50 Indigenous/non-Indigenous... becoming more Indigenous than non-Indigenous. That's a good thing, because that means students are attending. There are people coming in from other communities into town, which hasn't always happened in the past. While they are here, the kids are coming to school, which is a good thing. They are getting exposed to the idea that going to school and learning is the done thing. It's accepted. It doesn't matter where they go, they've at least had that experience and hopefully, that's what they'll expect of their children. Because not all of their families have had that opportunity...where you live, definitely family support, about being involved in learning.

There are all kinds of learning, but we are a society that has expectations of people when they are looking for work. It's basic literacy and numeracy but especially attendance. All those sorts of things school prepare you for. If you live in an isolated place, online courses are fantastic because if you want to access learning or if you are a bit of an entrepreneur, there are all sorts of ways that people can make a living.

A lot of students complete school not knowing what they really want to do. It's not for lack of information or opportunity, because schools are hugely busy with, not just learning, but people from outside agencies...universities to health agencies, to mental health agencies...people that nationally go around presenting all things teenage. Healthy relationships, safe risks. So, the information's there.

(Where do your students tend to go to university)? they get a little bit influenced by each other. Possibly, if one of the stronger personalities says they are applying for a particular university, the cohort tends to stick together and go to wherever. University of Melbourne, students frequently apply, but we've probably only had about three or four students who have actually taken up an offer. This year we've got five students who've registered to do the Flinders uni test. That is another incentive that Flinders offer. If students don't get as high an ATAR as they want, they can sit the uni test and try and get in that way. They say it doesn't disadvantage them, if they don't get a really good score for the uni test, because its lateral thinking, problem solving...it's not considered, but if they don't quite get their ATAR, it can help them get into a higher preference. Some students go to Queensland, example is James Cook (uni) in Townsville. In the ten years I've been here, not very many have gone to New South (New South Wales), and even less to WA (Western Australia). I'd say Victoria and South Australia (main uni destinations).

(What % aspire to uni) round about ten students that apply for university in the current year. So, the majority would do a gap year. Some even do two gap years and apply later. That's probably about 60%. VET...yes, we do have students who apply for traineeships with VET. NT government traineeships are out now. We'd probably have about ten apply for traineeships. One student this year wants to do the dual pathways, so apply to do a TAFE SA (Technical and Further Education South Australia) diploma and get into engineering with Flinders. The majority would go to work out of about 30 Year Twelves. Ten students out of our cohort of Year Twelves apply to uni. VET is less than that.
What % fail their SACE (South Australian Certificate of Education)? Don't have too many that don't get their Year 12. Few want to go to university straight away, it might be in six months or twelve months that they are still looking for something. Graduates are welcome to discuss their options and pathway courses is part of those conversations.

(training and Education Gap) I rang the literacy and numeracy people in Darwin to ask about the opportunity to provide that to our incoming

students from overseas...mightn't necessarily just be them but students with low literacy and numeracy skills to get them into a position where they could succeed more in VET. Because we've got students starting here that don't speak English. It's a growing cohort, and OLSH (Our Lady of the sacred Heart) said the same...probably be able to give me ten names of students in the same situation. St Philips said the same. So, the schools are finding that there are a lot more enrolments from places that don't speak English. Chinese, Thai, Sudanese, Nigerian. Most speak English...it's not their strength, their writing, analysing, comprehension, that sort of thing, but they are often the students with personal and family goals of studying and entering professions.

– (more education support) literacy support, definitely. Plus, support for our students with, not just disabilities, because there is a bit of a process with that, but students that have got complex behaviours that we recognise in schools...trauma and the range of mental health issues that students are dealing with. They are disadvantaged, or they're excluded, because of their behaviour. But we know as a school, that while we are working with them, as best we can, that's the kind of student you are dealing with...may be there could be a pre-VET course about what to expect when you go to VET...so students are better informed about the environment, and the adult learning area. For a student it's recognised that trauma is an absolute block to their learning and their trust. So you do a bit of theory, but then you do something practical. It's relationship building and it's recognising they are kids, they can only cope for so long or with so much.

(VET Start) That would be so fabulous. Even if they (students) did that in Year Nine, by the time they got here, they'd already established all those boundaries...pretty well knew what to expect, because they had that kind of introduction. That might even help the language barrier, because at least there is more introduction to the course. It is not all content. It's how to do it. We do make assumptions about students. We think that young people are all computer savvy, well they are not. The majority of our students wouldn't have WiFi at home. Their parents certainly don't have laptops. They don't have access, unless they are at school. The assumption is they know how to find their way around, which they do pretty well, but...we assume too much. They live in places where they can't get WiFi, but most of them wouldn't have a computer to access from home.

We've got the rental scheme, so a lot of students do hire laptops. This year is the first year they are introducing online Year 12 exams. Students are very good at two fingers or two thumbs, but they not necessarily have great keyboard skills...so I don't know how it's going to advantage or disadvantage Year 12's this year. We are having a trial to see how they go before the end of the year, because it's the first year that it's coming to practise...but it's a SACE requirement. This year it's English, and I guess they want to see how it goes, but it's going to be an online process, and if students haven't learnt keyboarding, I wonder how they are going to keep up. That's for the exam.

I mean, all year they're using computers to do their work. It used to be at the end of the year, come exam time, three-hour written exam, so that was a different disadvantage I suppose, because their handwriting is often very bad. Lots of hurdles they have to jump before they can be really successful. Time management's huge, because most of our students are working as well. So they are part-time employees. Play a bit of sport. They got to socialise. That's what we talk about with our Year Twelves. It's a little bit late by then, but we put it in a time management plan, and say to them, now you can see if you don't allocate that particular time slot to study, then where else are you going to do it...or, if your friends ring and say let's go for a pizza, you have to be able to say, well I can swop that with that...but if you can see there is no other time that you can actually physically rearrange to catch up, then you have to say to people, sorry, I have to put it off. Catch you later, which is not what young people tend to do.

(uni destination peer pressure) stick together, because we're all country folk from Alice Springs. We don't know anybody, so it would be good to go together. A lot of them are keen to go and try somewhere different, but the reality is they need company, or they need somebody to do it with. It's a big change, it's huge. The stats for dropouts in First Year is enormous. People aren't really ready. They take the easy road or the party road, or whatever, and don't complete their First Year or don't go back.

So, the high school in Alice Springs acts like another form of a bridge. The expected modules/units/individual courses are offered to reflect what a student may want to do in the future working environment. But also supporting this are connections or 'bridges' to the adult employability space that prepare students from the transition from school to work. As this preparedness is a work-in-progress, looking for further efficient ways to accomplish this is what else other education service providers external to the high school may be able to offer to lubricate the wheels of the transition. Let us see what the next education transcript, at a different high school, offers in terms of similarities and differences.

(Where do they tend to go to university) That's a really big issue and they go all over. Probably the most common destinations would be Adelaide, particularly to Flinders, Uni SA, and also to Adelaide uni (the three universities in Adelaide). Also to Melbourne. They would be the most common two destinations. Although every year, because of our location (Alice Springs), we get one or two students who would be looking at Perth, one or two who would be looking at Queensland, and some who would be looking at New South Wales as well. Obviously, a couple who are looking to stay here, and maybe some who are looking to go up to Darwin as well. It really is a complete spread, which does make it quite challenging keeping up to date with what's going on in all the different States and Territories. Some go to ACT (Australian Capital Territory) as well...But most look at Adelaide, because a lot of them have family that are there. All thinking about accommodation as a big thing about moving Interstate and looking at, oh I've got family there. It'll cut down on the costs of accommodation. So, they are looking at Adelaide, and also Melbourne to some extent as well.

A lot of them are looking at...they've been in a smaller town, and they are looking for a big city experience. We see a lot of them go and then come back. So, it's not a permanent move away. A lot of them perhaps move Interstate and then it's not quite what they expected...that's a thing we try and sort of prep them with, before they go about looking at what happens when they do move...to feel they can always come back if that's what they need to do, and not to worry about that. Even when they are in Adelaide, the number of them that will keep their Alice Springs contacts and live in a house with other Alice Springs people is quite strong...that bond...when they do move Interstate. There's not many that detach and then have no connection after that point. It's not always mates from school. They could be at other schools. They have their friends and contacts from town, which is good.

(what % aspires to Uni, VET or the Workforce) it's probably 50 or 60% will be looking at Uni, but most of them will be looking at probably working before they go. Again, a lot of that is to do with costs of moving Interstate, and a fear of not being able to find work. Sometimes if you look Interstate, there are more people, because they are at home, and that sort of continuation (stay in the same city to attend university where they grew up in) happens more than to make that break and go away. (British uni context)...No one stayed at home, and if you lived in a town with a university, you'd go somewhere else.

(face-to-face) A lot of them are looking at online options as well. That they can stay here and work and they have already got that position, that income, and are looking at online courses increasingly as an option. A lot of them don't think about it. They think they've got to go away. There's nothing to stop you enrolling and doing units online and staying here. You've got your accommodation at home, if you folks are happy to have you for another year. They've already got their part-time job that's already lined up. It's not for everybody, because other people want to get away, but if they are happy where they are, then it can also be a bit of a safer option. Some are looking at maybe doing a year here, and then transferring when they got a bit of money under the belt. They're already a year done, so they only move away for two years.

The VET and the workforce would be the other 40%, looking at either apprenticeships or looking at going full-time. That's probably half/half out of the remaining ones.

A lot of them move between work and apprenticeships. We haven't really got all the data, because they say they are looking for an apprenticeship when they leave school, and it is only if I catch up with them afterwards, to find out what happens. You know that they have got a job lined up, but it's not necessarily an apprenticeship at that stage. Then you bump into someone a few years later and they've done something completely different. We don't have as good a tracking data as we perhaps...that's something we are looking at...tracking our leavers to find out what they actually do. But we haven't got reliable enough data to share at that stage on this.

SACE results? Last few years we've had really good results and it's been either nobody or one student that fails SACE. It's really a very small percentage in that area. (pathways programs) We talk about that sometimes to international students whose English is perhaps not quite there. It might be worth them trying a pathway before they go (to uni).
Training and education gap? CDU are pretty good. They've got those different options, the VET side, the university side. Also, they are quite strong online. Always talking to CDU, particularly the people up in Darwin like student recruitment, because they are always concerned that there aren't huge numbers from here that go north. A lot of the kids do look at Adelaide more than Darwin. That they just got family there. In the holidays, that's where they go. They are more familiar there, than they are with Darwin. They are definitely trying in that area with recruitment. The only thing that would make a big difference at the end of the day, if there are scholarships for local N.T. residents. If that is something they can tap into. If they haven't got the family in

Darwin, it's a combination of expenses, travel, all of those things that are inhibitors. But ones who've got scholarships to go to Darwin and CDU up there, they'll go. They're not saying we won't go, but it's more...well, if it's the same Adelaide, Darwin, we are going to Adelaide, because we know it more.

The Aspire program is good, with the travel grants for schools to send students up to open days. We did that last year, when they gave us a $5,000 grant to take students and staff, fly them up and look around the open day (at CDU in Darwin), which was really good. The other thing that the students look at for the Alice campus, is they look at the courses. There is not the range they're after. Obviously, it's got to be financially viable to run the courses here.

(Service provider) I'm the careers advisor and the VET co-ordinator. Bit of a dual role. So, the VET side of things is mainly working with CDU Alice Springs. So we support the VET-in-Schools program, or VSS (VET for Secondary Students) now. We send a number of students over for the blocks in Year Nine and Year Ten and Year Eleven, and a lot of our students also come after school, for hospitality. My role is promoting what courses are available and ensuring students attend. Dealing with behavioural issues, if there are any. Because some of the students, particularly Year Nines, find that transition from school into an adult quite challenging. Also mixing with the students from the other schools. Suddenly they're in a class with students from all over Alice Springs, and that brings its challenges. They've got relationships outside of school that you're not always aware of...they were at primary school with someone, and there is something hanging over from that...those are interesting weeks. By the Year Ten, it seems to have settled down. The Year Ten blocks seem to be a bit more straightforward.

Then it's also encouraging students who've looking down vocational pathways, looking at apprenticeships, making sure they're doing courses that fit with what they are hoping to do. It's been the biggest developer in the last 15 years. When I took over the role about six or seven years ago, we only had five or six students doing VET courses here, and now we've got over a 100. The students are really open to learning in different ways than the school model. CDU have been really good at providing options for that, and have expanded the courses that are on offer for students in that space. It's been led by different governments, but also CDU have responded and put on courses that do fit...students want to go to automotive or construction, and there are pathways for them to go into work placements that also fit into that. That's the VET side of things.

I also do the careers, which is more of a flexible role in many ways. Half of my role would be looking at helping the school deliver the personal learning plan, which is a new part of the SACE. So, students look at career options and career pathways in Year Ten. They do assignments on that and it's a compulsory part of their school certificate. It's helping teachers to deliver that with the content of looking at career options and career pathways. It's also working with work experience. So, sending students out in Year Ten to local employers. Also working with students in Year Eleven and Twelve towards looking at apprenticeships, or looking at university pathways and meeting with them, one-on-one...looking at what's appropriate for them and what they are trying to do. Calming down the ones that are panicking. Looking at second or third options for ones that perhaps might be aiming in directions that are challenging to get into. That's probably the main part of the role.

(careers support) That's been a big changing area as well. Things like the Careers Expo are really good in town. That's another part arranging for students to go there and just putting them in contact with, and having those conversations with, people who are in industry...it's more about giving them the skills to approach people, and skills to find out information about careers. There is so much out there, a lot of them will do lessons with them on various career programs...they can create a profile, they've got videos and interviews with people in different professions about what they are doing. Students can find out that information without being told what it is that they should be doing. That's the key thing. Just to give them a sense that they are going to be doing different things. They are not going to be necessarily in one job for ever. Although, some of the older generations are more used to that. Increasingly...how are you going to deal with contact work, short term contracts that are becoming increasingly common. It's about giving them confidence that they can change, and there is going to be opportunities to retrain. It's about where to look for those opportunities and that constant up skilling that we're doing all the time with changes in technology, that our skills are not always in date. That's an ongoing process. I think they're quite open to that. That's certainly been one of the aspects of the role that's been interesting.

They're quite good at looking at the skills that they've got. A lot of them are working part time and they are looking at the skills they've already got working in retail or working in hospitality, where those skills can transfer. A lot of them are very much ahead of where I was when I was 18...there wasn't any talk about careers. It was just, off you go and you can go to work or you can go to uni.

(the job) Sometimes it doesn't end, because you'll get students who leave and then a few years' time they'll give you a call or they'll drop in and say look, this is what I'm doing, what shall I do next. (job position recognition) Validates...they feel still that they can come and talk to you about the next step for them.

Most of the students that I teach have got a pretty good view of themselves...relaxed without being too lazy. There's not so much that sort of panic, nervousness that's sometimes created and fostered in bigger places. They know themselves within their context and community and they feel comfortable with that, most of them. So, that's certainly a positive. Alice does not have the intensity and sharpness of cities, good to visit them, but nice to drive out. Somewhere like here attracts people who share those values and that way of looking at things...Cities likewise, attract people who have those values. Don't miss the unrelenting comparisons that kids made at schools, like the highly competitive schools in Melbourne and Sydney that I've been at. That was not always good for them that the kids who were doing quite well, but were not in the top 5-10%, were all feeling that they were failing. It is sad.

Whereas here people...whatever...it's a more realistic approach that not everybody is going to be in that top 5 or 10%, but their choices are equally as valid. We do have a lot of parents of students who are in trades, and they are doing very well with themselves, and students see that...there is a bit more valuing of that pathway, which is often difficult to suggest in other environments. There are also kids looking at options of doing both (VET and uni). Had a student a few years ago went off and she did an electrical apprenticeship. She's now a qualified electrician and now is going to uni and will do contract work in electrics...A lot of them don't see they need to choose between the two, and that they can move in both worlds...that's really good. Hopefully we are getting that message across that it's not a second-rate option choice (i.e. VET). We get past students, they're very good, they come back into school and talk about what they are doing.

There's a guy who left in Year Eleven to do an apprenticeship in construction. He's now got his own building company and he's employing lots of people around town. He is doing very well. He's great. He talks about he was glad he didn't leave in Year Ten that he did Year Eleven, but then it was time for him to go. (can earn lots of money in trades) the kids here are really good at seeing that, and don't view that as, oh I didn't quite get to that (finish Year 12)....that it's a valid option, can actually be the best option. That's what the town does, it opens up to these possibilities that there's lots of options, and people are doing things that they weren't necessarily doing interstate. That they feel they can change here and people give them a go.

The service of formal education 'bridges' to the capitalist system and is an integral part of that system. The motivations, procedures, and curriculum are driven by the essentialities of getting into work, just like the previous education transcript indicated. There is almost a blurring of movement from one education stage to the next one 'up', i.e. high school to VET or Higher Education or numerous employer streams. The movement from primary to high school, with its attendant preparation for the transition from one to the other, is part of that longitudinal education time/space service preparation to be a functioning member of society. Functioning in terms of being an economic asset for society, not a liability. The final education transcript from the third high school in Alice involves two respondents labelled 1) and 2).

(where do your students tend to go to university) (Respondents 1 and 2 were present at the same time for the interview)
1) I've only been here for a couple of years, but I would say the majority of them go to Adelaide...would you agree with that.
2) I think they would be...Melbourne would follow that.
1) It's really dependent on where a lot of them go, because they've got family or older siblings. There's accommodation support for them, and a lot of that is in South Australia. The students, when they are ready to leave Alice Springs, want to head south or to the big cities...there is not much interest in staying within the Northern Territory or going to Darwin. Most of them don't have connections in Darwin. If they are going to move, they may as well make a big move to somewhere with a lot more opportunities and connections. I would say that's mainly where they go.
There has been a handful of students interested in agriculture. A few last year went over to Queensland to an Agri college
2) They weren't Year 12, they were younger students. They went over to finish high school to be specifying in working on the land. They were simply moving schools, because they preferred what was offered. That's the family making that move.

1) The majority, from my limited time here, of Year Twelve students taking a gap year, a lot of them don't want to go straight onto uni...there is quite a few that will stay in Alice and work for a year. Hospitality or in the primary schools or whatever job they can get or will travel, whatever, but going to uni the year after. Applying for uni now but deferring it a year. There seems to be quite a pattern of students doing it.

2) Reaching exhausting point by the end of Year 12 and having a gap year. Although they don't kind of realise you have four months off anyway. If they did apply and start uni next year, they would have a break anyway.

(what % aspire to uni, VET or the workforce)
1) We have nine students in Year Twelve that choose specifically to either follow a VET or an employment tract. At this stage they are not interested in uni at the end of this year. So that's nine, and in the Year Twelve cohort there are 90, so probably between 8 and 10% will go down the, I'm not going to university, I just want to get a job, do an apprenticeship before that. But we also have kids leave in Year Eleven who have found a job. Our statistics get a bit skewed by the time they get to Year Twelve, because some of them have decided earlier to leave school and get a job or an apprenticeship.

(what % fail their SACE and would like a pathways option)
2) one failed last year and one the year before.
1) If they didn't get SACE, they're probably not looking at a pathway option...I'm over education at this stage in my life. So, they're probably looking at working. A pathway might be something a few years down the track.

(what Training and Education gap could external education providers be filling)
2) A fitness qualification. Childcare qualification.
1) Kids are looking for those. There is a demand for those.
2) Cert III or Cert IV in fitness. There is a Cert II in Sport and Recreation, and it goes nowhere. So it would be great to have even the next level in the Sport and Rec, plus some fitness options.
1) and childcare, there is no options here. We often have kids who...because our Year Ten's do work experience...there is quite a few that are interested in early childhood or child care centre work, and they kind of get interested and they come to the school career staff and say, can we do this here? No you can't, there is nothing here.

1) (as service provider) I work mostly with the older Year Ten, Eleven, Twelve. My role is to assist them with school-based apprenticeships, or to finish and successfully complete Year Twelve. I deal with subjects that have bit more of a practical focus and are based around employability skills. So I spend more time there than doing an academic subject. Teach nutrition as well for students interested in gaining that ATAR. So I work closely with my colleague here with kids who come to me looking for apprenticeships, or the kids that go to my colleague wanting out-of-school…can often be the same kid. So, they want out-of-school, but they're really just looking for other options. So we work together to help find the options to keep kids in.

(out-of-school) if the pressure of school is becoming too much or they don't want to go to university or don't know why I have to do all of this stuff…well, let's look at what else you can do…can you combine school with employment?…can you combine school with VET?…can you combine an apprenticeship with school? (is it similar to Gateway? (schooling for students who experience challenges fitting into mainstream tuition)) that's the closest thing to it.

2) My colleague and I have some common ground. Her official title is VET Co-ordinator. I'm Careers Advisor…is part of my role. So I not only work with the kids my colleague is talking about, who are wanting to make a mixture of work and school. Like we put together a jigsaw puzzle of what their situation could look like, but I also work with academic pathway kids who are like, I'm not sure about what university to go to or what subjects should I be choosing in Year Eleven to get on to doing a science degree after I leave. Or how do I have a gap year. At the moment, all the university applications are open, so I have different kids coming in saying can you help me with understanding the applications process. Also I do work with parents just explaining a lot of things to do with educational requirements and ATARs (Australian Tertiary Admissions Rank) and SACE (South Australian Certificate of Education) and NTCs (Northern Territory Certificates) and all the language of that as well. I also teach English to some senior classes as well.

1) We had work experience when I was at school. That's the other thing I do is co-ordinate the work experience for all our Year Ten students…but we had that at high school. I did one in Grade Nine and one in Grade Ten.

Understandably, and expected, that a commonality of purpose and similar/sameness of service provision is offered by the three high school offerings. Understandably and expected because that is their common purpose and deliberate societal design, as education service providers, and providers of transition towards the 'greater' societal environment. The three Alice Springs high schools are embedded into the network of one of the numerous microcosms of Australian society, namely the microcosm society of the Alice. Parents and care givers 'feed' their offspring into this education service production line, which, if the students can stay the course to Year's Ten, Eleven and Twelve, 'feed out' potential agents of mainstream society; both within the Alice Springs and environs and the wider Australian space, and for some, beyond that sovereign space. Not all offspring can get through or cope with the education service offering, and these are some of the ones in Alice and Australia wide in general that will find themselves, voluntarily or involuntarily, engaging with other services reflecting their circumstances and needs.

The education transcripts thus far have concentrated on servicing school age students, trying to make them 'battle-ready' for the capitalisms of society. The next education age group focusses on preparing adults for employment or return to employment. There are NGOs that are tasked with this in the Alice. Not-for-profit organisations, who are in competition for government tenders that provide funding, acting in the role of employer of apprentices and trainees. How this operates, for example, is that apprentices are employed to industries and workplaces, comparable to hire for labour, for the length of the apprenticeship. The NGO provides support services all through the training on a monthly or more regular basis. The character of these service supports involve mediation and mentoring at a general/generic level, both within a professional and personal context. Recruitment is filtered through aptitude tests and screening procedures.

> *STEPS Group Australia was started by Carmel Crouch in Queensland as she had a son with disability. He went through secondary school. Did a bit of tertiary and had nothing to go onto afterwards, so she developed STEPS as you see it today. It's got many facets. At the moment it's got the SEE program, which is an acronym for Schools Education Employment, so that's one. There's Disability Employment Solutions. There's the Northern Territory Aged Care program, where they concentrate on the Central Desert Shire and the Barkly Shire, and some of the MacDonnell Shire, delivering aged care units to people who are working in the industry. Just a new one that has come on just last year is the Employability Skills Training program for job seekers. Mainly young job seekers aged between 18-25 years of age. I started in the position in 2018, but I have worked for STEPS in a previous role as a skills and education employment trainer. So, next door there is a training room, and I work in the SEE program on Friday nights. I'm pretty well across the SEE program, and I'm just sort of learning other parts of the STEPS group, so probably devolve a little more knowledge of the SEE program for you. Some of the other programs I can bumble my way through it.*

The main outcome for us is to train people up to get them workforce ready. Some of them might come to STEPS for so many hours...they can do up to 600 hours in training. It used to be 800, changed now. New rules. New financial year. So, we've had a few people sit in that training room for up to 800 hours doing some non-accredited and some accredited training. At the end of that 800 hours, is to get them employed in a local business in town. If they're interested in working as a cleaner or working as a carpenter, we try from day one...we do pre-training assessment, and try and gear their units, their curriculum, so at the end they are going to go into some sort of employment. Sitting in that room for 800 hours, you'd think they'd get a bit of a break, and they can then go at get employment. Doesn't always happen, you get a few success stories.

The SEE program covers financial literacy, digital literacy, ready for work, those type of resume units. If you started on day one, it might take nine weeks intensive work, and you can pad it out. You can visit all sorts of other units to go over the 800 hours, but now just 600 hours. Previously, it was a lot of unaccredited training, and the Commonwealth government decided, that's not quite good enough, so they moved down to foundation skills, which is accredited. Just like going to CDU (Charles Darwin University) or IAD (Institute of Aboriginal Development). Get recognition for your units and competency, which is better. Sometimes the foundation skills might tend to lose some of the clients...this is not what I (client) really want to do, to sign up for. Prefer to spend my time in the training room, you showing me how to write resume, addressing selection criteria, because they want to get back into the workforce as quickly as possible. So, accredited training does not always suit why they actually joined up for the SEE program.

You had a little more flexibility, prior to the 2017/8 financial year. I was training for about twelve months, and you could really tailor it to the client what they really wanted. Now, you've got some units that we focus on in accredited training. Some people love it. There are some great units. Some people just want to come in and job search, look at their resume, learn how to grab someone's attention when they're writing a cover letter. Probably appreciate sometimes that the client you have in the room doesn't have the most extended literacy, language and numeracy skills. So, it's a matter of working on that, and sometimes the foundation skills need to be watered down a little bit. They're about Cert 2, Cert 3. So, that's the SEE program.

Then there's the Disability Employment program. So, people with varying disabilities can sign on. It's like a job active provider as well. We've got WISE Employment Solutions. We've got MAX Employment. Salvation Army have one called Employment Plus. Karen Sheldon Training has one over in Darwin harbour...there's a number of job actives in town here. So, if you get referred from Centrelink to a job active, they will try and put you into a job which suits you. STEPS have a disability employment specialist, so people get referred here for about up to 76 weeks, and they have a separate plan on how they are going to get back into the work force. Their referred by Centrelink, and after that 76 hours they default back to a job active, like MAX Employment, Employment Plus. 76 weeks is quite a while to get something in place. If it hasn't worked, you spin wheels for another 20/30 weeks, go back to your job active or Centrelink and then try again that way.

STEPS employment specialists will try and match someone to a position in town. They'll have a bit of coaching along the sides. They'll go and do the part-time work, but they always come back and visit their employment solutions officer, just to make sure they are keeping on track. Making sure that they got good time management, good self-esteem and taking their place in the workplace like a good worker would. (grief in the workplace) That does happen. Bit of a resolution to resolve if a client is being unfairly treated in the workplace. The client officer will go out and visit the person on site, meet with the relevant and necessary people to try and nip it in the bud before it escalates. Whatever the issue is at hand, they will try and get to it as quickly as possible. (employers keeping back places) not so much...whatever the client, if they want to work at Woolworths, the Town Council, or wherever it might be, STEPS employment officer makes those calls and tries to see what the position is...make them fit nicely into that role.

Aged Care is the other one. Units around aged care is providing support to people who are working in Old Timers or Hedy Perkins (both old people's homes), that sort of thing, and remote locations. So, they're actually employed and come and do separate units. I'm not across all the units at the moment. It's only a twelve-month program and it's funded around the twelve months. STEPS don't know until the eleventh hour if they are going to provide for the next twelve months, to provide that aged care training. (the remote side of things) So, it's Ali Curung, Tennant Creek, Lajamanu, Docker River...the more remote locations where they've got aged care facilities and rolling out units they need to be across if they'll be doing medication, medication management of clients or feeding, cooking. Making sure there's that food safety, food handling and so forth. There is a variety of units. Can't think of them all at the top of my head at the moment. It's been going pretty successfully as well.

The shires (Local government areas) see a great need for it. Just to make sure that people are competent in the workplace, especially around medication, first aid. Making sure that if you are the first respondent to something that is occurring in an aged care facility, having those basic qualifications to make sure that they can do the job safely and protected legally as well. If things go horrible wrong, you don't want to be giving medication to someone, and they're not supposed to be having that medication...get mixed up dosages...making sure it's all signed off correctly.

Employability Skills Training (EST)...employability skills are for 18-24/25-year olds, the young job seeker. The SEE program is for people up to 65 years of age. You can come here when you are 16...cater for 65-year olds. EST's, 18-25, so that younger cohort, school leavers and so forth. That's provided by a three-week block of study, and then they have a one-week break and come back and do a three-week block 2. That really focusses on job readiness. Learning how to mock job interviews, along those lines. So, they can get the job and present in a good fashion, when they are applying for jobs. Job interviews, there's an art to doing them, and just that practise of sitting down and doing the mock scenarios over that three-week period.

(high school support for job seeking) Never been approached to do that sort of stuff. There would be a great need for it. If I was a 15/16-year-old, sit in a room and you've got a recruitment panel...they're firing questions at you...I don't know how many 16-year olds would be really well prepared. They're going to ask you certain questions, set 10-15 questions which your bound to have when you go to a job interview. Being able to confidently talk to one of those questions you are definitely going to get fired at. Being able to talk yourself up, not shrink in the seat. You really got to sell yourself and demonstrate to them that you know how to do the job. Just the simple stuff...how to present in an interview. Common sense...dress in a tie to go to an interview...that is somehow missed. Making sure you are properly dressed. Got the right appearance. You don't have to get suited up like you're going to a wedding, just to make sure you've got the proper attire on, you look smart. Just expecting the questions from an employer, how to respond best to some of the questions, be practised at it. Not falling apart and going to butter, so to speak, and melt...I

have one, two or three people sitting in an interview...just making sure that you can clearly articulate why you are the best person for the job. We try and tell them that the employer doesn't know you, they're probably nervous as well. If you didn't go in feeling nervous, you don't want the job. If you go in too cocky and say this is going to be a breeze...a little bit of nerves is good.

If I've got students coming to practice to get that job interview right, you can actually tell the person whose interviewing you... 'I'm feeling quite nervous'...provide you with a glass of water...be upfront... good to lay the cards out at the start. At least you come over as half human, not try and be a robot.

Employability skills training are actually referred by job active providers here in town to STEPS. They're not run each week of the year. Run about three or four times a year. There has to be a certain number of job seekers involved in the program as well. About eight to ten from the job actives in town, to run it. Soon as we got that number, we go out and explain, 'rightyho, ready to go', get your job seekers ready for this day, and we'll see everyone on Tuesday.

Bit of natural attrition after that three weeks. I've only seen it once before, where we used to train them up in the Prime Minister and Cabinet second floor, here at Jock Nelson (a building in the CBD)...started off with 12 clients, and come the third week, down to about three or four, so it does drop. Drops all around Australia. Alice Springs runs it. Darwin runs it. Sunshine Coast runs the program. Cairns. Townsville. STEPS has got a few classes running. It's expected you start off with 12 to 15. Eventually by the fourth week, it's going to be down to four or five. Things might change a little bit now. Things being put into place this financial year. So, if you don't turn up through the three weeks, there's applications on computers where they are required to send through advice to the job actives to say these two or three clients that you referred, didn't show up on the second day and third day. That puts the onus back on them to get these job seekers to come back. It's not accepted that you turn up on day one and say... 'bit too cool for school, I've got better things to do, I'm not coming to the employability skills training'. Bit different now though. The 2018/19 financial year won't allow them to skive and disappear. There's a real mandatory compliance that is going on at the moment...you said you were going to sign on for these three weeks, you're expected to be here. All payments will be cut. Still receiving their benefits and so forth, and as soon as they start to drop off, they'll notice they've been cut off with their payments. A bit of motivation to come back. Consequence. It's the same with the SEE program.

The success of these programs is based on participation rates, so bums on seats. Some people don't like the term being used, but it is participation based. We can't get around that. The success of the program has to be that people attend, and in the past, it's been a little bit soft. Really don't like doing it, find you another activity to do with the 'work for the dole' maybe. They won't have that curtesy, as of today. So, if people don't attend appointments or come to training, or do the EST program, they'll find in a very short period, maybe two or three days, didn't come to training this week, payment cut. It's hard to get back onto your payments. So, there are some people out there who are going to find out the hard way, the payment being cut. Not too happy. Clients getting them into something that they are fairly committed to doing. To avoid getting cut off, come and do the SEE program. Do what you are meant to do in the first place. (notice on office wall portraying at risk students) Stay in the green zone, rather than flounder into the red zone. It's really up to the client. We can help them as much as possible. If they don't show up for an appointment, got to have a pretty good reason why not to. Reasons why they can't make it to an appointment, or come to training that day due to their disability or impairment, that's fair enough...but there is a small percentage of people who fleece the system...if they're required to come for ten hours a week, fifteen hours a week or twenty hours a week in skills of education and employment, signed on the contract that they'll come, and they don't, well!. We just notify the job active. Can you come and follow up with us. We try and make phone contact that it's good if they can come to class. Not so much has happened, as a result of that. They go under the radar. They might come in the following week and sit in the room for a couple of hours to browse. You don't see them for a little while, sort of cruise for a little bit. But they won't have that opportunity anymore. They've just got to come in and do their five hours each day. Have to be here, Mondays, Tuesdays and Wednesdays. Just depends on what's been allocated to their job plan, or work for the dole plan. Some have up to 20 hours. Some do a minimum of ten hours a week. We don't set that, mainly down to the job active who comes up with that number.

(typical client profile) Probably been out of work for a while. Last year in the room, had a lot of mature age students who for some reason found themselves out of employment. Been unemployed for maybe two years or so. They want to improve some of their IT (Information Technology) skills, which they can obviously do. That's a

fairly common one. Usually they have pretty good work ethics. They can turn up to training on time, got the time management skills...just want to develop a few skills on the IT side of things, which we can help with. It's not that academic either. It's real basic Cert 1, Cert 11 (vocational education training certificates) standard level. We're not too academic in the stuff we're doing. Basic language, literacy, numeracy support we provide. A lot of these people have had some good jobs in the past and held them for quite some time, and then they've been let go for whatever reason. Haven't been able to get work. A lot of it comes down to self-esteem. Their confidence is down. A little bit despondent. This is a bit hard. Been knocked back a few times. Try and improve their self-esteem. A lot of the job applications are now online. Making sure that they have the guts of the application, prepare that in class, going online and submitting their application...that can be a bit of a learning experience., if you're not quite across the IT side of it.

(Alice Springs saying) If you haven't got a job in 15 minutes, you're not looking for a job. I've been here since 1993, and that used to be the saying, now there's not the jobs there was. Bit more competitive as well. Things have changed a bit.

We try and encourage people to do voluntary work as well. Even though the goal is for paid employment, it is a way in. There are a few big businesses, places around town which, if someone would like to, we try and set them up to do some voluntary work, then those hours they're doing in a voluntary capacity cover their time in the classroom as well. If they do ten hours voluntary work on a Monday and Tuesday, they're still addressing those ten hours. If they have to do twenty hours in the classroom, those ten hours would work towards those twenty hours.

We've had some younger people as well in the SEE program, a government funded program. Might be an NGO out there who get support workers on, care workers, and all of a sudden after three years funding comes to an end, runs full term, and then the NGO says, we don't have that program anymore...sorry, but we'll have to let you go. Had a number of participants in the SEE program that come in and work quite well for a number of years, their employment is dependent on the funding from the Territory Government, or Federally funded. If that program doesn't role over, they're out of a job. So, had a few of those come in and actively look for work, and go back into the workforce. It might take a little while...the law of probability is you're not going to get the first job you've applied for, but for every ten jobs you've applied for, you're going to get a couple of bites...most times you won't get any receipt that you have applied...go to the interview and see how you go from there. So, for every ten, you might get one or two interested people who are going to get back in touch and say, come on in for an interview. We liked your job application, it was really nice, neat, and tidy. The cover letter as well. Not just your resumé, the cover letter speaks volumes of who you are. 'Do I need to write a letter to cover my application?'...yes, you do, because the resumé, that's just one part. There's a, not a culling process, but a short list application. So, if quite a few people are applying, gets them in the front door. If you can clearly, succinctly, write a letter, it's a good job skill. If you can sell yourself in a neat little letter, page to one and a half pages, then that will get you in the door. So, a bit of practice around that as well.

Free service, but generally got to have a CRN (Centrelink Reference Number) and be referred through a job active. Most people are Centrelink referred or come through job active. We've had the odd client whose come in, known them personally, and sit in the classroom, and you can help me with my resumé, covering letter, and just getting ready for that interview...what you have written down in your selection criteria, you can confidently talk in a job interview, and impress upon the people who are interviewing you, and get that job. It's harder to win someone over in a 30-40-minute interview. Stick to what the panel are actually asking, and not veer off on some other tangent which is not related to what they have asked you. Some people can talk the leg off a chair, but if you can succinctly demonstrate how you can do something, or how you've improved goals in your previous employment, always helps. So, try and get them to relate...when I was working at the town council or when I worked at Woolworths, I took it from this level and improved things a little. Really impress upon them that when you were in your previous role, you had an effect. Demonstrate that you improved things, rather than say, I can do this I can do that, but if you can give an example from your previous employment, or something recent, of how you are going to be of value to the job you are applying for, and to the organisation or business, whatever it is. Having that in the back of their mind, because some people just don't go well...they plan and rehearse when they go in for an interview...so, we can focus on that. Might get them the job.

So, a politician has got a set of advisers, who are going to advise. Like Scott (McConnell, Independent member for Stuart), he would have two or three advisors working for him. When he fronts the camera from the ABC or whoever it is, he knows exactly what questions are going to be fired at him, and he's going to have his advisor provide the right response. The same with a job interview. The job seeker will walk in feeling confident that they know the questions, the five to ten questions they are going to get from the employer on that recruitment panel. Knowing they are not going to be sitting there thinking what's my best response. They know that question...I've got a pretty good response here. Not come over as a robot, but tailor that response to what they've asked you...so they can feel a bit confident when they walk into the interview. I've got it all mapped out. Got it all well planned. I've practised with the other people in the classroom and with the trainer or teacher, and feel confident I can sell myself, so to speak. Much easier to have a pen in my hand. Just to stop fidgeting and so forth. Always hold a pen. It looks professional for one, and maybe have a think, make some notes, keep you focused, on track.

We don't actually have it at the moment here in Alice Springs in STEPS, but they do offer it around the other sites in Australia, and that's the AMEP (Adult Migrant Education Program). So, that might be offered in Alice Springs. I know it's offered in Darwin, Palmerston. In the SEE Program, we do have the odd language speaker who comes in. Might be a Taiwanese person who's come out to Australia, for whatever reason, they don't have a lot of English. Probably a few of those migrants who've come. Obviously we have got quite a lot of Aboriginal participants. Maybe there is a bit of a need for the AMEP Program here. We're starting to get a few people coming through here who want to improve their English language skills. See on the TV they advertise that Language Centre over at CMS (Centralian Middle School)...learn Western Aranda or you can learn French, Spanish, whatever. They might be offering something through the education system here. STEPS have just started a new learning premises up in Darwin, actually got a few students on the AMEP Program up there. We're a bit limited on space here, share an area with WISE Employment. It's a five by four training room, which is not...need to knock out this wall to make it a bit more enjoyable for the people...nowhere to hide in that room. I'd like to sit in the old Prime Minister and Cabinet training area offices upstairs, which they have now vacated, gone over to the new supreme court building. Upstairs it is nicely fitted out, nice big training room, which we actually do use when we're doing the employability's skills training. So, we just use it on a three-week basis. Go through L. J. Hooker (real estate agent) and rent that room out. Got lift access. So, people with disabilities, they got the ramp, can come up. (upstairs) Great view of the town.

So, firstly, a school of hard knocks space catering for the needs of clients who perhaps have fallen off the society treadmill, or are perceived to not retain essential base skills, both physically and mentally, to be competitive in the economic marketplace. This space provides a service to fill the gap between being unemployed and not employment ready, and creating opportunity to be employable. Secondly, the disability employment services involve support, training, and placement in the open labour market for adults and young people with disabilities. Thirdly, as an RTO, training is supplied in health, aged care, and community services. Lastly, the SEE imparts language, literacy, and numeracy training for suitable job searchers possessing skills deemed insufficient to capture ongoing employment, or aiming for further/future education and training.

Other support services, supporting the education service, for often services are multi-layered within the same field, create their own related agendas in a self-perpetuating system that hopefully sustains the 'wholeness' of the education service. These support services, in the Alice context, would assist the town's schools, and within the Alice environs. This may imply coverage as far up north (roughly halfway to Darwin) as Newcastle Waters, the Barkly Region, Tennant Creek, and down south to the NT/SA border. If the support originated from a government assigned education department, for example as with STEPS, there would be disability and higher needs help, operational advice and support, early childhood coverage, as well as the usual teaching and learning. As the service support is within a government context, truancy and attendance would be monitored. Also, since Indigenous student representation is overwhelming, both in town and out 'bush', an Indigenous education strategy is encouraged. For 'out bush', a Remote Schools support unit would support these remote schools. Additionally, school infrastructure is important, in terms of the actual building and services to the buildings, i.e. water and electricity, so maintaining the infrastructure is essential to ensure service delivery. If these are lacking, the 'superstructure' of the education cannot perform efficiently. Finally, in a capitalist system nothing works without money, and with all education establishments retaining monetary commitments there is financial service support.

Services just to do with education can be thought of as preparing, or arming societal agents (culturing the capital), to cope with challenges and demands to survive society and maybe get ahead of the game, at least for a while, until the game finally catches up. That goes for all of us, as eventually we end up as the reason for a church service, or profane equivalent. Agents, in the education context, can be all of the people in society, both teachers and students, young and old, male and female, all cultural groupings. All utilise the acquired knowledge accessed through educational services to perform, and to give that subsequent performance. Thus demonstrating that they know how to 'play the game' as Bourdieu adheres to and by. It is this service field that services all the others. It is a reference point and a comparison point to work from…to gain work…to gain play.

To utilise all the other services, both as a servicer and serviced, at an optimum level of engagement as possible, would not be feasible without formal education. For it is this formal education that trains its societal agents to learn and conform to the rules of the societal game, that allows all the other services to function. For how can they and it function, or even exist, without the laws, rules, norms, values, and expectations laid down over generations past and present, that have constructed education, which in turn constructs them, and all the other services, as to what society is. All are tarred with the same brush. The brush being, how society has been painted, and continually being touched up, within that basic, ever present, culturing the capitalism.

Chapter Five

Government/NGOs

> Specialised discourses can derive their efficacy from the hidden correspondence between the structure of the social space within which they are produced- the political field, the religious field, the artistic field, the philosophical field, etc. - and the structure of the field of social classes within which the recipients are situated and in relation to which they interpret the message. (Bourdieu, 1991, p. 41)

Even though government money comes from all tax paying societal agents, for services to thrive, prosper, and flow, in a type of circuitous formation, it is government that can turn on or off the tap of monetary issue. It is also government that is conspicuously one of the main drivers of capitalistic intent and profit generation. But it is also government that is a prisoner of capitalist intent, as societal agents, which make up the economic workforce within that society and beyond (in terms of corporations who may play off one society against another, to obtain favourable working environments, and who are also major drivers of capitalist aims) apply pressure to government to maintain, sustain and increase capitalism. Perhaps all in society are prisoners of capitalism...realised or not. These performances are shades of symbolic violence as the specialised discourse linguistics of government/capital language is constantly expressed, and agents in turn reciprocate that expression of capitalist interest.

The following transcripts and other narratives of government related services express their service provision of a commitment to capitalism.

Government shoulders the responsibility for particular services that other individuals or organisations do not have the capacity, or will, to address. A prime example is public health. Actually, government itself does not have the capacity to shoulder this exclusively, so the service is not carried out in isolation to achieve a more complete package, and the dispensing of resultant superior outcomes. The willingness to take on a challenging service delivery significantly assists with the functioning of society, and at the same time reinforcing and perpetuating the societal system. In relation to societal functioning and sustainability, quality control is part of the government filtering process of who gets to maintain or create a service. For example, the N.T. government is prepared to pay over the odds for contract work, with the proviso that the agenda is realised. Thus, procurement is strictly governed, to make sure that goods and services are supplied and delivered, backed up by in-placed mechanisms and levers with accompanying checks and balances to monitor the winning tenderer.

An N.T. government service support department is the Department of Corporate and Information Services (DCIS). It offers enterprise information and technology services, and shared corporate services to support Northern Territory Government agencies. It provides services to N.T. public sector organisations, the business community, especially the digital industry, and businesses that tender and supply to government (Department of Corporate and Information Services (DCIS) (2019). One form these services takes in practice is through training and training providers. One challenge for DCIS is to assess and realise the levels of public services offered, so consequently this is dealt with and established by the Competency Leadership Framework (CLF). This encourages consistency, and favourable panel contract subject matter. The favourable subject matter reflects skill base levels, determined target and the training to achieve that target. Since government does not retain the capacity to shoulder challenging services exclusively, the service burden is shared by panel contracts, who are a group of contractors providing services for government. Examples of these types of services are advocacy, plug the holes, leadership capabilities, ensuring rigour within the levels, and conflict resolution.

The education fields do not hold the monopoly over VET training, as DCIS offer various traineeship programs via its employment unit. Examples include The Northern Territory Vacation Employment Program, the Graduate Employment Program, and the Indigenous Employment Program. The programs cover trade to office skills for children and adults. Program duration is twenty weeks with an offer in industry of half to a year's experience. Qualifications cover the VET range of Certificates I to IV. Government money is wasted if there is ad hoc training, so there is a need to create an efficient way for this not to be so, of which a competent core of capability is already present (The Office of the Commissioner for Public Employment, 2019).

One of the roles of government in the N.T. is targeting those identified as Indigenous, and those perceived as disadvantaged. Hence the Indigenous Employment Program. Attempts to increase the Indigenous workforce have been ongoing for several years. One method to try and do this is the service provision of Indigenous preparation programs. Also, positive discrimination to enable easier access for Indigenous people, and others classified with a disability, to enter employment. An illustration of positive indigenous recruitment is, as part of the Northern Territory Public Sector (NTPS), the Office of the Commissioner for Public Employment (OCPE) which enjoys a sector-wide obligation to ensure an effective framework of employment for the development and management of the NTPS workforce/public servants. Its objective is for the workforce to be 16% Indigenous. Part of this encouragement is in the form of tender and contracts. To access the tendering process, the tendered must show three things; N.T. association, based in the

N.T., and has an Indigenous employee percentage in its workforce. Having these adds credence for the tender and assists with price competitiveness.

Established in 1957 the Chamber of Commerce NT is the largest employer association in the Northern Territory. It is an independent, not-for-profit and nongovernment body. The membership and offices span the Territory. For instance, it services the N.T. with offices in Darwin, Alice Springs and Katherine. It lobbies Territory and Local Governments, ensuring members views are presented to Government Ministers and officials:

> *"The Voice of Territory Business"*
> *We are proud to provide our Members and the Northern Territory business community an effective platform for lobbying on the issues that impact upon business, whilst providing services and support to business in a number of key areas including industrial relations, training, employment, education and training advice, networking and premier business events. The Chamber of Commerce Northern Territory is governed by a Board of Directors. It has both a General Council and Regional Executive Council in each region of the Northern Territory ensuring our Members have direct influence and control in the lobbying platforms and policies of the Chamber, in addition to ensuring the service provided meet expectations of business in the Northern Territory.*
>
> *We put on networking and premier events all year round from Corporate golf days in each region as well as Darwin, Customer Service Awards, Chief Ministers Export Awards, Mining Seminars, Defence Industry Briefings, motivational speakers – such as Ben Roberts-Smith, Allan Pease, Kieren Perkins OAM, etc. We host Prime Ministers and politicians, so the local business community have access to the high levels of Govt. through us campaigning and lobbying constantly. We lobbied hard for the DAMA 2 agreement successfully, we have programs for seasonal workers and the Pacific labour scheme to increase access to the labour workforce that local business wouldn't ordinarily have access to. Chamber of Commerce NT also have the Industry Councils, Manufacturers Council and International Business Council (chambernt.com.au).*
>
> *Chamber of Commerce NT is the voice of Territory business for the Northern Territory. So, this one is quite unique. In the Northern Territory, we're one chamber of commerce with an office in Darwin, Alice Springs and then we have a membership officer in Katherine. So, in all other states of Australia you will find there are a lot of small chamber of commerce's for different regions, that answer to a state chamber of commerce, kind of thing. So, we're quite unique that we're*

one chamber of commerce for the whole Northern Territory, and we're the voice of business for the Northern Territory, which is really cool. So, we are a membership organisation. We rely on the members to talk to us. Tell us what is happening in their industry. What's happening in their business. What they'd like the government to do more of, or less of, anything like that. We lobby NT Govt. on issues that affect NT business like red tape issues and the economy/population growth and employees. In the Regional areas we find it very difficult to maintain long term people in our jobs, we have a transient population that turns over every 3-5 years. It's hard to fill jobs and retrain. The cost to local business is very high in this regard. We also have an issue with housing, the cost of rent is high and the number of rental properties low. So when people do move here it's hard to find a place or they struggle with the high rent. You'll find some granny flats go for over $200 per week.

We provide training...if they say, 'look, it's been seven years since Health and Safety training', we'll organise that sort of training for members and non-members as well...right down to small training about social media. Large training for the defence industry or Federal government tendering for projects. So, anything like that which is assisting business. We provide HSR (Health and Safety Representatives) training twice per year in all the regions, as well as legal and governance training 2-3 times per year in the regions (as well as Darwin of course). We utilise our members who provide softer training such as social media/digital, empowering conversations etc. to our members. We always have a members and non-members price on all the training and events we provide, so it's inclusive to all.

What we'd like to see is those really big projects have a local and Indigenous component. So, we don't want to see the FIFO (Fly in, Fly out workers) coming in and out taking their money back to the eastern states. So, what we'd like to do is work with those really big projects for the little guy, and make sure in those projects there's components for the local business and local Indigenous as well. By doing that, we then have to work with the local guy to make sure he is compliant for those Federal projects. So, you have to have workplace health and Safety, building code compliance, all your tickets. You can't have someone turning up on a site that doesn't have a forklift ticket. Those little things. We need to make sure our little local guys are fully compliant when they tender for these big projects that they have a fair chance, and we are not having as many FIFO, which is really good. So, sort of the voice of Territory business, essentially. My role is very hands on. I talk to members. I've had a lot of meetings. It's learning about all the different industries...I don't come from a mining background, I don't come from a defence background, but learning about these projects and how the tenders work, I can assist these other guys to work with these. So, the voice of business.

Chamber of Commerce also co-owns ICN (Industry Capability Networks), so we work very closely. Industry capability is looking at those capability structures, we got our members, we then say, 'o.k. there is a big project coming to town, we need everyone to have building co-compliance for 2016', which is the latest one...then ICN will go through that data base and go, 'you know what, out of the ten business, only five have that'. So then we work together with those other five to make sure we bring training to town, bring them up to that standard. So, it is very much working hand-in-hand with NTIBN (Northern Territory Indigenous Business Network), ISACNT (Industry Skills Advisory Council Northern Territory)...hardest part of the job is to remember all the acronyms and what they stand for. So, we all work together to get these businesses to step up to those levels and be able to tender for that work. We work very closely with all sorts.

We're not funded at all. We are membership organisations, so our only funding comes from membership. Occasionally we might apply for a grant, or something like that. Like at the moment we've got our CBD (Central Business District) beautification project happening. So, business around the Alice Springs CBD...we've partnered with business, trade, and also with Alice Springs Town Council. So, between us, we have provided a grant, as such, so businesses in the CBD can apply for dollar for dollar, up to $5000, and they can get street art or Aboriginal art painted on the side of their business. The reason why that came about is night-time when you walk through the Mall, everyone pulls their shutters down after closing time and it's very unwelcoming. It looks secure but is not very inviting or welcoming for tourists going to restaurants that are in the Mall. Murals, art or street art or a splash of colour, or something like that, it's up to their imagination. They can choose the artist, but we'll match them dollar for dollar up to $5000. So, it could be possibly $10000 that they're improving the facade of their business. So, it's those sorts of little things as well. We can partner with the N.T. government to help our little area of the Northern Territory. We're not funded by the N.T. government at all, we're purely membership.

Our CEO (Chief Executive Officer) is based in Darwin. He's got an executive assistant. There is a vice CEO. Then there is myself. I'm the executive officer for the Chamber of Commerce for central Australia and Barkly region. So, our CEO in Darwin looks after the Darwin area. I look after central Australia and the Barkly region. We got a membership officer looking after the Katherine region. We got a Board of directors in Darwin, executive committee here in Alice Springs, executive committee in Tennant Creek. We work together as a team and we are building that strength every day. Because we have got that unique Northern Territory Chamber of Commerce, we try and work together for the Territory. Whilst Darwin has information about what is happening around the Darwin region, my job is to give them information about what is happening in this region. So, it is up to the members and non-members to approach me, and I approach them as well. If they have an issue and come to me and say, 'this is something we really need the N.T. government to have a look at, this is something we really need their attention on', or whatever, then I take that to our Regional committee. Also to the Darwin Board and then together we create a voice to the government and go, 'this is an issue that is happening in central Australia at the moment'. So, it's one voice taking it to government. It is stronger.

So together, we've got over 1300 members Territory wide, so that's a big voice. So, if I went to N.T. government on my own with just over 300 members, they'd be like, 'o.k., whatever'. So, we've got one big voice for the Territory. My job is to make sure Darwin is across what is happening in our region as well. So, we're pushing that perceived Berrimah line down.

A big issue at the moment is the Aboriginal Art Gallery at ANZAC Hill or the location. So, everybody in Alice Springs, well the majority of people in Alice Springs, want the art gallery to go ahead. It's the location being ANZAC Hill that is the contentious issue. So, again what we do is I go out to the members, which I'm currently in the mist of doing now, slowly getting through them all, and I talk to them one on one...how is your industry going, how is your business going. What are your thoughts on the location of the Aboriginal Arts Gallery? So, we've done surveys on that before and that gives us a general idea, but what we found and what the N.T. government have found is that the very small minority, that are against the ANZAC Hill location, have allowed a voice of the people for it. Simply because, when you go on Facebook and you say something whether you think it's right or wrong, you just get hammered, and there are some people in town, for their business reputation, don't want to go out and say, 'I think the ANZAC location is a good location', because they have fear of repercussion of their business. By me going out one on one to the members, we're in their office and I can say to them, 'what do you *think?', and I come back to our Board of Directors in our next meeting...I've surveyed 60% of our members so far, the majority are all for the ANZAC Hill location for the Aboriginal Art Gallery. So, it's not black and white on paper. It's not a legitimate survey as such, but it is having that private conversation, not naming companies...go back and say, 'the confidence of this business community for this location is quite high', or I can go back and say, 'look, there is one particular business I spoke to, and he's dead set against it for these reasons', but I still don't name names. In that particular case, I'm still going through that. Haven't got final numbers, but the majority I've spoken to, all are very confident that the ANZAC Hill location is the right location for the art gallery, but for Alice Springs in particular. The reason for that is vitalising the CBD.*

So, if we have it at the ANZAC Hill location, what you'll find is more tourists coming into that location. For instance, the buses stop at the bottom end of the Mall, walk through the Mall, possibly shopping on the way, get to the art gallery and the bus picks them up at the other end. Might have four hours free time, or something. In that location you'll have more tourists coming in. Some people will say, 'locals won't use it'. Locals don't use the Araluen Centre, they'll go for a show, not go and have a look at the art all the time either. So, you might find the locals go, once or twice, for curiosity sake. Might go when their friends and family come up, but they probably won't go every day. But the tourists will be. Tourists that are here every day, will go. The more people that are there, the less disruptions are in that area. So, when the building is there, the landscaping is done, there will be more lighting, so less anti-social opportunities. Less of that, simply because the area will be used more, and it can be used at night-time because if they incorporate into the design another function room, that just adds to more choice when people come to Alice Springs. Or a conference, or a get together, or an event...perhaps that will be used at night-time...there will be lighting, there will be people moving around, therefore the youth won't probably be there as much.

(effect of lighting on behaviour) It's like the big shopping centres that play classical music, like K-Mart had a lot of issues for a while, they started putting classical music on outside speakers really loud at night time...all of a sudden the problem went away. So, if the area (ANZAC Hill) is utilised more...at the moment you've got the rugby fields there, which is great, you've got the old high school (former ANZAC High...now St Josephs that help challengingly defined youth), which is not used too greatly...so, if we had an Aboriginal art gallery with a functional space, an event space, whatever, then we have those

gardens redesigned into a functional space with an amphitheatre and lighting, it would be used more. Which means the youth wouldn't be breaking windows, doing other bits and pieces like that, they might be throwing a footy around, or they might not be there, or they might be joining in on the events that are there, or something like that...

update THE NT Govt and ASTC are now negotiating a new site and in conversations with the Traditional Owners of the Arrernte Land – ANZAC site will no longer host the art gallery. It still needs to be in the CBD and majority of residents agree with that.

(Youth pushed to other areas) Then we can look at these areas. I just had a meeting with an outside company that had been asked to come in and have a look at the security of the area through the environmental design of Alice Springs CPTED (Community Protection through environmental design) report. So, what that means is, say your house for example, nice beautiful house with a big fence, you got gardens all away round the front...so you can't see out into the road, the road can't see into you, that's a prime way for someone to hide in the bushes to get into your house, because no one can see them. So, it's security through environmental design, and having a look at how the building are done, how the security is done, how the laneways are done, how the roofs...I used to work for a company at the end of Todd Mall a few years ago, and the only time we got broken into was through the roof, because our roof line was quite low. It was quite easy to climb up over the back and break in through the roof. So, if those things are implemented through design that we look at, instead of putting in more cameras and more lighting and anything else... have a look at the design of the CBD.

If this art gallery goes ahead, you would then perhaps go down the road and doing a bit more with Todd Mall perhaps, and making that a bit brighter, lighter, full of people. So, you would look at, as the youth would move, you would then look at those areas and implement that. Then overtime you would find, hopefully...

('they'...those pushing for the art gallery at ANZAC Hill) This is what they are doing with those coffee and chats, because they've gone ahead and they admit they did it wrong the first time. But now what they are doing, instead of going this is what we think, they are now coming back and having a chat with the locals...so, you're worry about the public parking for the staff o.k., what are ways we can rectify that?. You're worried about tourist buses going in and out, what are the ways?...actually talking to people in those industries and

have that information, and now going...we can tweak it here, tweak it there. That design they put out was just an artist impression. There was nothing set in concrete, but the uproar from that was people are going, that's what's going to happen...no, this was just an idea of how it may look, but now they're open to opinion. A tourist bus is coming in. They are obviously large, need a big turning circle. Let's look at designing that. But of course the architect they hired to do that, will then be armed with all this information that they are gathering from the public, to then o.k. we really need to get this right, first go.

They'd been talking about staff car parking in Alice Springs for decades. I don't know what the solution is to that. No reason why the car park out here (next to Alice Springs post office) can't be made a double story. There's no reason why the Alice Plaza car park can't be made a double story. There's ways in town where it won't look ugly. It can be done in a way that it's going to keep the town nice and historical and welcoming, and won't look like a concrete city. All those environmental designs need to be taken into consideration. Any sort of car park is going to have a dark corner, a dark staircase.

So, N.T. businesses get together and generate a collective service mouthpiece in the form of the Chamber of Commerce to create a strong voice to government. Not only is the voice directed towards government, but also towards the local community to maximise, or advantage, local businesses when encouraging potential consumers through their doors. The example of the realisation and locational negotiations of the Indigenous Art Gallery is a case in point. This Gallery can act as a service hub or focal point to draw in visitors, and the surrounding business service environs, i.e. proximity businesses can potentially benefit. A similar rationale to the established supermarkets in two of the prominent Alice shopping malls (Coles and Woolworths), that pull in customers, and consequently the surrounding small businesses can benefit, i.e. the big service providers directly and indirectly servicing the small. Continuing along the vein of one service provision servicing another, the following examples engage with delivery of business and industry development services, defence support, and employment and training....

Advisory service for skills in industry encourage development in workforce, training and skills. Government provides the running costs. Consultation is the key, targeting businesses, government agencies, registered training organisations and schools. The point is to discover shortfalls and challenges in the labour force of the NT., then recommendations and suggestions are communicated to government for them to apply some policies to address the perceived disadvantage. Current examples involve increasing skills levels to fill gaps in more qualified positions. Also, dealing with the National Disability Insurance Scheme implementation and the resultant adaptation of what is anticipated by health care workers in relation to eligibility. Additionally, considering the future, as there may be potential major mining projects in central Australia coming up, and how that work and economic expansion can be bolstered...essentially the service space of workforce capability.

Continuing with the theme of capability, another service-to-service industry example is supporting major projects. One method of support is working alongside the project exponent, in which understanding is created as to what the current industry capacity is, with a view to getting involved in its supply chain. Doing so identifies skills gaps and assists the enhancement or development with government, industry groups, and industry. Within this business level of interaction, there is engagement with the previous history of projects, licenses, certifications, insurances, employee numbers, are employees indigenous or not, and statistical information on business. This engagement assists project requirements. The physical business space may extend from Alice Springs up north to Elliot (approximately halfway between Alice Springs and Darwin on the Stuart Highway). Essentially, the push to favour local industry is a central motivation. Examples of involved industry groups are Master Builders N.T. and the already mentioned Chamber of Commerce. Essentially a collective group of industry associations.

The Developing Northern Territory White Paper...the N.T. government's economic development framework, contains many tasks and objectives that drive services, and when servicing industry in the N.T.. government funding and support is provided. The focus is economic development, in which development implies population growth and job creation. The framework may incorporate the geography of regional development or be motivated by the relevant government minister or other agencies. The focus is industry and sectors, rather than individual considerations or individual businesses, although by association individuals will be involved. In essence, innovation and trade are central to the economic process in northern Australia. Within the central part of northern Australia, government funding allows for business advisory services for small and medium business, and start-up and intending business. Government funding includes Federal government funds to service tourism business, and Territory government funds, which incorporates not only tourism, but all industry. In addition to Industry advisory services, diverse workshops are presented throughout the year as well as a referral service. For example, a business client may need contact with accountants or lawyers, so consultancy with specialists or experts in that field is arranged. Essentially, this is a non-for-profit business advisory service.

In these industry services, non-Indigenous and Indigenous people are regarded as non-distinguishable. They are simply people with skill gaps that require training over a range of industries. As a part of this, within the space of the regional economic framework, industries that are lacking required training are a priority to fill the skills gap. An example, Australian wide, is limited

Work Health and Safety skills competency, but particularly prevalent in the N.T. Thus, a natural step is to arrange for a training provider in the N.T. to teach health and safety. However, if a service cannot be sought for 'in-house', i.e. the N.T., an option is to bring in an ''external' service. In the case of health and safety training provision, an 'out-house' health and safety service trainer was 'imported' from Queensland and a course was run in Alice Springs. The Queensland trainer was an accredited deliverer, the qualification being a Certificate IV in Work Health and Safety.

These types of courses can run into the thousands of dollars if categorised as a 'fee for service', since providing services can attract economic costs. A possible result of paying for services means that they are not or cannot be used, as the serviced simply is/are not willing or unable to meet the cost. To get around service bills, money is subsidised from the N.T. government for central Australian employees and people to train in Health and Safety. A serviced trickle-down effect is then put in motion, as when these former trainees return to their small businesses, these become a safe place to work in.

Another central Australian training example is for remote communities, revolving around early childhood, and community safety and night patrol. Many employees doing that program live and work out in remote communities. So, again through N.T. government funding, enables the delivery of a skills set concerning workplace mentoring and training, gaining a Certificate III in Early Childhood or Community Safety and Night Patrol. Workplace supervisors are utilised by training providers to encourage employees are ready for the training, and working through the work and content at a reasonable speed. It is these hands-on services that aim for success, rather than failure, when the training provider goes out and assesses. Success in terms of experiencing achievements and being assessed, rather than training that dribbles along, happening, not-happening, resulting in non-completions and dropouts. Therefore, aiming to encourage better outcomes in remote area training by keeping the momentum moving along, through the Workplace Training and Assessing space. An N.T. based provider is used for Training and Assessing. At least that is the priority, to use N.T. providers if feasible. Examples of supported remote employers are MacDonnell Shire and Central Desert Shire Council. These types of services are concerned with sustainability and shutting the FIFO (employees flying in to work and flying out when finished, until the next set of shifts) gap as much as possible.

The N.T. government has a preference to limit the number of FIFO workers as much as possible and employ people in the N.T. instead. This preference is a baseline for all organisations in the N.T. to induce growth in population and job creation. This is part of the industry servicers role to encourage local skills acquisition, hence an enabling process. Thus, allowing locals to get some of the FIFO jobs in town, and out on site, i.e. in Indigenous communities or the mines. For example, there are five mining resource projects happening in the central region with capital expenditure running into the millions of dollars, and involving a couple of thousand jobs in the construction and other various stages. It is preferable, from an N.T. context, to not employ companies' interstate or people not living in the N.T. to carry out the work. This is because, on completion of projects, the money does not disappear out of the N.T., skills are retained in-house, and the demographic is increasing.

Target sectors to service are oil, gas, mining resources, and defence since Pine Gap is near the town. There are other projects on the skyline, supported by the service of Federal government funding, indicating millions and millions of dollars over the next decade are to be invested in the N.T. When attracting funding for projects in the N.T., i.e. to service the funding, skills and capabilities must be shown to be viable/adequate to do the job. As the Federal government are the paymasters, they need to be convinced that their dollar, or taxpayers' dollar, is going to be effectively invested for suitable return(s). Consequently, when money exchange is involved in any transaction, it creates a reciprocal service exchange. Money services the possibilities of action, movement, behavioural response, to create something that produces its own service capabilities. Or at least, hopefully it will do. The unknown results of a money service exchange understandably produce caution in the money lender or giver. The Federal government would not be an exception when targeting the N.T., as they require convincing that the N.T. retains appropriate skills and capabilities for work performance. To address this, the Canberra government is lobbied for the big companies involved, to breaks things down into a more manageable scope. So, attracting funding services requires subtle communication processes.

Another example of attracting funding is the international student market. As with most universities and their associated towns/cities, the international student cohort can bring in generous monetary exchanges, hence a money service for tuition to gain a qualifications service. In an acknowledgement of this, the Government Development framework wants to increase the 2,500 international students already across the N.T., to 10,000 by 2022. However, the implication of what international students are is not confined to the university sector. It may also imply short term placements, high school students, study tours, and at all levels of education, including adult education. There is an opportunity here to raise international student numbers in Alice Springs. In this fashion, increased numbers of humans and hence potential and realised greater numbers of consumers of services, stimulates the services in the place frequented, and perhaps produces new services to satisfy and feed human consumption demands.

Continuing with the theme of an international influx of visitors or indeed workers or the self-service of workers, the Alice Springs hospital is an effective example of a multicultural workforce. For instance, many of the doctors are Indian and many nurses are African. Also, in the laundry and housekeeping work areas, many people are from the Philippines, Asia and Indonesia. Returning to the FIFO challenge, if these people were not doing jobs, the government would have to implement FIFO in these areas. In this manner, self-service is the key here. The self is the self of the N.T., but the irony is to maintain the 'self' of the service, as the 'other' of external countries and cultures have to be actively sourced to fill in the gaps of employment.

For example, when actively sourcing external workers, there is in place the Pacific Workers scheme launched by the Federal government who broker between people from Pacific Islands and employers. Within this scheme, people come overseas to Australia to do seasonal work in hotels on maybe two or three-year contracts. There is generally a demand in the Alice for hotel employees. So, one could service the other for mutual benefit, i.e. earn a wage and sustain the hotel as a going concern. The Pacific Labour scheme exists because the Pacific population is growing but there are no jobs there. Since the Pacific workers usually have a qualification, employers would get qualified people. Thus, it is not just people wanting jobs, they also have qualifications to fill the local Alice employment gap. It is a real 'win-win', because they are able to provide for their own families, and give their children a future. For example, if there is no employment within the Pacific locality, they can send their children overseas to study in Australia. Accordingly, a service reciprocation!

Another area that requires workers is care work, and there are childcare issues in Alice Springs. Care work is low paid work and not recognised that well, so some people view caring as a vocation who wish to work in that industry. Consequently, to be able to work in childcare requires motivation and compassion to do so, but if the Pacific workers scheme was in the Alice, . it would fill a significant gap, i.e. fill a service gap. Childcare would be perfect for that scheme in Alice Springs, and an immediate fix for it. This in combination with bringing in people and have them in shared accommodation. Thus involving the big hotels and resorts, e.g. service rippling outwards to incorporate other services.

One other thing worth mentioning is the whole Indigenous space, as the Indigenous sector is scrutinised, because of requirements that project proponents seek for and want. There is a vast Indigenous population in the central Australian region, and if people are empowered and involved in the right processes, potentially the lifecycle of social issues can be altered. Proponents are assisted in this, because if an appropriate project becomes available to support Indigenous people, a level of funding would be made available. This economic stimulus is a positive inclusion, as project proponents have commitments. They want, and mean to, appoint a quantity of local Indigenous people through contracts or jobs, as opposed to taking a bow and having an Indigenous person from Sydney being involved. So, why not employ someone or somebodies from the neighbourhood remote communities, to try and create change from that. By doing so subtly changes the service environment to raise the local societal wellbeing for all that live in and around the Alice and N.T, creating a sense of welfare (relating to the next chapter).

So, returning to the N.T. government's Economic Development Framework, and the levers the government have identified in order to grow the population, stimulate the economy, and all of these different things, it is people that are one of the main things to produce and sustain connectivity. Alice Springs has many of those things, but acceleration is desirable to move into that space even more. As in government related NGOs, as with all services, people and individuals are the key to get services moving, and communication is essential for that to happen. Consequently, linguistic inquiry between fields and political fields has to function at effective levels of mutual understanding and benefits, for these services to operate and thrive alongside and for each other, and the service self; self-service indeed! Hence, the existence of one allows for the existence of the other, a mutual service partnership for the existence of both, allowing government to work within its service to its people. It is a Culture of Innovation, top down driven to encourage the development of ideas…powering and powered by a cultural of capital.

Chapter Six

Welfare

Core and periphery. Centre and marginalised. The voiced and the silenced. The haves and the have-nots. Society and under society. The servicer and the serviced. It can be imagined that the latter of each of these pairings would struggle under the demands of society, and require this thing called 'welfare'. Definitions of welfare can range from firstly…wellbeing, happiness, safety, health, prosperity, benefit, and good, to secondly…aid, assistance, the dole. The first group of definitions can incorporate all who live in society, as the positives of wellbeing, health and so forth is what all should, or may, wish for and for some hopefully realise. What each of these actually may imply or mean on an individual subjective level is a matter of perspective, and Bourdieu's class (or lack of class distinction) may supply some answers. The second group may only involve the ones that struggle somewhat within societal space, and it is not necessarily the same people or groups of people within each pairing. One's habitus is active here as Bourdieu indicates that individual histories are not identical, therefore no two individuals habitus are identical. So, no welfare service demands, or necessities, are the same for every individual. Nonetheless, welfare services are necessary for many people to achieve degrees of functionality in society. Now it is time to see what 'good', welfare services accomplish in the context of the Alice…firstly, the senior end of town.

> *Donations at the door. Get us some money and we'll be more than happy.*

> *We have been here since 1996. We opened up the workshops again, a senior workshop. You've heard about the Men's Shed. We are not the men's shed, we are the Senior Workshop. I suppose we do much the same sort of thing, woodwork, turning, carving, anything.*

> *(woman said) We are meant to be 50's plus. We do make allowances for people who are younger who want to do specific jobs or want to learn, but technically we are meant to be over 50. So, we got a range of people from 50 to 90 that come here, not just for the workshop. Inside they play bingo, they have a library, got a snooker table, they got computers, people play cards. U3A (University of the Third Age) come here to use the facilities. They have history sessions, people come here to discuss history, all sorts of things. When I say from 50 to*

90, there's one lady waiting to get one from the Queen, so she's nearly a 100. The facilities are used by a variety of people, for a variety of things. Bridge (cards) come here. Not just for retirees, for everybody. The council took down the Senior Citizens sign. There is a Fifty Plus sign at the front gate. They took it down, and they haven't put it back up. Fifty Plus doesn't mean much to a lot of people, it doesn't tell you what you could do here. There are men's sheds. The risk of sounding racist, the white men's shed used to be at Bindi, now moving out to Blatherskite, which I don't think they are quite set up for yet. The Aboriginal men's shed is on the way out to Santa Teresa, past the airport. We did Thursdays, because some people wanted to learn how to turn. On Wednesdays, we usually have ten to twelve people at least. It varies, people come and go, like they go on holidays. Around the ten to twelve mark would be an average number. Notice board on what is happening on what days and what times. COTA (Council of the Aged) is Fran Kilgariff (former mayoress of Alice Springs), doing it part time. She's organising seniors change, that's happening with the concessions, stuff like that. We have a church group on Sunday. Probus come here. They are more into public speaking. Snooker. NS committee. Australian history. When you see Games group, they play Mahjong and Barista... card games.

Alice Springs: Travelling through in 1979, came from the Rock. Travelling through. Tried to get away a couple of times. Then you find you buy a piece of land, have kids...end up being here for the rest of it. Quiet really, the weather is usually fantastic, even though I'm feeling the cold, especially if the wind is happening. The lifestyle is pretty laid back. The facilities aren't too bad, being so isolated. Some people complain they're on the north side, and don't visit people on the east side, because it is too far away. The health facilities and anything you want to do, is here. Beautiful country. Doesn't take too long to go to a swimming hole during the winter months, if it rains. Beautiful, East McDonnell's, West McDonnell's. Ellery Big Hole. Always find somewhere isolated to have your weekend.

We belong to Senior Cits (Citizens). Pay $20 a year to be a member of Senior Cits. Senior Cits used to run the place, then they were running out of money. Council (Town) owns the building and the area. They decided they needed more a management committee, which is the Fifty Plus committee. That, supposedly, is in the process of taken over the whole running of the facility and canvassing for finance. We used to get grants, but we don't anymore, from Home and Community Care. Then they changed their policy, or we weren't fitting their criteria, so *the funding stopped. We now have to apply to other sources to fund major works/maintenance.*

A lot of older residents don't want to move. Actually, some do move (leave town) and come back, because they found that having to move to a place, say by the beach, you still got to fit in with the community. Got to make yourself known, make friends...they were finding it difficult at an older age to do that. Also warmer here...you're in air-conditioning for most of the day, for the hot parts of it, and you rug up in the cold winter.

(Woman) (in the woodwork workshop). This was setup a long time ago. I used to come up here, when I first came here, I wanted to do ceramics on a Saturday morning. They used to have a family day, so it was running a long time ago. Then it was quiet. The people moved or passed away. It wasn't being used and Rosemary whose out there hammering before, she got a grant and started it up again, because all this stuff was here, well not all, some has been added since...the stuff was already set up, just not being used. Pay your membership and come and join us...more the merrier...

(Man) Used to get government grants. The last government that came in stopped that. The last two or three years, we have survived on savings. Savings have just run out and now we have got no income, apart from fees which is minimal, and we have to pay all the outgoing expenses like power and water, gas, electricity, all that sort of thing. It's about 25,000 bucks a year. That's just living costs, that's nothing for anybody to do anything. We've been trying to get money from the Council and the government to keep going, or we'll close shop. Which wouldn't be good, because a lot of people use it.

(women) I spoke to a chap the other day. He was saying he went to the Men's Shed, but he just said all they want to do is just sit around drinking coffee, where he wanted to learn and that's why he came here.

(women) The Men's Shed is set up differently though. That's for men to support other men that are out of touch and they can do projects as a bonding thing, or as a thing to give back to the community, whereas here it's come and do your own stuff. At the moment we are doing the drawers (chest of draws). Brought some chairs up here, we work on that. I've seen a couple of people coming through with bits and pieces that are broken...can you fix it. We don't charge. Ask for a donation for the building. Grant money started to dry up. Bit of argy bargy

between all the senior groups in town. Mediation was done, and all the groups are allowed to come here. Not all the groups have put money in. When you pay membership, it helps particular groups survive whatever they're doing...it doesn't contribute to the overall running costs of the building here. It would be good if the council helped out with solar panels, because that would take a lot of the money as far as power prices. You get the ladies coming in. They whack the heaters on. The heaters are gas now. All those things get used, the air-conditioners, the heaters as well as the power out here, hot water.

(man) There's going to be a proposal to council shortly, about supplying some sort of funding, paying some of the bills basically. Not sure what that proposal will be. So, an appointment with the council next month. Council lease it to us as a group. Here, there is three groups.

(women) Council does help out with fixing things. Council comes out and fix water leaks.

(man) council does the major maintenance. Tuesday there was water pouring out of the roof, pipe had burst, so the council got a plumber and fixed that up. We pay the garbage fees. The council may take that on as well. If we can get the council to pay, like on goings, power and water, gas, etc., and a little bit extra on top, we'll probably break even. Can't do anything special for anyone. The old days we used to take groups out, do a bit of Stuart's Well. Take them out for lunches, can't do that now. Bus registration, license. There are four associations, so got to pay for the insurance of the associations. So, by the time we get the council to pay for the public liability for the insurance...

(women) Needs to be talked about (services in Alice Springs), where people turn around and think, we're not just numbers, at least we are progressive. As long as children are brought up to be effective in doing things and learn to do things. People can get a bit of help in choosing what to have a go at. I think we all need it. I was the one who started this off, because the shed was shut down for five years or so because people had passed on. I'll get a $1000 grant to see if we can do woodwork or get someone to help us...Graham has just retired, and he came in and is still helping us. I lived on a farm. We didn't have all the things they have got now. It's just great to have the oldies around. I love being around them, spent a lot of time, nearly forty years around them here and on stations, and go out bush with Joel Fleming, he teaches four-wheel driving.

(women). We could run classes for women to do things, we could run evening classes.

(women) that's going to be a one-off thing though. People could pay for a one–off course for home maintenance...fix doors and hinges around the house...a lot of women living on their own. They don't want strange men coming into their houses. There was a woman at CDU (Charles Darwin University) who offered one course in home maintenance for women. We could do that here, because I think she's gone. I volunteer at the Aviation Museum, and the amount of people that come through, they spend one day here. They have absolutely no idea how many attractions there are in town. A lot of our wood gets donated.

(men) we got a whole lot of nice stuff that looked terrible from the outside, when you cut it up, beautiful timber on the inside...jarrah and stuff that gets donated. People keep bringing us stuff. People cut down trees...oh we got a cedar tree, different sorts with nice timber in it....come and say, we're cutting a tree, do you want some of it?

Service provision is ageless, as all, from the cradle to the grave, need the attention that services offer. The attention could be purely from the motivation to sustain or remedy health issues, funding to get through the day or week on onwards for years, or as human need to be social with other like-minded humans. Maintaining that feeling of contact, contact with others, contact with life, especially when one realises that the time of serving life and being served by life becomes more precious the less of it remains. Now, heading towards the junior end of town for those that may have all the time in the world, and hopefully can make good use of it. So, the next segment looks at a facility that offers shelter and guidance for young people who have been pushed over, or fallen off, the edge of society. It is called

'Proud of the Place'...

The age group of children and adults that come and stay at the facility in the Alice ranges from twelve to twenty-five. The majority originate from the Top End such as Wadeye and Darwin. The greater part admitted are referred by the Department of Health. The facility tries to create family support stay. Several sniff AV gas, which can be a petrol suppressant for hunger, and not automatically in addition to. At the present time one female and eight males are in residence. As part of the coping strategies that are in place, a choice-based program is available. The skills base to supply support is social work. One aim is to develop life skills, but not the 'life skills' of Facebook, as media protection policies are implemented.

Funding aspirations is common with all types of welfare service programs, and the facility is no exception, as holistic funding is necessary for the select programs. Alongside this there are funding challenges. To illustrate, limitations of staff funding, and limitations for the offered large camps (out bush). These camps can incorporate fifty to one hundred people, but receive no monetary assistance. In addition, exit strategy support is constrained. The young people, or clients, have a case manager, but sometimes it is more to do with looking after them, as some clients have no identification, thus reduced records to access and work with in assisting them. The local Alice Springs and environs children remain one month, with multiple entry and exit dates.

Several of the eighteen-and nineteen-year old's request to get involved in the facility. Reasons may be influenced by the following: a safe place, and free from alcohol and other drug related products. Clients are not judged and taken at face value. That is the reference point staff operate from. The place has energy and offers fun and sports. It has a gymnasium and computer room. Case workers desire to be here, and there is an on-site general practitioner.

About one hundred clients a year comes through the residence, with 600 Outreaches. It has been in existence for about fifteen years. For young people, this is good emergency accommodation, providing placements for up to seven nights assistance. The dream is to build a purpose built facility. The therapy philosophy is Art and Horse, an approach that supports personal exploration through creative practice. Accordingly:

'If the client is not calm, the horse will not be'

The calmness of service provision is vital for its success and 'running costs'. The 'costs' are not just assessing, measuring or predicting economic costs of running services, since the 'costs' or compromising quality of service experience and outcomes are also in terms of the mental and spiritual, not just the material. Along these lines the serviced or client, if agitated, threatened or disempowered, will not respond that well to the service encounter, just as the horse of the servicer also will not be tranquil and peaceful. Hence, the goodness of the service welfare encounter will not be so good. A calming welfare service environment saturates the next transcription, as it is very necessary for effective servicer/client connectivity and positive progress…

> *This counselling service is a non-profit organisation. Our head office is based in Darwin. Got offices here in Alice Springs, got one in Tennant Creek and one in Katherine, and we also do fly in/fly out services on a regular basis to Yulara and a destination up in Darwin end. Predominantly we provide counselling services, and the counselling services is provided to most organisations in the Northern*

Territory. The way it works is probably 55% of our customers are government. So, government and other organisations have contracts with us, and the contracts are employee assistance program contracts. What that means is by having a contract with us, the organisation enables their staff members to have a certain number of counselling sessions per year that the organisation pays for. So, for the government for example, they, and that's all government organisations, so all of the kind of sections that come under government, Public Health, Department of Education, infrastructure, we have working in Alice Springs...they can all have three sessions with us per year. As a Non for-profit organisation, we tend to have other organisations within us who aren't government based, who have four or five sessions in their contracts with us rather than three, which is much better for clients. Sometimes three, four, five sessions are not enough for our clients. What we then do is contact the organisation and ask them can client number 34572, whose comes to us for stress management, have extra sessions. That's all we tell them. We are huge on confidentiality, that's really important to us. We don't disclose details, names, anything of the client, or what they come to see us about. Very general, might be stress management or managing anxiety or work related stress or something like that, is all we would tell them, when we are asking for that extension request. Most organisations, 99% of the time, will come back and say yes to the extension request. So, a lot of the time clients can have maybe five to ten sessions depending obviously what the issue is, and at times organisations are more than happy to extend further than that. Sometimes they then may want further details, depends on the organisation. Some are more flexible than others.

So that's one of the services we provide. Other services we provide, and one that is very popular here, is mediation. So, conflict in organisations. My background and training is in conflict management and mediation services. I'm an accredited mediator in AU...National accredited mediation services within Australia, so I work under that kind of umbrella. I probably do at least one a month, sometimes two a month of mediation. Process to that would be the organisation sends in two people. Generally, it's a voluntary process, although some people say, if I don't come, it's going to go against me in the organisation. So, even though I'm coming on a voluntary basis, know that there is a consequence if I don't come. So, the process is they would come in. I would do individual sessions for each of them. Find out from their perspective what's been going on and what sort of outcome they are looking for. In an ideal world, I would also get them to explore, using conflict management strategies, around how might things be from the other person's perspective, and then in the afternoon, or the following day, we would then look at doing a joint mediation session, having a historical conversation about issues that have gone on. Chewing that out. Having some robust conversations, and then moving on from there to looking at some of the options. How can we work with that in the future and finally moving on to come to a kind of agreement, in terms of working together in the future. So, have some really successful outcomes from mediation. Can be two people on the same level. Can be from different levels in the organisation. Each one is quite unique, quite different. Probably out of all the roles I do here, that is my favourite, working in the conflict management and mediation field.

Other services that we provide, something we do is called formal referrals. A lot of the time we have staff members not working up to the levels they should be within their organisation. They might do performance management of some sort, and part of that performance management is to refer them to ourselves for some kind of training. Some kind of psychoeducational stuff around whatever it might be. Might be around work misbehaviour, intelligence, communication skills. So, we kind of amalgamate that psychoeducational stuff around stipulated topics, as well as doing some counselling work. What's their background? Where does that come from? What are their perceptions, their beliefs? and gently challenging some of that stuff in how it is brought into the workplace, and the appropriateness of that. What changes they might need to make. Perhaps looking at re-wiring some of the neural pathways in their brain, to make it appropriate and fitting to the organisation they are representing.
Training, we have a wide range of training topics. We generally do six to eight public workshops a year. So, one of the trainers here, who works with us, will go out, usually we hire one of the training rooms in one of the large hotels here, and put on training that is available to the public to come in, join the training, depending upon it is something that will be useful for them. We send e-mails to organisations around here and get quite a good response. When I initially came here, they were putting up one a month, sometimes two a month, and it really wasn't particularly effective. It's kind of like that when you drown people with too much stuff, so we cut it right back, and it's proved to be really effective now. The other training we do, is in-house training for organisations. So, we get called in a lot to provide specific training on whatever each organisation needs. Examples are counselling skills, and appropriate workplace behaviour, with the latter very common. Organisations are now not saying to new staff, 'now read the stuff on the computer and tick the box'. That is actually proven not to be very effective, although legislatively they can say, 'well you've read the

policies and procedures, therefore now you are responsible'. Organisations are finding it is not really effective, because people don't want to do it. So, they are now realising that to drum into people what appropriate workplace behaviour is, we actually need to train them on that, and make it fun and interesting. A lot on emotional intelligence, communication skills, time management, managing difficult people, conflict management. So, all the kinds of topics that really people face as challenging in the workplace, we can offer training in those areas.

Emotional intelligence is around knowing what's going on for you, and not just what you are thinking, but what you are feeling and how you manage that, and also knowing what's going on with the people around you. For example, 65% of our communication is done non-verbally. Someone might be sat there and not saying anything to you, and not saying you're talking a load of rubbish, but the look on their face and their body language might be saying, I'm not agreeing with what you are saying. Emotionally intelligent people will pick that up, sense what's going on around them. Without emotional intelligence, we would not know what is going on around. Consider the context of smart phones, tablets, in the workplace, if you don't learn those social skills....

Cyberbullying is absolutely rife. Cyberbullying is massive, particularly for youngsters at the time their brains are still developing. For us, as adults, a lot of the time we struggle with the rational versus irrational thinking, but for youngsters that has even more of an impact on them, because their brain is not fully developed. So they have not developed those resilient levels that we have, perhaps as adults, and so cyberbullying can have huge impacts, as we see in the news of the suicides and suicide attempts of youngsters, due to that kind of stuff. Just kids, you only know what you know, you don't know what you don't know. Couple of practitioners here that work with children.

Critical incidents is something we do, and sadly do too much of. So, not only in Alice Springs, I go out to numerous communities at different times, sadly if someone has attempted suicide or committed suicide or something's happened, there has been a death. Our role is then to fly in and do a kind of de-brief. Talk to the staff about what's going on for them and prep them for where their mental health might be over the next few weeks. What to expect. What's normal, what's not normal, and in terms of humans there is no normality. It's a big, wide range. So, we go through the de-brief with them. Things that they might expect for them in terms of what their reactions might be. From a brain and body reaction, I guess. Also talk about self-care, and then we'll do regular phone ups afterwards. Do follow ups to check how they are doing. Touching in with them for about six weeks afterwards. That's the kind of impact period that the brain can continue to react to some kind of traumatic incidents. To try and prevent some kind of post-traumatic stress occurring. That's the service we provide.

Your own experiences in life, I guess in the role I do, we get better at it in a lot of ways. Enables us to develop our empathy and understanding around other people and ultimately, sure there are skills and knowledge attached, that's really important, but first and foremost our job is about being able to walk alongside someone else, walk in their shoes, and understand their perspective. Not try to put it from our perspective or I've been there too, and I get it. Looking in their shoes, and that's the difference between empathy and sympathy. That's one of the skills that we specialise in, is being able to do that, and help them work. One of the important things, and my background is working psychoanalytically, which means someone lies on a couch for three years, comes three times a week... and it's great!...we don't live in a world like that anymore. We live in a very solution focus world. You've got three sessions, come in, let's fix your problem, stick the plaster on, and out you go. That can be really challenging, because three sessions isn't enough. In my world you need three years, so it is about trying to juggle so this is the stuff, that's old stuff, we can't focus on that, what can we manage here and now, what kind of solution focus methods can we use. Cognitive behavioural stuff we can use, that's going to help you manage stuff, here and now.

We do provide a service here that can sometimes take more sessions. We can continue to provide. If the organisation will not extend, some clients do continue paying for sessions to come here. So that is an option for clients. We provide a therapy, a type of work here that we call eye movement de-sensitisation reprocessing. Bit long winded that sounds...the way it works...we've got an incident that happens. We reflect on it. We dream about it. We talk about it. That's all our brain's way of processing it. So, that when things go into our long-term memory, we are not holding onto that negative emotion, that might be attached to it. Some memories don't get processed properly, and so the emotion and the memory itself don't perhaps get separated in quite the way they should. So, when we reflect back on something, we still got that urrrr, and that kind of emotion is still straight there, when we go back to it. When we look at post-traumatic stress, people who've had historical traumatic incidents in their lives, that way the brain hasn't processed in quite the same way it would, in a kind of normal, everyday incident. That's where the de-sensitisation reprocessing can be really useful and effective. It's now actually almost kind of stepped up to be the platinum, stage one way of working with historical trauma. So that is a service we do provide here. We have a number of practitioners trained, and work in that area. The difficulty is, it takes more than three sessions. When we offer that service to people, check with your employer to see if we can get those extra sessions for you. If not, are you willing to pay for the extra sessions yourself? A lot of the time, clients are more than happy to do that. So, that's our services really, what we do.

Reporting to employers: what we send out at the end of three months is four of your employees came to see us. Two came for anxiety, and two came for work related stress. That's the feedback employers get every month, or three months, depending on when the report is. All of our customers in Alice, we would do the same in our Darwin office, we get calls throughout the year saying we have got a new load of staff in...can you come in, introduce yourself, can you talk through what your services are, can you let them know about the confidentiality.

Servicing the brain or the psychological wellbeing of someone of stresses and strains that societal performance throws at them, is a challenging and often open-ended procedure. As referrals come from employers, the motivation for subsidising or paying for counselling services may not be of too much consideration for the wellbeing of the client, but an interest to get them functioning enough to perform their work duties adequately, thus, sustaining and maintaining the economic wellbeing of the business. Servicing the dollar line is perhaps the bottom line in societal serviceability. Servicing members of society in terms of their objectively or subjectively perceived 'abnormal' psychological characteristics, is maybe too big a nut to crack in purely social caring terms. Too many numbers may be involved to service effectively and economically. If the complexity of multicultural considerations is added, service welfare provision becomes more complex. Hence, next the welfare of multiculturalism.

Migrants who enter Australia holding a spouse visa, permanent visa and other types, are eligible for English classes of 510 hours. The duration of completion varies of one to three years depending upon engaging daily or once a week. Other support services for migrants may come under the umbrella of Settlement, Engagement, Transition (SETS). These are funded by the Federal government, and referrals are steered towards English classes. Other practical knowledge deal with social issues covering renting workshops, domestic violence (clients are referred to experts in this field), health (Community Health offer talks concerning prevention and inoculation) and employment challenges. Also, 'work' shops helping people seeking for jobs, résumé guidance, addressing the selection criteria, and keeping jobs. These services assist immigrants who are new to Australia and experiencing early settlement challenges. Additionally, immigrant groups/cultures are informed of diverse services to obtain knowledge of the workings of the new society they have entered. About seven information sessions occur annually. Examples include what the Alice Springs Town Council delivers, a CDU one on demographics and census, legal such as family law, and parenting. Essentially, a One Stop Shop for all things migrant.

For those immigrants who have lived in Alice Springs for at least five years, different service support is available Community groups are an example. These are important for cultural identity, especially living in a country in which one's culture is not the dominant one. There are about fourteen immigrant associations in the Alice, including four Indian versions. Other cultural association examples are Hindu, Malayali, Sikh, Kenyans, Christian, Sardinian, Indian, and the Carrion people originally from south of India. There are also, Nepalese, Fijian, South Sudan, African, West African, Samoa, and Shi Lankan. Assistance is offered to celebrate their national days and other cultural events. For example, Harmony Day involving activities, readings, hair painting, food stalls, performance from Samoa, India, Philippines, Ethiopian coffee ceremony, Zimbabwean Ladies choir, costume parade, and Taekwondo. There is the Islamic society also. Funding for immigrant groups is based on census numbers, so if there is underreporting of numbers on census night, the funding model is underrepresented. Of the 25,000 population of Alice Springs from the 2011 census , 23% were overseas born,. That is almost a quarter of the local population, so a significant leverage to attract funding.

For the children, there is a homework club run once a week, led by a management committee. Volunteers supplement the tuition support as well as ex-teachers taking the homework tutors role. For the even younger, a playgroup is run. This space goes to the heart of multiculturalism, as it is an access place for migrant children to mix with, not just other migrants, white children of five to six years as well. So Australian children can attend also. It is a good way for the young, the future of Australia, to mix with diverse cultures. Hence, helping to shape the form and type of multiculturalism in Australia in years to come, so servicing the upcoming-ness of Australian societal future. Giving it a chance for a feasible sense of wellbeing, amongst the complexity of cultural groups vying for position in society's complex web of power plays and identity construction and sustainability. A wellbeing of communicated comprehension amongst common misconceptions and missed communication processes and performance. Australian society is multicultural. Whether it is multicultural in tolerance, is a work in progress, but attempting to service multiculturalism in a supportive manner, services society in a supportive manner.

Roughly, half of society is male, the other half female, if traditional gender definitions are upheld. This traditional is in the binary sense of one or the other, and not along the continuum between both 'extremes'. For society to function well, in terms of all given a 'fair go', adopting Australian vernacular, these gender(s) across its societal presence should enjoy a fair share of the societal voice. Voice in this sense or context is a metaphor for equitable access to society as service, service as society. Next is a gendered service space and place:

Working Women's Centre has been working in the Territory for 23 years. We're an NGO funded partially by the NTG and Fair Work Ombudsman and we're here to support woman who require advice, advocacy and support for workplace problems in the Territory. So, the main workplace problems we deal with are unfair dismissal, discrimination, sexual harassment, workers compensation and problems with pay. With discrimination, pregnancy apparently is quite a significant issue we see quite a lot here, with women telling their employees about their pregnancy, and perhaps they will have their hours cut back, their role may change to their detriment or they go on leave and their job is 'made redundant' whilst they are on maternity leave. So, these are issues we see quite a lot. Bullying is almost systemic, comes up as a secondary issue with most issues that come into our centre. Bullying within the context of the workplace, but we also do deal with issues of domestic and family violence. So, the directors who work in Darwin worked really hard over the years to create a program that is really starting to pick up now, called the Domestic and Family Violence Awareness Program. This was developed in response to the new domestic and family violence laws that were put in place through the National Employment Standards and most Modern Awards. The program teaches employers and managers how to effectively respond to a Domestic Violence discloser from a staff member at work, and the best practice guidelines about how this can be managed.

The Northern Territory government have just written into the Enterprise Bargaining Agreement, domestic leave, for their employees to access if they are affected by domestic and family violence. When a person is supported in the workplace to have some time off to either see a lawyer, move house, go to court, if they've got the security of the job and paid leave, it can give them a better opportunity to get out of that relationship and hold secure work...continue to support themselves and their family, and move forward. So, our organisation's training government at the moment, through human resources, to know how to deal with family domestic violence so people can be effective in the workplace. That's really exciting, and it's something that hasn't been done before. Hopefully it's paving the way for something that could go across the nation one day. Domestic and family violence just isn't physical violence, it's psychological violence, or interpersonal violence. When we look at what is interpersonal violence, it's not just being harmed, it can be financial violence. It can be social violence in terms of isolating somebody from their workplace, their friends, their family. It can be psychological and emotional violence...all sorts...technological violence. Psychological violence is something that's probably not talked about enough, spoken about enough, in our society for us to recognise that it is occurring.

We talk about EASA quite a lot in our clinics here with our clients. We don't have actually much to do with them. They are the Employee Assistance Program in place for people to access counselling, and we always suggest to our clients to inquire to their human resources whether they've got access to those programs. We always encourage people to use them. We really focus here on industrial relations. We are such a small service. There are only six of us in the Territory...two co-directors and four liaison industrial officers. So, two industrial liaison officers here and two in Darwin. Work all part time as well. It's a three week wait at the moment to get in to see us, which can be a bit problematic, because if someone has been unfairly dismissed, you've only got 21 days to make a complaint to the Fair Work Commission. So, when we've got a three-week waiting list and someone calls up who's just been terminated, it can be a bit of a challenge, but we do make it work. So long as they lodge their compliant form by the 21st day, they are covered. If they come here on the 20th day and potentially they are very vulnerable, perhaps low literacy reading and writing skills, that also can be a bit of a challenge, because you've got to assist this client to get the form done to be sent in. It can be quite technical and complex sometimes, ticking the right boxes and understanding which section of the Fair Work Act has potentially been breached.

So, there are only a few small sections of the Fair Work Act that we work with here...Section iii Act vii, which is unfair dismissal, for example. I think the way I have learnt to do this job is because I have done teaching and had to do so much learning through uni, that I guess I've had the skills to pick it up. Some of the women who work here, who have been here a long time, do have a legal background. They are a wealth of knowledge. I have been here a year and a half. All the other ladies have been here, at least five plus years, six plus years. It's really a fantastic organisation to work for.

We assist women that are working, and the demographics and areas of work vary vastly, from backpackers, to people who worked in the same role for 30 years, to young casual employees. The oldest person I have assisted, was in their 70's...we work with women from all walks of life. We also do quite a bit of work with N.T. Anti-Discrimination Commission. So, it's unlawful for an employer to treat you differently based on an attribute...that might be race, sex, age, gender, social origin, religion, injury, illness, disability, so a wide range of issues....parenthood, pregnancy.

We're not funded to assist men. That is because statistically women are in a worse off position than men in the workplace. I guess that is due to women being more vulnerable in their roles at work – women are employed in more casual and part-time work in contrast to men – their gender bias (conscious and unconscious) and then there is the gender pay gap. It's systemically entrenched in our culture still, and there's quite a lot of areas of work where we see a lot of discrimination, even against women based on their sexuality and gender. Really sad and really hard for a lot of women trying to succeed in the Territory.

Masters of Sexual Health degree is not recognised as a Commonwealth supported degree, in contrast to something like nursing, teaching or social sciences. The government won't support sexual health as a subsidised degree at present. Hope over the next few years that the mindset will change. Sexual health is a part of health, and it affects everyone in different ways. Concerned about sexual health in the Territory. Professional practise concerned about, why isn't sexuality education being delivered, particularly in Year 11 and 12. If you look across Australia, most people do not receive any education in Year 11 and 12 about relationship and sexuality education. It's all taught by Year 10. Statistically, when you look at young people, the age of their first intercourse is happening around 17 years. So, it's interesting to me that we are teaching this quite complex notion around Year 6, Year 7, and then nothing's happening, Sexual education is not marked. You don't receive a grade for it. Drugs, alcohol, sexual education are all extra curricula things that it is up to the principal and management to decide whether, or not, it is able to fit in with the school year. It's also a subjective matter. Teachers really haven't got the capacity to deliver it in terms of their time pressures.

Need a lot more work to be done in the Territory to deliver culturally competent sexuality relationships education to cater to students, particularly in public schools, because our public schools are 65 to 70% Aboriginal and Torres Strait Islander students. It is important that we do deliver in a way that resonates socially and culturally and is appropriate. There is a lot of work to be done.

Cultural competency is so important, especially in our context here. Gen Z now, they are a technology-based generation, and they are really selective in the information they want to consume. It's something like kids or adolescents look at their phone and within six seconds of what they see on their screen, they've moved onto the next thing. So, their attention span is very quick, limited, they want short bits of information and they are onto the next. It means that the way people are learning is really changing now.

Decades ago there was a psychological observation done on young kids. They were just coming into their primary school years, and they were given a paper clip each. They had to write down how many uses does this paper clip have. How many things can you do with it? How many things did you make out of this paper clip? Some of them think of hundreds of things. When they got these children back in their teenage years in high school, they said do the same activity...how many things can you do with a paper clip?...some of them could only do up to ten ideas. So, we've got these amazing imaginations when we are young, but we're quickly squashed down in our imaginations and think within the box. Think of Pink Floyd's The Wall...we are placed in a factory and think in a certain way...cuts our imagination. It cuts our options back of the way we think, quite sad.

Alice Springs is such a unique context with such a diverse range of backgrounds here. An urban approach with everything in this town just doesn't work. It's really important to understand the demographic you're working with and the different types of literacy or cultural competency. They both come together. Not saying literacy in terms of reading and writing, but ways of communicating. There are different ways of communicating in this town. Really important that people come here are mindful about different ways of working, and you've really got to understand the populations that you are working with. It's different to the urban scene.

Communication is common. What that implies is for society to service itself well, communication, and communication in a mindful capacity, has to enjoy a level of linguistic inquiry that can recognise and react to, in a positive manner for all concerned, what the other person is feeling, thinking, and experiencing. The 'commonality' of communication should spread across all levels perceived and/or positioned in society, to allow the 'Wall' of society to be porous so gender differences or multicultural differences can be bridged, at least to a 'serviceable' sense of mutual understanding. The welfare narrative will conclude with the theme of marginalised services in the Alice that serve the welfare of society...

Four primary service streams categorise what Headspace does within the mental health of youth (12 to 25 year olds); physical health, psychological, vocational, and alcohol and drug support. It is a space that these services could be enfolded around. The serviced demographic would be roughly a fifth Indigenous, one twentieth from other languages, and the remainder non-Indigenous. Other welfare services are Communities for Children, and Anglicare, providing lists of social services, legal services, and youth services. N.T. COSS (Council for Social Services) offers an up to date services directory covering the N.T.. Bushmob supports young people who have a lack of accommodation or current unsafe accommodation, many of whom have alcohol and drug issues. Alice Springs Youth Support Services also offer accommodation and run other programs, as does the Gap Youth Centre. Legal services in town add to the mix. These are formalised youth services for those not coping too well within the 'headspace' of 'formalised' society.

Service quality is a fluid concept. A number of provisos can influence this. For example, some of the bigger welfare NGOs attract positive robust programs. However, funding dictates the duration, which may only be for one or two years, then a new program will begin. A challenge is to keep attracting funding. Rationale for some of the funding is sensitivity to community performance, accordingly some organisations respond to after-hours youth issues occurring in the Alice, as well as government responses. However, the performance within the Alice environment concerning community services can change rapidly. Also, changes in personnel running programs. People get used to dealing with a familiar face, and creating layers of trust and confidence, then that person leaves. A challenge when this occurs is that a replacement may be from elsewhere, with the time delay of meaningfully appreciating the local context and cultural safety. The local context is one of movement, so 'sameness' is rare, thus a demanding local context to service. It is the limited number of individuals that have dwelled in the Alice for an extended time, which are the ones that retain effective and quality information concerning the place.

People with disabilities (disability is defined as physical, mental, or intellectual) in the Alice sometimes require advocacy services, to liaise with service providers. Within this process, there is a sense of individual advocacy and systematic advocacy. For instance, the serviced may struggle to access the services they might require, or the servicer may require a 'nudge' to service appropriately. These 'deficiencies' can be remedied somewhat by having an effective voice that advocates by standing beside, standing with, rather than standing for. In this manner, the servicer is assisting the serviced to have their voice heard and expressed. However, the extent of whose voice is heard, varies, depending upon the ability of the individual serviced of how their capacity of articulation and expression performs. The bottom line is endeavouring to achieve the desired outcome, which can be a negotiated process for the stakeholders concerned.

The NDIS (National Disability Insurance Scheme) is a current prime example of demand for advocacy services. The conception that drives it is having an insurance scheme that provides individuals with funding to purchase the services they require. The NDIS places service choice onto the individual, a client centred approach, but one that results in grey areas of service entitlement. Consequently, some clients may think they are entitled to certain services when putting their service plan together, but in practise may not be so. An aspect of quality is in the entitlement expectation, which when generated by the individual serviced, may not have an equivalent in the bureaucratic make-up of the servicer.

For instance, the bureaucracy of the NDIS, as with the nature of all bureaucratic spaces, will have inbuilt design and capacity limitations. Also, the plan by the individual may not have been rigorously thought through. It is these human factors and perhaps frailties that can influence service quality. Although as a safety valve, plans can be reviewed within the NDIS framework; a grey area work-in-progress. Although, many other applicants do genuinely lose service funding. One aspect of this is the time delay of moving people from the Office of Disability to the NDIS, which can be a vulnerable time, and it may come down to the individual servicer strength of character to offer funding during the transfer. There are many service consequences going on for individuals, their families, and service providers during this 'grey' time, so, advocacy service is key to assist people to attain what they need, but perhaps not what they want.

Understanding what welfare is, is positioned by cultural perspective. This positionality can produce a misassumption of what actually may be going on from the behavioural pattern(s) shown. This is a misassumption driven by a lack of 'insider' cultural intimacy. Paradoxically, the misassumption may not be recognised as such. An illustration is the dearth of 'right way' relationships. Within an Indigenous context, this has markedly dilapidated much of the kinship system of young people. As a consequence it also effects domestic violence. For instance, if two people get married, the husband may insist that she dwells in his community. Thus by proxy, she has wedded the community and his family. If, by some unfortunate incident between the couple, he is sentenced to prison time, the violence continues by his family towards her, since she is blamed. It is difficult for her to leave and not return, because the consequences are unhealthier as compared to remaining. Also, a spiritual element of interaction within and between families adds complexity. This cultural process would produce misassumptions from the non-Indigenous gaze, as it would misunderstand these layered interactions.

In this misunderstood fashion, 'whitefellas' would judge and label the process 'relationships' and miss the rest of what is happening. Therefore, they would not realise that if the wife left the community and did not return, the only option is to leave town. However, she would be losing her country, her friends, her family and go to an unfamiliar space. Her identity would be mis-placed and mis-spaced, hence her spirituality would suffer. As the cultural perspective of 'whitefellas' entering community space would not understand what is going on, this example is a microcosm of many non-Indigenous people in society (mis)judging the Aboriginal 'mob' for their performance. Some of what welfare services are, are partially based on this missense of understanding, however good the intentions are for offering the services. Not necessarily 'mis-sensing' the violent aspect as an upfront physical act of harm, but the layers of cultural meaning that cause it and result from it. Thus, understanding not of what is physically happening, but acquiring a depth of comprehension of why things are, and utilising one's imagination as a lived experience to do so, i.e. mindfulness.

Therefore, be mindful of the young roaming the streets. It may be safer there than at home, as parents and families may be 'on the grog (alcoholic beverage)'. The young can express themselves on the streets. That space is more secure, as they feel more in control of what may occur or develop. For instance, if police or security arrive on the scene, the youth presence dissipates, as their survival skills are finely tuned. Hence, the potential for self-welfare is there, and there is capacity to release positivity and service oneself. This may be in the form of altering or adapting one's approach to events or experiences. However, peer pressure to not alter or adapt is immense, as peers equate to families. Finally, when seeking for a 'safe' place to practice welfare, mindfulness is needed to appreciate that it is difficult to achieve a sense of connectivity and rapport when displacing youth from the street and placing them in a synthetic space of counselling. Instead, services perhaps should alter or adapt and meet them in their headspace.

Chapter Seven

Indigenous

In colonial and post-colonial societies, there are movements of development, evolvement, and progression. The ongoing tensions these three movements represent, can simultaneously depict positive and negative perspectives, which are dependent upon how one's place in society is affected and effected. For some, these movements enhance one's profit, power and self-performance, and for others the opposite may occur. For every action, there is an equal and opposite reaction. This may be so in the space of physics or chemistry, but in the space of human society, the 'equal' portion of the equation can be questioned. For instance, 'social equality' may imply the following in terms of; who has access to societal resources, one's limits of decision making, one's limited access to service provision and service usage, and limited involvement in setting the societal agenda or reacting to it. Thus, for some groups in society perhaps the famous equation should read...For every societal action, there is an unequal and marginalising reaction.

It can depend upon the strength of resolve and character of the marginalised group or culture, of how the reaction is played out. This may run along a continuum of total acquiesce at one end, to total resistance at the other. The majority of reactions would lie somewhere in between, and be in flux as movements of development, evolvement, and progression happens. In the Australian societal context over the course of its colonial and post-colonial history, a very prominent presence of a marginalised group or culture (or should that read multicultural) are the Indigenous language groups. These groups have been subjected to acting out the role of serviced, in perhaps a passive sense, but also in the active role of service provider, creating, maintaining and sustaining Indigenous identity. The following looks at the fluid usage of Indigenous service provision, beginning with an adapted narrative from an Indigenous researcher and a couple of Indigenous ladies, whose identities will remain hidden.

When researching within Indigenous contexts in the past, there has been a tendency to 'voice over' Indigenous opinion, perspective, attitude, from external 'vantage' points. This method limits first person or first culture involvement to the advantage of the agenda created by those doing the research. Hence distorted or manipulated findings and conclusions result, which may bare scant resemblance to what actually goes on, practised, and believed. To circumvent this, movement towards decentralisation by occupying a greater Aboriginal researched based role, can neutralise somewhat communication disparity of the research service of researcher and researched. In a profound sense the researched and researcher become the same to minimise miscommunication and mishandling of the cultural product. Of course the communication challenge has not been negated, since the researched product has to be read afterwards by those external to the research process, perhaps resulting in miscommunication and mishandling at that level. Thus, cultural differentiation in research has not been eliminated, but pushed along to a different space within the research communication chain. Nonetheless, at the coalface of the research process, Indigenous presence is acknowledged as a contributing factor to limit miscommunication.

As with many research projects, funding is vital to the process. If there is not operational funding, a social enterprise is promoted to contract partners to support research endeavours. This may be on a project by project basis and there may be numerous projects occurring alongside each other, with some acting in a minor role adding to a much bigger project. When carrying out Indigenous research projects, the method utilised is participatory action research. This may involve participant observation, interviews by Indigenous to Indigenous, and applying specific research questions. So, ground up research is cultivated to encapsulate Indigenous perspectives. The process is assisted greatly by researchers being Indigenous language speakers, thus leverage to involve Aboriginal people in the research process, and not as passive participants.

When servicing the research service provider, it would be appropriate to create some form of payment to them in return for their imparted knowledge. For instance, there is an extensive history of interaction between Indigenous Australians and Australian researchers, mostly a one-way advantage process favouring the latter. To balance this out, two mottos suggest that…'Researching ourselves back to life, taking ownership' and 'Survey without Service'. The first relates to Indigenous self-service, which has already been adhered to in this Indigenous segment, the second refers to researchers interested in town camps and specifically housing. Within this context, the focus is on infrastructure and repairs, but as part of the exchange of information, it would be good to receive 'service to repair'. Not just Survey without Service, since producing an honourable service exchange can be difficult in a space of Survey without Service. Within the Indigenous research domain, it is problematic to gain project support from Indigenous stakeholders. Thus, in this social enterprise space, efforts are applied to not compromise Indigenous principles and values, so procedures are practised to navigate through that. Accordingly, the premium projects are partnerships with ongoing relations encouraging collaboration, rather than a funder coming in with their set agenda and fieldwork requirements, creating disservice.

Servicing a research story within the Alice Springs and environs Indigenous context, often returns to land ownership as the mitigating circumstance. Even during colonial imposition the Traditional Owners of Alice

Springs would have retained some control over central Australian land spaces. For example, when 'outside' language groups came into town, they may not be recognised officially (by the State) but recognised by Traditional owners. Accordingly, they request, from the Traditional owners, to inhabit land outside of the town's area. This is the origins of town camps, and camps relate to particular language groups, their Dreamtime stories, and connection to the country story. Hence, everyone has a diverse connection to the Alice Springs area. There is much history that exists well before 'white man' recordings. When the colonial presence occurred, there was limited space for Indigenous groups travelling to the town. For example, allocating people army tents for those dwelling on the Alice peripheries before these evolved into town camps, but since living in humpies and cardboards require the services of power and water, this is one reason for their evolvement into camps. However, when describing these living conditions, a generation gap appears, because communicating to younger generations the living space back then, they just look at you, it is just like another story. Therefore, a missed understood or acknowledged space of 'landed' service provision.

There is background and cultural history with town camps. For instance, there are a few temporary camps, camps that are made up, but the majority on the peripheries (of the Alice) retain stories and history, connected to culture. These places become much more than perceived homeless sanctuaries, by becoming missionary spaces, as those choosing to live there are connected to what is in that area. This goes beyond dwelling practicalities, as they are holding that camp in order to keep everything in 'place', with authorisation from the old Aranda (traditional owners) generation back then. Authorisation to stay and live in the Alice area was through verbal agreement and gift exchanges. This is how the majority of the town camps were 'earned' from outsiders, i.e. people who do not have their place in Alice Springs. Traditional owners can relate to other Indigenous people's stories, country, and story lines, when these other people speak to them. The present generation grandparents connected with Traditional owners and brought that connection down the story line, to keep it in line to the present, e.g. the 'line' of looking after this place, as a cultural obligation. Examples of story lines are the story of the dreamtime Such as the Caterpillar dreaming. Every camp has its own, for example, Dog dreaming for Larapinta.

Examples of Indigenous cultural and language groups coming to the Alice are; the Warlpiri language group, who travel as far as Warlpiri town camp. South camp serves Luritja, Alyawarr, Pitjantjatjara, and Old Timers. Little Sisters serves Luritja and Hermannsburg. Hidden Valley is for the Eastern Aranda family, and many traditional owners are here. Morris Soak is also Aranda family, with connections to the artist Albert Namatjira. Finally, Charles Creek was a small Catholic mission, which relocated to Santa Teresa. Even though the camps are outside the town, they still connect to its Dreaming. There are many Dreaming sites here, and can be used for cultural applications for language groups to abide by. These applications are set up to control their respective language groups, or own clan, if misbehaving. Therefore, Facing the jury of the rest of their language group. At least this is how it was meant to be when the camps began. It is all mixed now.

For instance, the little language groups are all mixed up. Now it is difficult to control and handle people. There is lack of choice due to government rules, which exposes vulnerability and mixing language groups up into the same town camp as people are placed wherever. Vacant houses make it difficult for local long-term residents to say new occupiers are not the appropriate people, as they are troublemakers. These people are not for the camp's wellbeing. If there is an incident, the main long staying residents must absorb the burden. Then the camp is tarred with the brush, labelled as trouble. When one is on the Territory Housing list, and your name is on the vacant list, there is a choice of town camps or urban, but there is no choice for the people already in the camps as to whom they want or do not want, i.e. there is no say if Territory Housing places someone. Service provision has to have a 'pureness' about it to create a holistic sense of wellbeing, but if there is contamination in the way it is implemented by the servicer, the serviced often wears the consequences. Movement from service contamination to service pureness relates to understanding. For example, when the Dreamtime story is utilised as a pureness space of arbitration,, accusations or false statements need to go to the right people to discover the accurate, true story, since people will be speaking of diverse things relating to the one Dreamtime story. Thus, the aggregate of diversity, when joined, produces a good idea of what it is, i.e. there is a sense of pureness.

To bring back a sense of service pureness, and perhaps cultural pureness, to Indigenous language group interaction, the Men's Four Corners Council has been introduced. Four Corners represent Traditional old men coming together to address cultural problems. If action is required, for example payback or ceremonial (boys become men), the old men get together. They also meet if there are camp apprehensions or anxieties in a traditional context. They are there to encourage young men to take more responsibility, to be counted more. If a person is given responsibility, behavioural changes result, i.e. 'change my ways'. Service pureness is not gender bias, as a Women's council also exists. This carries out similar roles to the Men's, but prevented from carrying out certain things, since that is men's responsibility. Conversely men are barred from being involved in women's responsibility issues, although there are many things which are carried out together, but for gender issues, separation is the norm. As a consequence of these councils, people are beginning to respect the rules and regulations of living on a town camp, and respecting other town camp members.

Land fulfils different service roles for Indigenous people depending upon where it is located, which is produced by memories of the past and holding onto threads of traditional identity. Although, remembering heritage and history of a region can be incomplete, especially when people move on, with many of these 'ex pats' still attempting to cling onto traditional memory, and traditional cultural identity. The 'wheres' are maybe out Bush and urban behavioural expectations. For instance, many Indigenous people still travel to the Bush for picnics and Bush hunting, whenever opportunities arise to go. They sleep out in the open, under the stars, and experience life as it was back then, but when returned to town, they are transformed to the 'other side'. Within the other side of the urban space, they are unable to see the stars and tell the stories the stars represent. It is a struggle for some that live in town. Communities have more access to traditional ways, but in urban life, it is different, as one cannot practice tradition in the backyard and cannot practice traditional cultural service. The next transcript looks at the Alice Springs environs 'backyard' and how it services that space:

> *We can only talk about what we think of Alice Springs and so forth, in terms of programs that we do. We do the Connect Program, Family and Mental Health, Age and Disability, as well as Social Enterprise. My two colleagues are in that. (Social Enterprise) when people are stuck in town, they come in. They do diary covers. We purchase some of these items, and if they're stuck in town, we do that. We pay them a certain amount, so they can then buy food, whatever they need for essentials in town. From those sales, goes back into the Emergency Leave Program we have. So, it's just recycling that money. (Emergency Relief Program) Helping everyone and anyone from all communities that are stuck in town. Or even out communities. So, if they need support in terms of food, fuel, accommodation...anything of that we provide support, if we're able to.*

> *Community members that come to town, we provide support to, but those that actually live in town, we don't. Because Tangentyere and all those other service providers, provide them that support. We service basically, nine language groups in the scope of the program, and over 30 communities, depending on the funding we receive...it's decreased. Got a whole lot of funding as well as Federal (government). Competitive to get the funding. (fellow competitors) depends on which program...I don't see it as competing. I think we all work in partnership to provide a particular service to a particular participant. If they can't do it, they call us up, and if we can't do it, we refer...try and fill in the gap where each service provider can.*

> *(media offerings) Funded by the Team Fairfax Family Foundation, couple of years. We go out to the communities and engage with the children out there that's not going to school. Teach them a bit of media...camera work, still shots, using a reflector, that sort of stuff...good response. Next couple of weeks, starting to get back into it,*

had a couple of weeks' off. They like it. Have a lot of fun. Movie clips. All different things. Bushtucker is the next one. Doing a series for NITV (Indigenous television channel). That one's out at Naramba. Try and finish that one off. Get the interest for disengaged students. To create that interest, and if they think media is an area they are interested in, they can follow it up.

Got the Hub out at Santa Teresa. They work with iPads. Making videos. The new ones are really great now. Take nice photos. (Drones) got one here. Kids love it. Seen them once out at Finke, people went there, government people, with the drone of ours. They (kids) loved it. Tried to jump up and grab it. Dancing in front of it. Have to do that actually. Start taking the drone out.
A lot of small programs. The media one's mentioned. We got the Young Parent Program as well as the boarding school. So, that's basically supporting kids, traditional landowners, their kids from Areyonga and Aputula.

(How did the organisation start) Last year, October, was 20 years of Waltjas existence. Started off as a resource centre, and when the funding got pulled, women came together, no, we are going to start up an organisation. Started in 1997. That's when they got incorporated as an Aboriginal organisation. (reason for existence) more because of the women. They wanted their voices to be heard more from each of the communities. Because all of our directors are from different communities, it was all about what they wanted to share with each other. Come together and come up with ideas for their communities. For their families and their communities. It's a service. Back in them days, not enough services out on the communities. That's what we're in here, I suppose. (lack of services) disability, childcare...Christine...she would go out and start up all these child care centres. Some, like Utopia, maybe doesn't have that service, that's when we step in and provide it. Find out where it's not. They need help. Only last year we donated those big old beds. Made out of steel. That's really hard. Sent those out for the old people. Just to get off the floor, ground where they're sleeping. Humpies and that. I think they like them beds. Cyclone beds they call them. CAT (Centre for Appropriate Technology) made those up. Got funding through CLC (Central Land Council), got CAT to make them. We got them out to communities in Troopes (four-wheel drive vehicles) and trailers. Lack of some services out there which government doesn't support.

> *We put in for funding, went through the Federal government. I'm sure if you are going to get it...you get it, you usually get it....95% of the time.*
>
> *We're working with a program with disengaged youth. Basically, bringing them back to country, strengthening that relationship with country. We help with school applications sent to me. Anything to do with the well-being of that particular person, we try our best to support. Am I missing anything out...school re-engagement, Centrelink support, banking. It's not just working with the youth, we work with the whole family to work with the youth. Reconnect staff work closely with all the youth services in town, and even out bush, even in the Shires to provide that ongoing support. So, even if they have gone to Adelaide for school, we provide that support if they calling you wanting to speak to family. We provide that bridge, basically.*

Servicing the Indigenous Alice environs is challenging. For a start, the remoteness, i.e. the logistics of providing meaningful service support in terms of direct interaction with communities. Next, funding uncertainties, which encourage alternate ways of overcoming community needs by not necessarily using economics to 'pay' for services. For example, the service generated in-house from the collective formidable female voices of Indigenous ladies, a powerful weapon of advocacy. A service that 'bridges' the urban and bush/remote/environs that allows for access and connectivity from one to the 'outer' other, and brings the youth 'back to country', maintaining the 'beyond backyard' imaginary and practice that characterises Alice Indigenous service experiences. Essentially the Indigenous Alice Springs and environs as part of a oneness of spatial immersion of people moving back and forth between the two.

To continue the service bridge between Alice and community and oneness of spatial immersion, one utilises the key phrase of Alice and community, hence looking at a community development organisation (CDO). This may be a non-government organisation which is not for profit. Communities within the Alice environs are generally Indigenous communities, so the CDO work with Aboriginal communities and Aboriginal organisations. The definition of 'work' is realised through planning, strategic planning, workshops, community development programs, and supplying volunteers. Volunteers in this context relate to people who wish to go to Indigenous communities, offering their employability skills, perhaps absorbing an authentic Indigenous experience and at the same time giving something of themselves in return. It is this reciprocity that characterises the community development process, in conjunction with communities themselves propelling projects. Demonstrating Indigenous ownership of projects creates sustainability, self-interest, and an in-built natural willingness to see projects through to a successful conclusion. Within this ownership, relationships are key, and in a sense Indigenous interests own the relationship, a relationship driven process involving communities, volunteers and CDO.

Although projects are space and place specific, they are not time specific, as they range from a matter of hours and days, to years. They also may be sequential. The community tempo sets the time, or lack of time structure. Accordingly, time integration with a CDO and community is influenced by availability, which in turn is influenced by what is happening in the community life at that time. The implication of community varies from being on an individual basis, an organisation, or actually the whole community. An example is Papunya or an organisation in Papunya, or a family group in Papunya. The Yuendumu space is another illustration of community variation. So, services are timed within the space of service relationships.

Since service provision is characterised by flexibility and miscellany, projects are also diverse. These range from building construction, gardens, renovating structures, to long-term challenges. Diversity also extends to attitude. For instance, the project model ignores shortfalls and welcomes potential and realised assets when working. This generates capacity, and not negative fault-finding, thus accomplishing the projects aims alongside community members within a partnership. Also, several CDOs can partner together if a project is beyond the capacity of any individual one. Or refer aspects of it to another CDO. It is a shared service.

Service quality, short or long term, requires a sense of self-policing. This implies that significant time is devoted to evaluation monitoring, which confirms or denies work effectiveness, also confirming or denying quality effectiveness. In a CDO context, quality equates to making a difference in communities. Quality service provision can also equate to funding characteristics. One type of character is from government coffers. For instance, Prime Minister and Cabinet may offer a two-year funding deal. The deal funded might incorporate community safety, remote school attendance, and a common one, literacy. Achieving functional (whatever that may imply) literacy standards in English is challenging across many communities. Also, prison to workforce. Another funding character is freelance. The imaginary of 'free' in freelance allows degrees of 'freedom' of practice through voluntary contributions, which would be limited more by government involvement, i.e. do it to their agenda.

Sustainability is important as another bow to service quality. Consequently, building capacity and marking the difference made in communities, i.e. achieving the 'marked' service footprint and enlarging the foot size. Hence, consolidating the track record by working with the same community again and again, rather than as a one-stop visit. This creates a strategic community approach with projects here, there, and anywhere in the Northern Territory and northern South Australia. Sustainability is also stability of communities, in the sense of community buy-in, as it is the community with the project idea, and not a project with a funded limited lifespan that dies at funding's end. Thus avoiding the community reaction of...what's been done to us, what next! Sick of seeing government cars coming to community and saying they are going to change the world, and they leave.

Assisting the buy-in is the act of listening of the CDO. Good listening is an art form of actually hearing and understanding to one's optimum ability of what is being spoken. From that verbal comprehension evolve considerations of how can the CDO assist, and who else can be brought in to help. It is essentially a philosophy of communities already retaining many of the solutions, but lacking resources to realise them, and CDOs may be able to service the shortfall. Sustainability is seeing it through, not promise that which cannot be delivered. For instance, there are many promises offered to the communities, advocated by the N.T. government, but these projects may be pulled, along with their funding. As a result, the service network that was built up, breaks down, and whole departments in government may be dispersed and re-structured.

An Indigenous community space is a difficult space, as numerous cultural factors influence service success or not. Instances include seasonal factors, sorry business, cultural business, what else is occurring in the community at the moment, and the motivation of a community at that particular time in getting involved in a project, i.e. the community must be keen. Also, when dealing with this difficult space, a softly approach should be adopted that begins small and slowly, always looking long-term. Consequently, operating at community pace, a gentle pace, because communities also can change as well as organisations.For example when building up capacity, people are lost, the direction changes, there are economic challenges. Additionally, it is a sensible idea to keep the planning map up to date, thus remaining at the forefront of where people are at, e.g. map mindfulness. Also, CDO mindfulness, i.e. what are you doing going in there, avoid stepping on toes, and generating a good understanding of the serviced landscape. Basically, ensuring the community is on board through the whole project process, and for them to speak about their stories concerning the project. This may be through videos or photographs, and interviews during and at the project completion.

Service provision commences with a conversation, which to be effective is ongoing throughout the process. The focus is on building capacity within the Indigenous service context, hence refocusing away from a skills transfer model of just conveying skills, to a community development paradigm. This produces a sustained, better quality picture concerning development and not just a stop gap. This is applicable to whoever is involved in the community work platform, i.e. government, semi-government, and local government, large organisations, and not for profit NGOs. The government participation in the service process can be rigorous and inflexible at times, when 'helping' a community, but it is the flexibility of CDOs that can lead to a greater success rate. Accordingly, in the CDO service field most projects do work, because of what they are. They are not unreachable. Not heavy handed. Not a top-down service scenario of doing it my way or the highway. Most importantly, Indigenous community people have a voice on how to treat and inspire the service. That is the key. Finally, returning to relationships, which encourage an equal service partnership to raise a project from the ground, i.e. a three-way cycle or tricycle watermark of CDO, volunteers, and the community(s).

Chapter Eight

Tourism

Tourism is a predominant public and private service industry. The public can be thought of as what the paying customers experience in full view of each other and encouraged by each other, for example in adventure hands on tourist pursuits. Also, there is the public face of marketing, devising the products. Any space and place that can be marketed out of the 'ordinary', and even those that are perceived as ordinary but are cleverly constructed as worth experiencing can, and are, sold as such. It is just as well consumer tastes range over the whole tourism offerings, of which new products are constantly being introduced or reimaged as 'new'. What drives the process of the tourism space is both what the consumer wants, which influences the tourism service creators to satisfy, and also what the creators 'advertise' tourists or the serviced should be experiencing. It is an osmotic process developing along fluid lines within the playing field of tourism. The private is the creative agenda that constructs the tourism space, but also the private wants, needs and desires of the tourist who wishes to indulge in that space.

The tourism service industry is a local to global performance, and as with the majority, if not all, of society's service industries, is competitive. Perhaps more so than most, as it does compete on the world stage, since the world is the touristic place of choice. Indeed, for some very affluent individuals, off world brief space travel is now offered. Choosing where to go in the world, or off it, is limited only by costs of what can be afforded. So, Alice Springs is contending with other places in Australia or overseas, to attract people in. Within that globally spatial competitiveness, its field of touristic services is but one amongst countless vacation/attraction/place of interest/leisure creations. The following narrative shows something of how it performs as an attraction service to maximise its potential, bring in the greatest number of service consumers as possible, and play the tourism tune.

In Alice Springs a touristic starting point for many tourists is the Tourism Visitors Centre. It orientates and guides the tourist consumer of what can be experienced in the Alice and environs. The Centre has existed for many years, located formerly by the Town Council building situated on the periphery of the CBD (central business district). This 'marginal' periphery location was the reason it moved into the Todd Mall about five years ago. The N.T. government encouraged the move, since the new location was more central, more local, and enjoyed greater access by vehicles and being on foot. As a Tourism Visitors Centre or Tourism Information Centre can attract many visitors and potential consumers to nearby town services (shops, cafes, eateries, as well as tourism products), another economic reason for the relocation was to draw more visitors into the space of the Mall. Consequently, tourists may then frequent some of the small businesses on route to or from the Visitors Centre.

Climate determines the ebb and flow of tourist visitor numbers to a region or place. Subsequently, climate regulates the level of tourist services. The summer months in the Alice of roughly October to March are the hotter times of the year, with temperatures reaching constantly into the high thirty degrees and into the low forties. Accordingly, tourist visitor numbers decrease as a result although, during the winter months of the northern hemisphere, people escape the cold and come 'down under', some visiting the Alice. The visiting cohort are essentially middle-aged Europeans and backpackers. They are the bulk of the summer customers, but generally tourism is a lot quieter than the cooler months. Thus, during the cooler winter and running into spring months of roughly April to September, the peak of visitors is realised. One reason, echoing northern hemisphere rational concerning shying away from wintry places, is that the weather is cold in the southern areas of Australia, and many people, particularly retirees, travel northwards for a few months to escape the chilly days of their home cities and towns. So, the majority of visitors are generally Australians. The demographic, as well as the already mention 'Grey Nomads' (retirees), are families who frequent the place during school holidays.

During the peak season of winter, 500 daily visitors may go to the Visitors Centre seeking advice, sometimes achieving the 1000 mark or over (the Centre has a one-way visitor door counter, so perhaps can be thought of as having a finger upon the level of tourist service visitation pulse in town). Visitors arrive from overseas and interstate and target the Centre, as they may have a lack of knowledge concerning tourism products on offer. An example of tourist visitors who come, or ride, into town sometime during the cooler months is Ulysses, an over fifties motorcycle enthusiast's organisation. They spend a lot of money, so the whole town benefits. Tourism service is not just about the direct benefits gained by tourism service providers, since other 'non-tourist' service providers also benefit. Mechanics are an example. During peak time they are fully booked. For instance, people may have attempted the long drive from down south or the east or from the north. All involve 1500 kilometres excursions. Consequently, vehicles can suffer wear and tear from the extensive road trip and require a service or other type of repairs. Or visitors damage their tyres or suffer cracked windscreens, when circumnavigating the Mereenie Loop (road between Alice Springs/West MacDonnell Ranges and Uluru/Kings Canyon). So, tourist services are not limited to hotels and restaurants or tours, as doing the tourist experience overflows into what else can occur, unforeseen or not, during that tourism time.

When mentioning the 1500-kilometre excursion to reach the Alice, the place is in a sense a driving half-way point of service. For example, the self-drive market, which is prevalent in the Alice, may be returnees to the Alice travelling up from the south who like the place and the central region, and stay for a few months in their caravans. Then at the end of their time, turn around and head back south. Or for others, who stop briefly in the Alice before heading 'upwards' to the warmer climate of the north and ultimately Darwin. For both, the place is literally the half-way mark on the road to and from their point of origin and destination.

For those who have not driven to the Alice, but arrived by plane or train, car hire is available to visit local and regional tourist destinations; Alice Springs, Uluṟu, Kings Canyon, west and east MacDonnell Ranges, and up to Tennant Creek. For those who do not have access to a vehicle for travel within Alice Springs, a hop on hop off bus is available. Navigation helping what to see in town, if 'hopping' or walking, is assisted to the tourist industry by signage provided by the Town Council. The importance of powered transport is vital for tourism to function, both for the tourist service providers and for the tourist serviced. Indeed, for all services in society and for those that are serviced, as without the modern day fundamentals of power generated by fossil fuel technology, electricity, wind, wave and solar, many services would not be possible, exist, or presented and culturally understood in forms which have not been seen or discovered as yet. The same dependence upon powered transportation would also have been applied to services offered before contemporary technology, based on previous technological levels.

Those who do not have self-transport options or occasionally do not wish to utilise them can book tours through their accommodation stops (hotels, motels, caravan parks), the Tourism Centre or online. There are many tours, events and attractions offered in the Alice and central region. Examples include the Casino for food, beverage and gambling. The Finke Adventure Tours situated at Hermannsburg offering ATVs (all-terrain vehicles) driving experience, in which the customer can be driven by the tour guide, if not confident in doing four-wheel driving, or follow the tour guide, each having its own vehicle, through Palm Valley. Next, the Ron Tour, a three-day camping excursion, AAT Kings at Yulara (Uluru) and Uluru Camels. Finally, the SEEIT Tours. Others touristic examples of 'non tour' attractions include the following; for those who have an interest in dinosaurs, the Megafauna Central is a recently created museum. It looks at Alcona and the megafauna unearthed there and about prehistoric times in central Australia. Alternatively, or as well as, attending the annual events of the Alice such as the Camel Cup, Henley-On-Todd (racing on river of sand, rather than water), Red Centre Nats (classic and tuned up vehicles) and the Alice Springs two-day show.

Tour operators suffer or thrive, depending upon prospective, within the competitive tourism field, as services overlay or replace or supersede previous services existing in the field. In the Alice there used to be many small tourism businesses, but some of the bigger and more powerful companies have bought them out although small businesses and private operators can do well and grow and become one of the bigger versions. To illustrate, Emu Run Tours began small, but purchased the Alice Wanderer, and expanded. Adventure Tours started as a one-man band in the Alice and now are international in scale. Additionally, a man began with one vehicle and now has three, focusses on the Italian and Spanish market, since being fluent in both. Thus, in Alice, it is possible to be successful in the town and avoid being a tourist tour operator casualty.

To ensure that success is contagious, or at least sustainable within opportunities to expand the local and regional tourism service market, a broader strategic space of the N.T. is considered...

Recently, the recently elected Labor government formed the Department of Tourism and Culture. Beneath that umbrella bureaucratic structure resides Heritage, Parks and Tourism, Arts and Museums, Department of Sport and Recreation, and principal happenings that occur in the N.T.. From this, N.T.s tourism or Tourism N.T. is endeavouring to expand the attractiveness of the N.T. as a destination of choice for travellers. Motivation is economy and profit making, so the outcome is for people to remain in that N.T. space for longer and hence boost spending levels. Thus, holiday campaigns are marketed, both for long and short-term visitors, as a 'must see' destination. Some of the campaigns focus on the Red Centre (central Australian) outback, highlighting adventure and ease of accessibility, and place uniqueness.

The Northern Territory Government created Tourism NT as a commission under the *Tourism NT Act 2012*. It is commissioned to market and guide NT development as a competitive visitor destination for sustainable Territorian advantage. Under the *Tourism NT Act 2012*, the functions of Tourism NT are as follows:

- Market the Territory as a desirable visitor destination.

- Facilitate the sustainable growth of the tourism industry in the Territory.

- Tourism NT works with the following main partners and stakeholders to achieve these following outcomes:

- The tourism industry to market the Territory interstate and overseas as a visitor destination.

- The travel industry to influence and coordinate partnerships with wholesalers and retail agents to facilitate distribution of the Territory's tourism product.

- The Northern Territory Government, through the Minister for Tourism, by providing policy and other advice.

- The Tourism Board of Commissioners, on strategic issues facing the Northern Territory's tourism industry.

(Tourism N.T. Corporate Website, 2019).

Thus, marketing is key to attract in consumers, boosted by partnerships and relations within the domestic and international space. But these dual contexts need to be serviced by monetary investment (utilise money to make money), otherwise the touristic intentions reside in 'empty' space. A current prominent example of funding investment is 'Tourism Turbocharging'. In February 2018 the Northern Territory Government released the Turbocharging Tourism Action Plan, a $103 million tourism stimulus package to attract more visitors, create more local jobs, and put more money into the pockets of Territorians. Rolled out over 18 months, across the 2017-18 and 2018-19 financial years, the Tourism Stimulus Package delivers an additional:

• $26.57 million for smarter and more targeted tourism marketing, allowing for increased promotion of NT attractions, more marketing campaigns with key airlines, more focus on targeting niche markets and to attract lucrative business events.

• $56.24 million for new, critical tourism infrastructure and related tourism programs that create more memorable experiences for visitors and drive demand, particularly in parks and reserves.

• $20.78 million to enhance existing festivals, events and other tourism experiences, to cement the Territory's reputation as a vibrant and exciting place to live, work and visit.

(Operational Plan 2018-19, p. 5).

Since there is a government commitment of 103 million dollars, it is a substantial sum of an uncharacteristically generous amount. The lavish rationale is based on a government prediction of economic return of one dollar invested can generate thirty-seven dollars (this can be justified by 2.5 Billion dollars spent by tourists over the past year (TurboCharged Tourism, 2019). Central Australian tourism would access some of the 103 million. For example, the restoration of Hermannsburg would be assisted by roughly three million, and perhaps five million for Tennant Creek for revitalisation and raising the quality of visitor experience. In Alice Springs, nine million for CBD revitalisation, the Cultural Centre, national Art Gallery and Megafauna museum. Beyond the 103 million is a further five million targeting the growing India and China visitor potential. These monetary offerings stimulates the central Australian economy, or services the economy, and from a strong 'Northern' voice.

To facilitate sustainable growth of tourism in the N.T., improving its infrastructure is fundamental. One infrastructure focus is roads. Road networks must be in a good state of repair or upgraded to bitumen. Roads coming in and out of the Alice to and from tourist destinations, of which the Alice is a key one, should allow ease of travel and traffic flow. For example, in the region of Hermannsburg, the road between Glen Helen and Hermannsburg has been sealed. This allowed for a transformation in who could drive 'out there'. Therefore, from the four-wheel drive market, the two-wheel drive market was added to the mix. Two-wheel drive vehicles cannot negotiate dirt roads that efficiently, but when the bitumen loop road flowed past Glen Helen, Hermannsburg, Standley Chasm, and Ormiston, a different touristic environment was created. An environment that could be accessed easily to immerse the tourist in Outback nature, its expansive vastness, scenery, and mountain ranges.

As well as the physical element of tourism, the cultural element presents itself. However, the authenticity of the cultural element can be treated with caution, since paradoxically, it is created within the tourism space of place production. Therefore, a sense of artificiality can dilute the product, as the very act of touristic transformation of a place does 'transform' it beyond what it previously was, i.e. from the 'real', to an imagined 'real'. To illustrate, a European cultural story and Traditional Owner story exists in the Alice and its environs, and the tourist challenge is to tell both stories. The challenge is for the tourist industry to service those stories in ways that are stimulating for the tourist serviced consumer, but not 'colonise' the stories too much. However, 'too much' is an arbitrary term, and a work in progress for cultural sensibilities, but for the tourism industry when marketing and marketing regions, there has to be a product to market a sense of serviced compromise between the stakeholders within the tourism field. The touristic Outback cultural interaction depends upon that.

The Stuart Highway 'feeds' Alice Springs both from the north and south. Along this vast road bisecting the Australian continent are many roadhouses and roadside stops. Every one of these is a gateway. A 'gateway' of tourism information, as drivers stop for the night and perhaps exchange gossip on what tourist destinations to head for and ones they have already experienced. In other words, word of mouth is a powerful driver to make or break tourist services. These roadhouses and stops tell a story to the driver of what is my next stop, what to do next. Many in the driver market travel around 200-300 kms per day and reach one of these stops about mid-afternoon to stake their parking spot. Sometimes 40 or 50 caravans can be set up in a roadside stop. They set up camp, get the chairs out, enjoy a beverage and absorb the outback 'infinity' that surrounds them. By eight or nine the next morning the travelling process begins all over again, and again the following day. These 'repeats' echo the north/south repeater stations on the old telegraph lines, with many of the roadside stop destinations having historical association with the repeater stations. For instance, instead of passing Morse coded communication along the telegraph lines, tourist coded communication is passed along the road stop network. However, the trick for the tourist industry is how to inform people, when doing that journey, of what is there for them to see and do and spend money on in the process, e.g. slowing people down to smell the tourist roses.

Passing on tourist stories to consumers can enter the virtual world. This creates a layered representation, as the 'real' of the tourist location is artificially overlaid by selling it as a tourist product, hence transforming the place to a representation of it. Then extending the representation further by 'placing' 3D goggles on tourist heads. Speedily, the tourist viewer is transformed to an imagined place of the past, an 'historical' journey of discovery. Perhaps the journey is about Central Australia before colonialism; no Western buildings, roads, shopping and monetary workplaces, and Traditional Indigenous language groups living within a pre-'white' influence. In the background resides the MacDonnell ranges (of course they were not labelled that then) standing majestically for geological eternity, indifferent to the games of human cultures, in whatever forms these take through time. The 3D visual narrative then flows to an interactive part with an Indigenous elder on community, walking through their land expressing their heritage and identity. The tourist can be a time traveller, whether being within a pre-colonial or colonial period, and partaking of a story that is being articulated, whilst looking and listening.

To ensure service quality, the story should be articulated well. Even though stone and cement and transport access routes are essential to get to the story and be in comfortable surroundings when there, if the story is poorly presented or represented, the tourist product is devalued. The story may be poor, for example within an Indigenous context, if there is no engagement at the community level. This may be due to the heritage of colonial exclusion, and the modern forms of 'post' colonial imposition of a community, and the constant need to nurture the economy. A form that this nurturing may take is attempting to run VET certificates in tourist programs or tour guiding, to grow a local workforce 'out there' in the Alice Indigenous environ. This will also involve training teams, so fashioning employment possibilities including small business enterprise.

When creating a small business enterprise (one example is Bush Foods), skill levels, or more precisely the lack of them, can equate to a lack of tourist services, or services in general. As a result it can be problematic to take a 'leap of faith' from being unemployed to overseeing that business. However, what will assist a business to sustain and grow is training through support programs. The government departments of Education, and Trade and Business can encourage these. A challenge though is within Indigenous contexts, a negative attitude may prevail that this is yet one more agency of government promising a product that will not be delivered. But, if this initial barrier is overcome, and if investors such as the ABA (Australian Bankers Association) or IVA (Individual Voluntary Arrangement), who do co-invest with community, come in and service the business, and if after two or three years the business is still a going concern with Indigenous involvement…many ifs…there is an expectation to community that they purchase the business off the government after training and knowing what to do, and operate it themselves.

When addressing Indigenous related tourism, or at least trying to acquire some meaningful capacity to get it off the ground, there are several cultural challenges to address. Firstly, there is Indigenous community participation. Who is or are the appropriate person/people to talk to?, as there may be six family groups, so a need to ensure that all are contacted. Second, are they happy about what is being proposed? If they do support it, then the 'trick of gathering them all into one place at the same time to describe what is being offered is not easy. Also, there will be some in the community that do not want tourism. That should be respected, but at the same time trying to avoid forcing tourism upon them as well. Thirdly, which probably pre-dates the first, is government level communication and negotiation. For instance, there is an overabundance of government agencies out there, both within the N.T government and Prime Minister and Cabinet. How well these interact with each other is a significant factor in producing strong initial and continuing foundations for Indigenous tourism, and non-Indigenous tourism service viability.

At the higher end of the tourism scale is the $100 million Arts Trail project. Its aim is to develop the Northern Territory into the premier destination to experience Australian Aboriginal arts and culture, and is expected to attract more interstate and international tourists to the N.T. (Arts Trail Project, 2017). One recent topical example in the Alice is the proposed building space for the national Indigenous art gallery. One discourse was for the gallery to be located by the ANZAC Oval. This is now not the case, due to some local resistance. However, from a tourism space context, the discourse is not necessarily the location, but if the Alice community actually wants the gallery. If not, it will go to another tourist location beyond central Australia. Hence, depending upon one's perspective, a service opportunity will be lost from a tourism perspective and as a by-product advantage for local businesses, or an 'undesirable' service opportunity will be avoided, i.e. someone's service gain maybe another one's loss. Thus, it is not always an economic return when 'measuring' service returns on service investment, as the social return is part of the equation, e.g., perhaps not just focusing on tourist visitor spending, but also taking into account of what the social return is for central Australia.

In the N.T there is a tourism policy called China Ready, as a preparatory capacity to attract Chinese visitors. For instance, China is number two in the inbound visitor arrivals, and number one for spending and accommodation. Going as far back as 2004, Tourism N.T. has networked the Chinese market, and in 2012 established a China Market Activation Plan with partnership in industry. The goal was to bring in 30,000 Chinese visitors spending 25 million dollars by 2020. The N.T. receives about 18,000 of the roughly one million Chinese that come to Australia. They wish to visit Uluru and the Outback in the central region, rather than the Top End. Thus, to achieve that 30,000 plus visitor numbers, a combination of what does the consumer want and is there capacity to delivery that service, are sensible considerations. Essentially opening up the Chinese market depends upon demographic demand.

So, training through support programs to gain the necessary service skills is offered to meet the 'promoted' demand:

> China Ready Online Cultural Training. Tourism NT has partnered with a China customer and market specialist, China Ready & Accredited (CRA) whose CHINA READY® training program equips clients with cultural insights and understanding that are essential for successfully engaging with Chinese people. Their training also leads to Global Accreditation which shows Chinese customers you are a reputable business that will meet Chinese traveller service expectations. The online training portal is free for NT based tourism, hospitality and retail staff. The training comprises of 12 cultural modules and three specialised tourism modules. Tourism NT encourages all NT businesses whose front line staff may come into contact with Chinese visitors to have them complete this accredited training. (China-Ready, 2019)

As one country's economic development expands, along with its increasing service capacity and resultant surplus cash flows, it can service other countries service capacity, and subsequently increase that. One result of profit surplus is the expansion of what can be termed the 'middle class'. Traditionally the Chinese upper tier could only pay for travel, but contemporary, literally millions of 'middle' Chinese can now purchase travel. They may be free independent travellers, making their own choices, discovering the world on an annual basis, and creating their own service portfolio.

To measure service excellence in N.T. tourism, aiming for the Brolga Awards is encouraged:

> The Brolga Northern Territory Tourism Awards (Brolga Awards) are the official tourism awards program for the Northern Territory. The Brolga Awards recognise and encourage tourism businesses that strive for excellence in every area of their operation. The Brolga Awards are open to tourism operators, industry suppliers and outstanding individuals, who prepare a submission in response to a series of questions and criteria that measure business excellence. Winning a Brolga Award is the industry's highest accolade and the recipients represent the best products and services in the Northern Territory. (Brolga Awards, 2019)

What the Brolga process does paradoxically, through the course of submitting or applying to the awards, is investigating business and marketing plans, thus a sense of business health check. As 80% of the N.T. tourism industry is small to medium enterprises, perhaps consisting of a married couple supported by two or three staff and working seven days a week for twelve hours daily, the luxury of time to self-reflect is rare. However, the awards process makes them do that, since by default, the businesses focus on what they do in a critical manner. Hence, a self-reflection on quality of service.

To encourage the quality of service, there are many support programs for businesses; Department of Business, Oz Trade, Oz Industry, and the Business Enterprise Centre. Business enterprise is vital for success, particularly as social media impacts about three-quarters of tourist consumers decisions about what to do or where to go,, i.e. the Trip Advisor carries weight. To influence communication traffic of social media, the bottom line is product quality. If there is naught to market or the product does not possess quality, or re-marketing the same fifteen or twenty products year after year, even if after investing tens of millions of dollars on advertising, consumers will look at alternatives. So, to keep the service fresh, stimulating, and exciting, development of the industry should be devising new products, packages, and experiences.

There are staffing challenges in the tourism and related hospitality industry in the Alice. It is rare for locals to work in hotels, and many people working the 'front desk' would be international visitors. Also, local Indigenous workers would be rare or non-existent. Basically, recruitment is arduous in town, and there is a recurring story of cannot find somebody, or somebody with the required skills. As the government is the biggest employer in town offering good salary, generous superannuation and six weeks leave, the private industry of tourism and hospitality, to compete for workers and even to be competitive, need to offer more than the government. Particularly as Alice is a regional town and pretty remote, and a testing environment to build employee capacity.

This employee capacity of industry can fleece Peter to pay Paul. To illustrate, a tour guide does not like the company where he or she currently works, and for whatever reason moves onto the next guiding company. Also, knowledge and intellectual property gained of the previous company moves as well. As a result, the former owner has to begin the training again with someone new, affecting product delivery quality. Another example is a waiter may only work for a few months at one restaurant, then onto the next, and the next. There is high turnover across the whole industry, and employee capacity, for many, resides on shifting sands. The service capacity likewise does as well.

Accordingly, not only does government service a positive spin on selling the N.T. as a tourism space, it also constructs affirmative reasons of attracting employees into the Territory, such as job opportunities, lifestyle, and minimal commuting time. But, whether the communication is effective is questionable, as there may be a case of a stereotype, trapped in time. In other words, an image of the N.T. as a place without tarmac roads, and a piano that ceases when slipping in through the swing doors into the pub, as everything goes quiet for a few seconds, resulting in bar brawls. An imaginary bygone era, which may still be perceived as such from other places within Australia, and overseas. An irony is perhaps some tourists would find that 'old world charm' attractive, but it cannot be marketed as the product does not exist. For services to perform, there has to be a product. To find out what the tourism product is, both from an industry servicer perspective and from the consumer serviced, can be a service discovery or service creation.

There is an agenda for finding out the tourism product generated from the needs of the community or an organisation (commercial or government). Firstly, at a State and Territory level, government needs depend upon which party holds power for its term of office. Secondly, the party then defines the product research parameters. The definition is assisted by National Visitors surveys and International Visitors surveys, of which both influence what the agenda is and what the agenda can become, within an ongoing trajectory. Finally, the quantity and qualitative data generated is utilised as a level of service comparison between Australian States and Territories. Paradoxically the N.T. demographic is the lowest in Australia, but tourism as an industry is highly important, perhaps more than how the States' view their tourism industries, since it is due to the level of economic dependence upon it. Therefore, the N.T. government agenda is to make the tourism product even more extensive. A reason for that is to spread the economic portfolio, to lessen the risk if one or more major products 'fall-over'. This is a prudent and sustainable course of action. To illustrate, the N.T. does have a history of favouring mining, so if that stops, a backup tourist plan is already in place, rather than facing an economic void. For any society and its space within, a main service consideration is the ongoing maintenance of what it is.

A tourism product such as Uluru is an established mainstay of central Australian tourism. Other places in the region can and are 'touristic' but are not as well known. In the domestic market, people are generally not aware of the N.T. in terms of these other places, thus an unknown quantity, so N.T. awareness needs to be developed. If the domestic market does not know what the northern Australian tourist product is, international tourists would be at more of a loss. Even though the traditional Western markets may have greater awareness of N.T. and central Australia, the growing markets of non-Western cohorts require awareness education. Australia itself as place has awareness, but places within that place do not, except for the leading ones such as Sydney Opera House, Great Ocean Road and Uluru. Therefore, placing services is just as important as the services themselves, since without location, services are 'used less' or 'useless'.

Increasing competition between places; country to country, region to region, local place to another in that same place, drives the tourism industry. Since many countries now welcome tourists, this may result in having twelve countries to choose from, as compared to the former range of six, and that is just the international market. To add to this competition between places, the

Australian market also can choose between domestic and international, for example selecting Indonesia and the countries around that region. Essentially tourism services contest for people's money and time and their space of performance. Part of the contest process is discovering ways to make the product more attractive, by marketing as not just as a broad product sell, but focussing on particulars, i.e., sections of tourist populations may prefer adventure tourism, so sell hiking, mountain biking. Others are mature, such as the Grey Nomads (self-driving retirees) who flow in to the central and northern regions of Australia for much of the year, so are a significant niche market. Also, there are those with an interest in N.T. Aboriginal cultural activities, so how can these be engaged with, which is not the same thing as engaging with Indigenous people in the N.T.. The latter is a throwback to a colonial exclusion and cultural curiosity. It is a sensitive tourist service space, with its inherent historical tensions, which must be treated with touristic caution and respect.

Another significant tourist particular are backpackers. They occupy the greatest tourist space, time, and spending, simply because they will visit Australia for months, as compared to the two-week tourists. A backpacker may be perceived as being money 'tight', however they do visit key attractions. They also can work. For instance, there are many backpackers in Alice Springs within a diverse range of jobs, particularly in the service industry, i.e. hospitality. So, some earnings get ploughed back into the local economy; rent, food, and local entertainment. Others that may not work, but do spend, are a new type of backpacker in their thirties trying to 'find themselves'... 'I'm not sure about my life, just going exploring'. They can stay in a hostel, but also three-star hotels or Air B'N'B, as preferring the more 'finer' services on offer. They do travel for extended periods, but have a closing date to finish.

The serviced tourist industry in central Australia does provide jobs for many, and also jobs for those support services that offer food and shelter to visiting tourists. However, the paradox is that local businesses who depend on the service industry of hospitality and tourism, have requirements for a talented, capable workforce, but since the N.T. demographic is small, locals in these tourist related spaces are not filling vacancies. Even though the N.T. government does encourage locals to seek employment in the N.T., and not depart from the N.T., it is difficult to get them to stay and take on jobs. Basically, it would be preferable for locals to be trained in tourist services, since they provide local insight for tourists, and hopefully stay in the employed position for a reasonable length of time. Thus, the time/space and investment of locals within the Alice and environs is just as important as the time/space/spending of the tourist visitors. Finding local solutions is an ongoing space of inquiry and challenging, i.e. short-term solutions are doubtful, public and private funds are limited, and no population boom is going to abruptly happen.

The tourist service 'circle' of serviced and servicer sometimes does not complete the circumference of societal aims, which causes challenges, in terms of demand and supply, i.e. the supply may not be able to efficiently deal with the demand all the time. Since service peaks and troughs are the order of the day, no services, touristic included, can maintain constant peak performance and resultant maximum output during the service transaction. Thus, to struggle and aim for a reasonably aggregate level of service performance and output, to create solutions, may be the only practical outcome. However, even this may not be feasible due to demographic limitations, such as in the N.T. and the Alice, and intentional limitations placed upon those who advocate, on behalf of the local population, for change. Thus, the last service chapter looks at political service and its advocacy, voicing the service of society to try and construct circles.

Chapter Nine

Politics

Politics is an integral aspect of fields and political fields. Politics create connections and break connections along the time and space of the roller-coaster communications they inhabit. This habitus is endowed with beliefs, principles, dogma, theories, and philosophies, driven by the human and physical geographical locations the political advocate dwells within. The human geography of that dwelling is saturated with societal endeavours striving to live the capitalist way, a way of work, profit, dominance and subordination, multiculturalism, and a sense of class differentiation. Class may be defined as an aspect of 'in-house' cultural structural hierarchy, i.e. within the same cultural sense of identity. Class can also be defined as an 'out-house' diverse cultural hierarchy, i.e. different cultures co-existing within the same space and place. Within characteristics of both, some voices are 'louder' than others to champion selected agendas, but generally accompanied by resistances that go along with that. Thus, competing cultural voices to stake claims upon the dwelling space.

These are power plays that draw from the abstract to create a concrete reality, be it one of fluidity, as the cultural players in the game jostle for position within the backdrop of the physical geographic space, in an ongoing performance. A performance of politics in a physical backdrop, in the Alice Springs case, of surrounding ancient landscapes of mountain ranges, vast open uneven plains of bushland, unending blue sky interrupted by the occasionally storm, both rain and sand, flies, and extreme temperatures of summer, and occasional freezing temperatures of winter. The physical backdrop also includes the urban environment with residential suburbs, town camps, CBD, industrial areas, the rural environments of communities, tourist locations, mines, and stations. All play a part in the political fields of Central Australia and all overlaid by political representations. Within the context of this physical backdrop, the following advocate politics of Alice Springs and environs.

The demographic character of the Alice has altered in the last decade with increased presence of African, Asian sub-continent, and Indian people. For example, Indian workers range from the unskilled to professionals, of which some work at the Alice Springs hospital. The town has evolved into multiculturalism and reveals a plurality of cultural behaviours and practices. Hence, there is an evolving cultural climate, one that drives acclimatisation of both the established cultures and newer ones coming in. Within this process, everyone's perspective of themselves and each other develops, and hopefully not to breaking points, from efforts to maintain societal integrity. Accordingly, the functionality of the town has changed. For example in homes, people dwell with their extended families in numbers beyond the suburban average. Additionally, English may be a second or third language, with the children learning English at school. So, business methods alter, reflecting the greater multiculturalism. This is a positive for Alice Springs if measuring the economic benefits of more workers. The multiculturalism is apparent during Harmony Day celebrations, when cultural diversity is on show. Also evidenced in the construction and running of the new Migrant Resource Centre, located at the Alice Springs Youth Centre about two and a half years ago.

The ever present, past, and future traditional culture of Aboriginal people defines the central Australian region in various ways. They are a prominent aspect of the community and also as an employment attraction, since many individuals gravitate to the Alice to work with Aboriginals. This may take the form of law enforcement, public service, or health. Accordingly, the Aboriginal presence in town and environs create significant business. Additionally, the noteworthy engagement with Aboriginals may be due to the fact that 30% of the Alice demographic is Indigenous, and for a town of roughly 25,000 people, that is not an insignificant proportion. Along with the substantial percentage, questions of racism can be considered, and Aboriginal people do experience it, but generally the cultures do get on. Perhaps that has to do with the small population and remoteness/isolation from other major settlements. For instance, it does not pay to be too aggressive in the Alice space, as people tend to know each other, or a friend of a friend does. Essentially, the majority share similar goals, hopes, and aims as a community, and individuals and families are just trying to perform their lives in the best way feasible. Essentially, people are generally social and outgoing, and mingle and enjoy themselves.

However, Alice Springs as a dwelling place is demanding. There is a hard edge to it. The climate is arduous with excessive heat and cold, and a dearth of humidity (mostly). Also, many Aboriginals live in poverty, adding further to community hardness. There are realities of deprivation and social challenges that go alongside it such as children being affected and not sleeping soundly, problems with behaviour, and not being fed. Therefore, an environment of exceptionally disadvantaged backgrounds, with parents having difficulties from various causes of getting their children to attain primary and high school, so the youngsters simply abandon the education process. To address the abandonment, the St. Joseph school, located on the site of the closed ANZAC Hill high school, acted as a safety net for 'abandoned' children of the mainstream school education system, and offered support with social issues, and taught youngsters rudimentary literacy and numeracy. A decade ago, twenty children joined the Edmund Rice centre at St Joseph's, recently there were ten times as many children signed on. Unfortunately, the site has now been bulldozed.

At the other end of the economic continuum from poverty in the Alice, is that the place comprises amongst the highest income capability of the majority of other Australian centres. For instance, an inconceivable amount of people earns above 150,000 dollars annually, so classified within the top ten percent of Australian income earners, living agreeably with an equivalent quality lifestyle. It is a place of contradictions and contrasts, not least Indigenous contrasts. To illustrate, over the last couple of decades there has been a developing and increasing middle class of Aborigines that are part of the well-paid segment of Alice society. Within the moderate income levels, more Aboriginal people are in ordinary jobs, just getting on and along with their daily lives as a working-class performance, similar to the 'white' families. Thus, there are many Aboriginal trades' people operating around the Alice; young men who are doing good, which is a good sign. One reason for the wellbeing is that the government does offer positive discrimination towards Indigenous tenders. Another reason is that these families are stronger, wiser, more educated than previously evidenced in the town, and encourage their offspring into occupations that have a genuine future. There are also a group of mainly migrants who juggle several jobs at once. These may be three or four jobs in number, adding up to many hours worked in a day. This is because the migrants are in the Alice to earn and save money, and then move on. For some, the Alice is a steppingstone service place to something 'better', and/or to get way from something worse in a previous dwelling place.

Returning to the other end of the Indigenous contrast in terms of economic scarcity, town camps can be a challenge for those living there. For instance, some families are confined to that lifestyle, being vulnerable to the poverty cycle. To illustrate, due to the Indigenous culture of supporting extended family members, perhaps to a degree well beyond Western family cultural expectations and obligations, attempts to move beyond that cultural normalcy is thwarted. This may be because family members are involuntarily pulled back into the family structure by instilling unfair and unrealistic requirements upon them through money requests and support. Also, in town camps and on communities, hunger is a significant issue. One cause may be due to the exacting nature of the Work for the Dole Scheme, for it is challenging to tick all the boxes for the scheme program. As a result, welfare payments are being restricted, with less money to go around, and less money for food. Inevitably greater crime and social dysfunction result. Consequently, rules set by a service provider can be so stringent that paradoxically the service cannot be utilised, which results in societal suffering. Thus, the connective flow between the servicer and the serviced can break down, and creates place tensions due to political decisions made that are problematic or impractical to follow.

The identity of a place, and what it stands for, can create the service identity of that place both through its natural resources and human resources. The two combine to service identity, both in the present and future possibilities or continuities. For example, Who is Alice Springs! Is the place a contested space! Is it in transition! The next part attempts to answer these considerations to assist with future characteristics and directions of the N.T.

In terms of Members of the NT parliament, Alice has two urban members and two rural members representing its political space. The Alice is also represented at the Federal level, being part of the Lingiari House of Representatives. Furthermore, The N.T. as a whole has two senators. From these representatives of the people, a holistic approach is required for the Alice and environs, as the significant in-migration of multicultural backgrounds (as already mentioned) has added difference to the traditional 'black and white'. Once the Alice was white people and Indigenous and very little presence of other nationalities, but the town's face has shifted. Also shifted is the dynamic between Indigenous and non-Aboriginals, so it is challenging as to where Traditional Owners situate themselves within the societal fluidity.

Disparity between the Indigenous community and non-Indigenous community perhaps is widening, not helped with non-resolved issues concerning disadvantage. A factor contributing to this is an all too human one of mutual suspicion of one's 'other', bred by a lack of communication. This can cause suspicion fed by ignorance of the other. For example, crime levels may be elevated well beyond the actual occurrences, and demonisation of the suspected perpetrators rides the cultural rumour mill. As a consequence, the social heart of the matter of people who are angry with perceptions of society being beyond 'normal' patterns and behavioural limitations, can produce fear, some of it irrational. However, a significant driver of this is lack of relationships between 'white and black'. For instance, those non-Indigenous who do connect with Indigenous and are active about going forward together, did enjoy former relations with each other, as they were local Alice dwellers growing up in the place. Perhaps these non-Indigenous individuals played football with the Indigenous 'Mob', so both related to a range of things. Alternatively, some people who arrived in the last half-decade to a decade, have minimal or no relations with Indigenous families beyond paid service provision. They did not work together with these families, having not grown up with them, no sport was mutually played, hence disconnection. Consequently, a 'fee for service' is not necessarily a holistic service.

A societal serviced space, for it to function along that holistic vein, should incorporate all groups, be a shared space, thus creating a conciliatory process. Alice Springs and environs have historically been a shared space, but perhaps not too conciliatory. It is challenging to achieve a shared space during the present time and indeed the Alice dwellers of the future may face generational tensions and agendas. To illustrate, people who are at retirement age and have been in the Central Australian region since the 1960s to 1980s, have done well out of the place. They have been serviced efficiently. But their offspring who are also doing well, ask where do we fit in this town? What does the future hold? Do we wish to raise our offspring here? Again, how does that spatial generational environment effect Traditional Owners?

Will Alice Springs remain within the longstanding methods of doing things, as being dependent as a service deliverer, based on the funding of

Indigenous disadvantage. For example, the Intervention (a set of policies introduced by the Howard government in 2007 in response to the The Little Children are Sacred Report, which claimed that neglect and sexual abuse of children in Indigenous communities had reached crisis levels) in the N.T. produced an environment similar to a 'mining boom' as wages and house prices increased, and people were priced out of the rental market. For instance, Centrelink would literally reserve a hotel, regardless of the rooms being used, which is an illustration of the Alice's reliance on disadvantage. Within this context, The Alice can be thought of as a thriving space of Indigenous demerit.

There is an intimate connection to Indigenous people in the Alice in terms of economic benefits. But perhaps they do not fully share in the monetary spoils, as the benefit of sharing is normally wage and grants for the servers and none for the serviced. Therefore the serviced context the sharing resides within is important to spread monetary economic value around for the general wellbeing of the locally 'placed' society. Another example of serviced sharing/non-sharing is the local mining escalation, since numerous mines are beginning to come online, especially towards Tennant Creek (rare minerals mine, phosphate mine). If the fly in/fly out workforce develops, local people looking for work and the local economy may or will be bypassed. The community services for fly in has existed for a considerable duration for out bush mining, or in remote communities for nurses and teachers, however local Indigenous people do not necessarily get offered jobs. Or perhaps, in terms of traditional gendered roles, nor do women, for mining and grazing. There are exceptions to this, within the roles of 'male' jobs, and the traditional female dominated roles in health. Thus, depending upon employment context, some people can be excluded from service provision..

Government funding dictates service levels to a great extent, i.e. the federal government provides funding to the N.T. government, and private funding partnerships, and the current policies and characters of these dictate flexible service deliveries. For instance, one; cuts to GST (Goods and Services Tax) have significantly influenced the N.T. budget structure. Two; Horizontal fiscal equalisation, will create a significant issue, if modified by the Federal government.. Lastly; the INPEX (International Petroleum Exploration) is a vast capital investment that motors the N.T. economy, with the point being that the N.T. economy is not fully formed. Thus, it is a young economy vulnerable to highs and lows and is inconsistent. Also, much of the economic infrastructure is government workers, with many public servants accompanying that portfolio and of which their sustainability is uncertain.

Reconciliation and shared spaces in the Alice are a work in progress, particularly within the realm of the young. They can feel excluded from the community, which is reinforced when media coverage significantly covers youth crime. Few other positive young perspectives may be voiced, hence there is social exclusion. However, it should not be ignored that some youths do perform unacceptable public behavioural displays, but as part of the holistic approach, inclusion may be advantageous for all. This is because they become part of the community, become productive. Alice Springs then develops a mutually serviced town incorporating all facets of human geography, and draws the dark spaces of the town towards and into the light, for all to comfortably share. Thus, creating a constantly reconciling system to maintain a healthy society.

The next segment also has in its background a mindfulness of aspiring to a healthy wellbeing of those that dwell in central Australia. Hence, encouraging voices to be heard and creating wellbeing from that, or at least having opportunity to express opinion, which in itself is a societal safety valve, literally letting off societal steam, letting the hotness cool down to allow the flow of society to move over calmer waters:

From the beginning in my role as a member of Parliament, my constituency is the electoral division of Namatjira. In summary would be basically everything that is located on the southern side of the MacDonnell Ranges, falling into the electorate of Namatjira. Scott (McConnell) takes in a portion of Hermannsburg and Areyonga, up to Katherine. So, Scott I believe, has the first or second largest electorate. Namatjira is the third largest electorate in the Northern Territory. It's roughly the size of Germany, with a population of around 6,000, but there is a higher population because the electorate itself is quite a young population, with a large number of people who are under the age of 18. Or, who are 18, but they are not on the electoral role for a variety of reasons. It's not my job to make them. I constantly encourage them, because elected numbers place significant roles on electoral redistributions. So, changing of boundaries.

My electorate is south of the Gap (Heavitree Gap), but it does shift further east and takes a bit of a bend up. I have Harts Range and Gowalla to Utopia and Ampilitwaja. They are my northern parts. My electorate is the electorate of which Alice Springs, the two town seats, sit within. So, I basically have 75% of the town camps in Alice Springs, falling in my electorate. So, it's a very interesting electorate. It's a hybrid seat in the Northern Territory. One of only two. I've got rural residents who commute in and out of Alice Springs every day. Town campers. Remote communities, and tourism townships such as Yulara (Uluru/Ayers Rock). I go down to three borders...to the western Australian, south Australian and Queensland borders.

It's a very interesting seat to hold, because no day is like any other day. It's fantastic. (work travel) I probably average on a year, roughly 55,000kms. I see my role in the Parliament for that particular electoral division more around advocacy, lobbying, governance, and being a supportive conduit for the people who I represent. Making sure the views, the voices, the aspirations of the electorate are heard in Parliament. But also within government, because currently the party I am affiliated with, is the party in government...there is an added layer there of making sure government policies, government initiatives and incentives, those types of things, are reflective of the views and aspirations of people in my constituency.

Without getting too much into it, that can be difficult. Because in particular with my seat with its many conflicting views, you've got the rural residents who are affected by decisions which happen in Alice Springs, because they come into Alice Springs every day. I got remote brothers and sisters who don't come into Alice too often, and their focus is on making sure there's remote programs and service delivery to build capacities and strengthen communities. What is interesting is at times there are cases where you need to support your community, and that might not be a position that the government takes. But, as a parliamentarian representing that, you need to make sure that people are aware of the views and concerns of the people in the electorate.

A large number of my day is out bush sitting down with people. It's about someone being an interface. If I'm out bush, I will take down constituent concerns or ideas. It's not always a negative thing. Sometimes you are out there, and people are talking to you about positive things that we could do moving forward. But an average day is talking to people and if people raise issues with housing or there is some repairs that need to be carried out on their property or around developing community or sports infrastructure, I take that on board. Record it in written formats...come back and make a formal approach or correspondence to Ministers offices to raise those concerns to get them done.

I probably take a different approach to most members. I don't like to stay in government accommodation or community organisations when I go out bush. I tend to stay with people in community who I've got a relationship with...whether they're friends or family, because I think that itself is really important. We talk about the issues of overcrowding. We talk about the repairs and maintenance that are required. Family units. Child protection and those issues. I think there is no better way to understand those, than to actually place yourself in that environment, to see how it happens. Because there will be times when departments come back to you and say, we've gone out and done surveying and there's not that significant level of overcrowding...and from that experience you can go, well I disagree, because I've been there. Sometimes it's because people are afraid to actually record just how much overcrowding there is, for the fear of being a victim, for the fear of having to be disciplined in some shape or form. So, it is different. So, that's one aspect.

Being a remote or bush Member of Parliament is not just about pulling up in the car, talking to people, and going back. We do a lot of community events. Community barbecues. Try to be as across the electorate as much as I can and try and put myself in situations where you can experience the electorate from different avenues, because it's such a diverse electorate. That's the best way to understand it. So, we'll go out and camp on peoples out stations, to get a view of life on out stations. So when they talk to me about services that they need, I know as well of those services.

The electorate of which I represent, I don't like saying mine, because it's our electorate...between the people who elected me and me as a representative, I am always honest with them, even if it's not going to be good news, because they respect it either way from being told what's happening. Sometimes there's going to be houses that you are just not going to be able to deliver in a particular time frame. But it's about people knowing that you're working for them. We've had times where communities have been told that clinics are going to close...so we get together, and I am supportive of the communities' views...that's the view I'll go out publicly in media, or to the government, my government, or to the parliament that I represent. That's always going to be a challenge, but it's how you manage it. That's the remote part.

The rural area is different again. People move rural because they like to have a rural lifestyle. (rural space in the electorate) Ilparpa, Ross Highway, Connellan, out near the airport. They are my rural properties. People choose to live out there, because they like to be in a kind of Outback environment...it's beautiful. It's constantly at risk of industrialisation from people operating commercial businesses out there. That's one of the challenges with that area. That's an area where you hold regular meetings, where people can come and talk about any local issues that they need you to take up and prosecute.

My role is not limited to Northern Territory government responsibilities. I advocate support and lobby on constituent's behalf in local government, Territory government, Federal government, and community organisations, for the benefit of my constituency. Recently, we've been petitioning the Federal government for better NBN (National Broadband Network) telecommunication services in the rural area. It's not a Territory jurisdictional matter, but it's an issue that effects my constituency. So, it's an issue that I am more than happy to take up.

At the end of the day my role is to be a strong voice for the constituency, and is to...I don't like the word fight...is to get down and try and push and pressure people to get in and support my constituency with grants incentives, programs, good policies...those types of things. No day is ever the same day. I try the best I can to work in a bi-partisan manner for the benefit of people in my electorate. It is a challenge my electorate being so close to Alice Springs that quite often I get brought in on Alice Springs matters. Of which I'll always try and work with the two members. One of the members, Dale Wakefield, is a member of my team, member of my government. Robyn Lambley is a constituent of mine, but she is also a member of parliament for Araluen as an independent...I have a good working relationship with the both of them, and if it is in the benefit of Alice Springs, then I would always jump in and support them or their constituents on community matters.

You've got to have that holistic approach, and being Aboriginal and being the only Aboriginal member down here, I get a lot of people from Braitling and the Araluen electorates come here, because they know I am Aboriginal...and they want me to take carriage of the situation or an issue they are having, because they fill comfortable talking to an Aboriginal person. Having grown up in Alice Springs, being born and bred here...having family any which way for a 200kms radius or more, people know who I am, and they are comfortable with me doing that.

So, they come into the office, we never turn anyone away...have an astronomical workload because of that, we will quite often assist as much as we can in taking care of those issues for people. It's not just restricted to the Aboriginal population in those two electorates...being born and bred here and my family being well connected to everyone in sports events, will be people who will come here because they'll say, you're Sheryl's son or you're Barbara's grandson...we want help. We always offer in first instance, your local member is the member for Braitling or is the member for Araluen, they're the people you can speak to, however we are always happy to help, and if you want to, we are happy to work in with them on the situation. So, quite often if they come to us, and they want us to look at it, we will, but we will always give the other electorates the heads up...such and such has come, just taking care of an issue for them, just wanted to let you know.

Quite often, and it would be the same for the member for Braitling, and the member for Araluen, people in the rural area might know either one of them on a personal level, and might feel comfortable talking to them, before they come here. Or they might know them through dealing through the member for Braitling's ministry, or through any kind of connection, because my electorate has a lot of community organisations in it as well. They might know either one of those. So, whilst we have divisions we represent, being based in Alice Springs, of which itself is a service hub for remote communities, there is a constant cross over all the time of talking to people.

This is the funny thing with politics though, many of my family and friends share the same value and affiliation with my political party, which is the Labour party. I've been with them for 11 years, but a number of my family and friends are also members of other political parties...whether or not you are in this party or that party, at the end of the day we strive to see people have better lives and live better lives...we just have potentially different values, which we believe are the values which will get up to this utopian ideal. We choose different roads to get to the Land of Plenty. We believe, across all parties, every party believes they have the best road to get there. That's why we ask people to join our party and vote for us, but at the end of the day I believe that, everyone believes, we are doing this because we all want better. It's an interesting way to look at it I suppose.

Organisations will do this, because they want people to be better. Their organisation believes they have the best to get there. That's kind of refreshing in a town like Alice Springs, because it's still a good size that you can actually see and hear people talking about why they want to do particular things they want to do. For me, it's quite special. People tend to go to different people here for different issues on a political level, because our electoral boundaries change all the time...the eastern side of the river, which was formerly the electorate of Greatorex, no longer exists anymore...a third seat for the Alice Springs township was removed, because the population declined. So, Braitling and Araluen had to take on, absorb, that part of the electorate. Alice Springs people, central Australians in particular, quite often they don't confine themselves to an electorate or a boundary, they'll talk to numerous people. My parliamentary colleagues are always pretty good if they've had a conversation with someone who's from my electorate...they'd just let me know they have had a conversation with them. That's across all party levels. It's never a dull moment.

You can measure a town's vibrancy by a number of considerations. Tourism is one of those...people coming in and out, but also Alice Springs puts on a range of events, and they're not just catered for the tourist market. There are a whole range of events which have started off for Alice Springs people, which we do tap into tourism, but they've actually been created for the love of the community. That's really special. If you would ask me to summarise Alice Springs, it's a hard task to do...Alice Springs is the Land of Enchantment, really for me. I've grown...I'm a fifth generation central Australian, that's as far as we can go back. There are more generations obviously, but it's a place like no other...Alice Springs is a town...well central Australia in general...it is a region that gives you what you put in. If you want to be bored and not enjoy the place and not put in, then that's what you'll have. But if you want to be active and involved and share in the spirit of a community, you will not be home every night, because you will be part of a community group doing something, whether it's in the arts or the motor sports or the creative industries or sports...there is something for everyone in this town. You will be rewarded in many ways, whether it's a reward in developing wonderful life-long friendships, or actually the reward of seeing what you do on a large scale when community events happen, and everyone talks about it. Or you see the final product. There are so many ways of measuring how successful your input is in the local community. You can't put a price on that. It's really rewarding to see.

Often people will always talk about making friends, and they're gone again. That's actually quite a positive element about Alice Springs, we do have a transient population. But it's positive because if those people can come through, enjoy every minute that they've had here in their contributions, well you've got people to stay with when you're interstate...but you've got people who go away and talk up the town...that it's not just this place that people hear about, every now and then, but it's a place that has a pull. Whether or not they go away and talk it up, or whether or not they'll come back for the yearly events like the Beanie Festival or Finke Desert Race, whatever it is, it captures you. There is no denying that Alice Springs and central Australia have a spiritual energy that gets into the soul of anyone.

When we, as Aboriginal people, talk about connection to country, people on the east coast don't understand that...but non-Indigenous people that live in central Australia understand that connection to country, because there are a large number of people who are non-Indigenous who have that connection themselves to place, and that they understand. I've got lots of friends of mine who go away on holidays, and by the end of it they long to see the Ranges...they're longing to be back again... (a significant Range landmark that says you are almost home, are the three transmitters on the hill near Heavitree Gap seen afar from the north and south) you see it and talk to them, and they have an overwhelming satisfaction of knowing that they're home, that they're back.

Alice Springs should be a Rite of Passage for anyone in the country. Anyone should have to come through the interior of the country, of the nation, to experience it in all its glories, but also to experience some of the areas we do need to work on. We cannot, and should not, deny that there are things that we need to do to make Alice Springs even better than what it is, and those things are things we need to work on as an entire community to overcome.

(Spirituality to place and experiencing Ulu̱ru looking at me, rather than me looking at Ulu̱ru) Having Ulu̱ru in my electorate, I go there a lot of times a year, but it still doesn't take away that tickling of my heart when you see the place. It's the energy. That's the same about Alice Springs. People will often talk about it in a negative manner...I can understand sometimes why people do that, because they feel like they are pushed to the extreme and that's the course of action they have to take, to get some remedy. But it's hurtful, because this is my home. I was born here. I moved away for a couple of years, as every young person does to experience the big wide world. I came home. I bought my first house. Did all of that stuff and we all talk about going on holidays and stuff, but I know that Alice Springs is my home, and it's a place where I will probably live forever. Not denying there might be times in the future where I may duck out for a little while, but I'll always come home. It's a place where it doesn't matter if you were born here or come here, you will ultimately have that connection or that vested interest in making it a better place. (travelling up from the south, seeing the artificial Welcome to N.T. sign when crossing the border and driving in the road train troughs to Kulgera (first roadhouse encounter going north in the N.T. on the Stuart Highway) glad to be back). They are all things that are quintessential central Australia...they're great.

Another thing about Alice is because we are in the interior, we're smack bang in the middle, we service remote communities. We are very fortunate to have infrastructure that no other town our size would have. We have key pieces of infrastructure that are state of the art that if you would look at towns of our size on the southern, eastern and the northern coasts, you wouldn't find a town that has the infrastructure that we have. But you probably wouldn't find a town that has the diversity that we have here. The multicultural backgrounds. The experience...the tertiary experience, the lived experience. We're unique in that all these different experiences are all kind of crammed into Alice Springs, and we all, for the most part, seem to get along harmoniously together. I find that quite fascinating.

Everyone has a story, and it's a different story, but we can all get along...for most of the part. I love Alice Springs...it's a mixed bag. There's everything and anything here. I probably haven't experienced as much discrimination as I probably would have if I lived in a town of similar size to this on the east coast. As a gay, Aboriginal person, I've had limited negative experience with people here. It doesn't matter what side or what views or values you have, 80 or 90% of the people in Alice Springs...if someone says something bad about the place...we'll defend it. It's kind of very patriotic towards Alice Springs. I've known people who themselves are critical of the town, in a group of local friends, but the minute an interstate person says something bad about the town, they will be the first people out there saying...how dare you, do not talk about my place like this...it's fascinating to see how that unravels.

That is the interesting thing with Alice Springs is when people come to cover a story, they'll always get the story they want, because there is so many different views, there are so many different energies that have drawn people here, that if a journalist or researcher comes, if they got in their mind what they want, they'll most likely get it, because there are so many different views and community groups who have different ideas and different values. It's very hard to get a true reflection of Alice Springs, because it's always changing.

This town pulls together when tragedy hits. It's always quite heartfelt and refreshing to actually see how the community pull together to support one of our own. I really find that heart-warming when I see that. If something happens, within a couple of hours there is a group of people out fund raising or dropping stuff off to help...that's one of the reasons why I love it here, but I love the lifestyle as well. Where else can you live where I can jump in my car or jump on my bike or walk the dog for five minutes, and I'm looking out at the Outback...like I'm the only person there. Or you jump in the car at night and you drive out, five or ten minutes, and you have crystal clear night skies. I recently did a section of the Larapinta Trail. I'm out there by myself...you're walking it and there is so much time to reflect, cleanse the mind and just absorb the landscape...it's indescribable, and pictures, photographs just don't do the landscape any justice. It is so beautiful to be able to do that and live in a town you can.

But that leads into another section. One of my passions is about planning and town planning. You don't want to lose that feel. Quite often, as a government, we talk about population growth, because it is good...more people, more taxes, more revenue, more development, more services for community...but people of Alice Springs sometimes don't want that. They say, we don't want to be a big city, we want to be the way that we are. That's the challenge for a town like Alice, we acknowledge that there is industry and economies that need to be created to keep the place sustainable, but that can't come at the cost of losing the character, the features, the uniqueness of the town. I've always, never been successful at doing it, I always thought that the town should have particular characteristics in planning. As a town, we should have a palate of colours...the colours of buildings and development...that are representative of the Namatjira water colours. We don't go seeing buildings like the courthouse, which just disrupt the feel of the town, the view. We need to look at things that blend into the landscape, because that's why people come here. (courthouse height restrictions circumnavigated) That was an exceptional application...the previous government's minister got to make a decision about it. They are some of the challenges that we face.

We have this most beautiful site in Alice Springs, being the Todd River, and the town's being designed that it's closed off. We've got our backs to the River. I would have liked to see that's the heart of the town. There's shops and Alfresco dining along the river for tourists. That's what you can't conceive. Obviously that was planning done years and years ago.

Being a member of parliament there is no job description on how you run your office, or what you do. There is a basis of being a strong voice, lobbying, advocating, and helping develop your electorate, but basically as a member you work with your office and your constituencies to benefit them...to benefit the people of which your division represents. No day is the same day, but there is nothing that we can't do. That's the really important thing for people. It's like, there is no stupid question. There is no stupid request. People don't ever feel like you can't come to us...come to us, if we can't help you, that we will always make sure that we steer you in the right direction, or go with you on that journey to find the outcome. It's about facilitating the needs sometimes of the constituency. It's probably a way of doing it, because there are times when it is important that people still keep that grass roots connection to issues...that's where we facilitate them, so they can have the satisfaction for delivering for their community, or delivering for a cause...it's a mixed bag.

You look at my predecessor, Alison Anderson (an Australian politician. She was member of the Northern Territory Legislative Assembly between 2005 and 2016, representing the electorate of Namatijra (known as MacDonnell until 2012) *she is such a fascinating individual. She's my aunty. But her role...people believed in her, because they followed her. She started off as a Labour politician, she went to the Country Liberals, Independent, sometime with Palmer United party, finished off her third term as an Independent....that's the important thing...I believe central Australians go with people they think are going to represent them, and they're connected to. Her (Alison's) process is fascinating for a study like this, people weren't bound by political views or particular political values. They follow her, because they believe she was the best person to represent them.*

There are people in Alice Springs who support me (Chansey [Paech]) for that reason, who support Robyn [Lambley], *who support Scott* [Mcconnell], *who support Dale* [Wakefield], *because of that factor. I know there are people who have voted CLP (Country Liberal Party) most of their lives, who voted for me in the election, because of my connection to place and my connection to particular community groups and interests. Alice Springs is very unique in that regard. In a demographic sense, that's healthy. It's healthy that people are not restricted by political views or values...that they're able to look at things and go...this is why I'm doing this. I think that's important. Yes, some of it is down to how it is portrayed in the media. There is no denying that. There is no denying that there are people who are members of particular parties, who fuel social media posts targeted at defaming one party or the other. Those people of particular views don't agree with the other ones, pushed by gossip. It is interesting to watch.*

It is interesting to watch because our elector numbers, our constituents here are probably the smallest in the country. 5,500 is the minimum per electorate. So, you actually get an opportunity to meet all of your constituents, within your four-year term. So you have a relationship with them. Whether it's a good or a bad one, at some point or another, you'll have interaction. There are people who represent constituents in all other capital cities, or in all other states, and the constituents never even meet their member of parliament. So they are having to look at various other ways of interactions, or hearing those kinds of stories. The Territory is very unique in looking at its political factors.

(asking 20 questions...yes...no...maybe) doing that doesn't actually allow you to have the in-depth conversations around understanding.

The other area that is interesting is local government. My electoral division has the Alice Springs Town Council, part of the MacDonnell Regional Council, part of the Central Desert Regional Council, part of Barkly Regional Council...my electorate and I could be seen as being bias. If you would sum up diversity, you would just have to look at my electorate. All those areas, I've got pastoralists, agricultural businesses, mining towns...everything in one area. I think I have the best job in the Territory...but probably my other three colleagues would say the same thing.

(Scott) you get Scott to talk about particular issues...housing, Indigenous economic participation, and he can talk for hours. It's constructive, empowering, and you just go away from there going, wow. You talk with the member for Braitling, same thing...very strong in particular issues, particular causes, as with the member for Araluen. It's about understanding where people's areas of strengths are on particular issues. I am not afraid to say to people, look, I don't know the answers or I don't know the issue very well to say I don't know about that, but I'm happy to go away and find out and come back to you and have that conversation.

My areas are around conservation, land management, horticulture, planning, Indigenous Affairs, and local government, because I spent six years on the Alice Springs Town Council. I'm always happy if people come to me...I will say, we can do this two ways...come to me and talk about your issue and I can go away and find out more or we can set a date, let me know what you want to talk about, and I can go away and do some research...so when we come together, I'm not wasting your time.

There is an added layer onto that, if and when you are given the opportunity to be a minister as well, because then that is not restrictive to a particular constituency. You've got jurisdiction of all of them, and got the jurisdiction of the Northern Territory, to make sure that portfolio you have, you are able to deliver on in a fair and equal and evenly supported way.

(Politicians constantly adding to knowledge and experience base) That's quite often why there is criticism when people leave parliament, they end up in particular areas. This job you learn every single day, more than just something, you learn a dozen things a day. That is really exciting, but also channelling where you go to get the best outcome for the constituency is sometimes a challenge, but a good learning curve as well. But the most important thing is, you have to make time for yourself...that's key...you go home after work, or you're in a swag at night looking at the stars, it's a bit of quiet time, but I always find you have to allocate yourself some time...I try on a Sunday afternoon to go horse riding for a couple of hours, because we've got horses out on my property, or go for a hike. Go and walk a trail somewhere, by yourself. You don't realise, but sub-consciously your mind is processing all these ideas and concepts, and actually giving you time to clear your head, so when you do go back, you do read things again...fresher eyes, different perspective. Just helps you to be grounded. When I don't get the opportunity to do that for a while, start to become a bit tense and irritable...just to get away, refocus, regroup...

As a politician, you need to learn to listen...even if its stuff you don't want to hear, you need to listen. I don't turn people away who I know we are going to have a different view...it's probably going to become a little bit warm, the conversation. They need to be heard and it helps you manage the issue, and work through it clearly. There are times when some of my colleagues will be like, I'm just over it. Whether or not you share the same view, you're voted in to represent everyone. That's something you need to do is be able to sit and listen. A lot of the time when I'm out bush, I'm sitting down with people, you're just listening...they are taking the opportunity to be heard. You speak when you are asked or when it's appropriate. (listening) That was one of the things I had to learn when I came into the job, because there might be stuff that you know and you want to talk to them...it's not my time yet...there are a number of public servants and politicians who are very uncomfortable with what they consider awkward silences out bush with remote communities. They need to just fill in the gaps to talk, because its silent, and you have to say, no, that's o.k. So the Western way of doing things, when it's awkward you try and just talk about the weather or you find something. It's o.k. to have the silence and the time to process...there is communication happening when there is silence as well, at some level. It's about acknowledging that and letting that happen.

Stop people looking at communities in a deficit model. That's often what happens in the mainstream...oh, there's this or there's that...they are issues that we need to work on, but we also need to acknowledge that these are places where people call home. They are full of love. They are full of ideas. They are full of strength and full of resilience. They are things we need to work with the community to share those stories, because if we want people to come on that journey with us, they need to feel valued. I don't think we do a very good job at the moment in that narrative, because quite often it's always talking about them in a deficit model...not as a value adding to the Territory's economy, the Territory's lifestyle, the Territory's identity. They are the kinds of things we need to look at.

People feeling valued and being appreciated is key to societal wellbeing and positive functioning. Doing so brings in and welcomes people along that journey of societal landscaping, and being inclusive of redesigning that landscape in subtle and profound ways and means. Or keeping parts of the landscape space as it is. Thus, servicing society's service capacity to keep it vibrant and equitable, is just as important as the micro service components that constitute it. The next segment concentrates on servicing Indigenous Australians in the central region and how they, in turn, can service the region...

Alice Springs is fundamentally an Indigenous place, which frequently is regarded in a disapproving manner. This pessimistic perspective requires reversing to regard N.T. indigeneity as a net asset, as a marketable product of diversity. If one stops and listens whilst being in the heart of the Alice street traffic, many Indigenous languages are heard. It is a living example of First Nations people living on their country, an uncommon performance in a world of displacement, absorption, and dissolving of original human place presence. For example, an uncommon electorate such as Stuart, adjacent to Alice Springs, exists in the context of First nation presence that still retains much of First Nation identity and practise. Stuart is, from north to south, 1600kms in length, located west of Katherine to west of the Alice, to the WA border along the Stuart highway. Within that 'First' space, people dwell on their ancestral lands, converse in language, and perform their culture and associated law. This performance can be perceived as constructive to business, by making ethical investors aware that this is a welcoming place to do business, of First nations people who hold Native Title recognition under the Northern Territory Land Rights Act, i.e. retaining ownership of space and place is fundamental for decisions in that spatial location, including business decisions. In essence, utilising Indigenous 'natural' advantage.

Paradoxically, the essential item that powers the economy of the N.T. is Indigenous disadvantage. To illustrate, in the Alice the 'normal' ratio of police to public is 1:1000. Therefore, there is an expectation of around 30 to service the roughly 26,000 local dwellers, but there are over 200. The cause and affect of this significantly lower ratio relationship may be attributed to Indigenous presence, a politically problematical call to emphatically make. Also, the very well equipped and funded Alice Springs hospital. It is one of the global leaders in its field, but on the flip side, there are many young Indigenous people who are admitted to the hospital for extended periods in conjunction with an over representation of Indigenous admissions. These are illustrations of Indigenous powered economy. Other examples are the many community controlled NGOs such as Tangentyere and Ngaanyatjarra Corporations aided by public funding, which also 'powers' the Alice economy. Even though the Alice and environs have tourism, pastoralism and mining extraction as significant economic drivers, the Indigenous service dwarfs these somewhat.

Gauging society for many is looking at the outcome of people at the 'base', not those at the summit. The 'base' of society is currently Indigenous, with outcomes meagre. Ironically, Indigenous people can offer something positive of themselves to the N.T. economy, being on their country and the resources that may involve, but also inadvertently offering something of themselves to the N.T. economy in perceived negative ways. To encourage positive economy, educating people to understand the negative system more would be advantageous for Indigenous people, but perhaps not so for non-Indigenous people (not all) who benefit from the current economic state of affairs, or affairs of state.

Focusing on Alice Spring's demography, the Indigenous numbers of the Alice is thought to be roughly a third of the town's population. This is based on the official census figures, but perhaps misrepresented. To illustrate, many Indigenous also retain a bush address and regard that as their base of operations, but actually may live in Alice for eight to ten months of the year. Therefore, the third proportion is appreciably surpassed. Of the non-Indigenous presence, it is uncommon to find people born and bred in the Alice. It is also atypical to find people dwelling for more than a decade. Additionally, the rotation of non-Indigenous utilising a half a decade timeframe would be about two-thirds of the population. Therefore, the majority of those who have frequented the Alice in excess of a decade would equate to 75% Indigenous. From that perspective, Alice can be thought of as generally Indigenous. If that number crunching is accepted, efficient service delivery and acceptance will efficiently work if the place is integrated, where cooperation and collaboration is key, rather than following separatism.

Funding Indigenous disadvantage for the Alice's long term 75% and across the N.T. is powered mostly through GST and the horizontal fiscal conversion. However, a significant challenge for cost effectiveness when investing in Indigenous demerit, is paying the wages of the twenty thousand plus N.T. public servants who service the disadvantaged. This would be a generous part of the funding budget, and understandably unavoidable within the established 'welfare' structure. Paradoxically the servants' agenda is to help Indigenous people, admirable though that is, but the irony is if there is too much success within that help, some of the servants would be vulnerable to job losses. 'Some' is an arbitrary amount. It may be more or may be less. Thus, Indigenous disadvantage self-perpetuates. If a service becomes too successful, the servicers risk being servicers no more, at least within that field context. However, the twenty thousand would not just service Indigenous disadvantage, as all who live in the Alice and N.T. are 'disadvantaged' to an extent, since all require government services, mitigated through the public servant system, i.e. roads, education, health, power, water, and building infrastructure.

To maintain service levels, wealth retention has to be maintained at a certain level and hopefully above it, both of which can be problematic. As an illustration and returning to the issues of fly in/fly out, much wealth is locally lost through it exiting the N.T. through service delivery. Apart from the prominent mining example of workers being in the N.T. for their shift rotation of a week or two or three and then going interstate on their downtime, many in the public sector are fly in/fly out. Remote nursing illustrates this. The majority of remote nursing placements out bush, examples include Mount Liebig, Harts Bluff and Papunya, are occupied by agency nurses, of which the majority reside interstate. High level policemen, language specialists and teachers are often fly in/fly out. Therefore, the cumulative 'flying' numbers affects the service performance of Alice. It would be advantageous for the place to attract more 'permanent' workers, however, supply and demand are strategic. For example, remote places require public services, and if these cannot be supplied locally or from the 'service' centre of the Alice, outsourcing is one solution. Be that not appreciated by all, depending upon geographical location.

Not necessarily fly in/fly out, but perhaps drive in/drive out, are retired people travelling through the N.T. These 'grey nomads' can remove wealth from the N.T. greater than contributing to the economy, as many nomads work in communities, roadhouses and cattle stations and understandably save their money for essential future purchase demands, which may be outside the N.T. space they are working in. The key thing is un-regulation of these workers. Whereas, backpackers can only work for six months or other employees do subsidised employment visa programs that are also heavily regulated.

If the cultural service infrastructure of a region, such as central Australia, is generally focused on one settlement, such as the Alice, the environs can be marginalised in terms of service levels offered. Literally five minutes travel beyond the urban Alice of its – 'third' percentage Indigenous population, the Indigenous numbers become predominant, reflecting the remote communities structure. Within these remote communities, literacy and numeracy levels are lower in adults as compared to the basic national measurement. Influenced by this, school attendance may be less than 50%, perhaps down to 30%. So, building economic capacity and skills set is limited, if people cannot engage in English and numeracy to the level 'expected' of to function effectively within a capitalist system, and also, to offer competition for the 'flying' fraternity. This is not to say that services are not present on communities, but the cultural capacity of them will equate to the capacity of the community, as it would for any community. The difference being, as compared to the service capacity of the Alice, is in the smaller range and quality of service capacity that can be, and is, offered.

Even if a remote community retains a reasonable capacity for service potential, the pull of the Alice still dominates. For example, Hermannsburg is just 130kms away from the Alice. It is a former Lutheran community, so traditionally it retains a higher education standard than many other remote communities and has more resources for people living there to utilise. However, to get ahead in Hermannsburg, Alice Springs is the destination of choice. If the aim is for a decent job, do a trade, get involved in sporting activities, visit the theatre, purchase a house, eat fast food, and utilise health support such as dialysis, then there is migration to the Alice. Therefore, due to the partially operating economy of remote communities, even the more 'established' ones, in terms of Western cultural similarities, a brain drain occurs as locals seek employment and quality of life elsewhere, which limits community service and associated economic functionality somewhat. As an illustration, the GST (Goods and *Services* Tax) provides $4.60 for every dollar collected in the N.T. As a comparison, Western Australia receives 30 cents for every collected dollar, and much of the income that goes to NT. communities is for welfare, totalling 40 million dollars annually. However, that money is literally 'driven' back to the Alice to purchase services there. So, local communities economies experience limited benefit, although the Alice economy benefits.

To change and sustain a community, remote as well as the Alice, equity of opportunity is welcomed. One opportunity aspect is investing in infrastructure and creating employment opportunities. Education is another aspect to achieve a semblance of equality. Also, public housing 'ownership', which creates a greater hegemony of housing by individual owners, tenants and residents. It is these 'ownerships' that encourage a better say and concern for one's community, encouraging development and capacity. A challenge to change the physical geography of a community is to also change the mindset of those that dwell on community, since generations of people are part of the Indigenous deficit model. They are victims of the system that surrounds the living space, a welfare space of 'assistance and of public servants holding the responsibility for community performance. To profoundly change, one must help themselves. However, a difficult thing to do in practice, especially if one is not used to it and subjected to the service will of others representing the dominant cultural form. Essentially, issues of complexity and of long-term dependence need to be addressed.

Addressing dependence requires community strength to help themselves, which resides in the majority population being permanently Indigenous. Outside interests who wish to invest in the place should recognised the Indigenous presence, as they are entering a space of Indigenous rights via Native Title, and 66% of the land rights mass under Land Councils administration. Also, there are opportunities to utilise the local Indigenous demographic, as they are an underutilised labour force, but also intimately connected to place. As a consequence, this connection can be used if business interests wish to 'connect'. A challenge emerges when companies do come into communities, is that the bulk of these 'connections' are short-lived when they leave. Their priorities are not the same as the permanents. Nonetheless, when companies invest in the enduring human Indigenous capital when getting involved in the N.T.s mineral or grass resources, or the stunning landscape within tourism resources, there is an opportunity to help the community 'self', which in turn helps the investor 'other'. Thus, serving each other for mutual benefit, and the benefit of others who purchase these resources.

A work ethic is fundamental to achieve service attainment for those who wish to help themselves. However, some people do question the work ethic of Indigenous people, but historically in some stock camps, these were operated completely by Aboriginal people, working 12-15 hour days and maybe up at 3am chasing cattle. Or Aboriginal women working at the stock house from 6am to 8 pm plus. So, the legacy of hard and long hour work is there. A contemporary challenge to obtain work on stations, and hence stock camp work, is the historically required Indigenous workforce of 100 is now only 20. This is because the job has diversified from tailing cattle to radio use and reading the Human Resources manuscript, in conjunction with modern technical advancements. Basically, having a workable level of literacy and numeracy to even apply for the job. Therefore, local community residents, due to their lack of education achievement and ingrained welfare dependence, experience difficulties obtaining employment. Fundamentally today, the collective community attitude may be one of a lack of work ethic and the systematic societal service performance perpetuating this, but within individual Aboriginal people, the work ethic exists.

Systematic societal service performance can make or break society and/or segments of it. The balance of service delivery and who delivers that delivery is politically charged and sensitive to too much change. Paradoxically, educating the Indigenous workforce may markedly alter economic processes. For example, if the economic working capacity of Indigenous people is to increase, dependency upon two hundred plus police and other support welfare services reduces. But, if employment prospects reduce, governments become unpopular, and within a three to four-year electoral cycle, that matters. Thus, governments can be caught in the middle of servicing society, i.e. robbing Peter to feed Paul, and long-term policy change talked over and acted upon with civil society, academia, business community, and community leaders like the church, is challenging. Also, governments are limited in what they can do, as they cannot govern everything that society throws up.

However, the government can control much of a dwelling place, with its policies overpoweringly transforming life choices; advertently or inadvertently. In remote communities such as Papunya or Haast Bluff, for example, modifications in housing policy or alterations in supporting sporting activities. Also, there is involvement in CDP changes and updated welfare regulations in communities that 'steer' users to a space of dependence with these government services. Services that would perhaps be used sparingly in more urban settings, and with a lot less significant affect to daily living practice and performance. Fundamentally, the 'same' service offered in different living environments can create diverse causes and responses that vary in effectiveness of life change.

In terms of servicing Indigenous people, getting the service balance right may rely on a shifting and flexible 'mainstream' societal gaze, one that regards Indigenous capacity as individuals, i.e. moving away from separatism and collectivism, and Indigenous being the same, but different from non-Indigenous. An awareness is required that appreciates that Indigenous people have different relationships to culture, law, and country but still as a part of a common future. In this manner communities can enjoy self-sustainable practices of property and employment tenure, which empowers individuals to run and organise their own lives, that in the long-term empowers society.

The N.T. has tiers of politics that empower or disempower; Federal, N.T, local council and the individual, public services, land councils, shire councils, and NGOs like Congress, but only one percent of the Australian population. To put it into spatial perspective, dozens of city councils across the country are larger than the parliamentary representation of the N.T. government. However, it is that spatial perspective of the N.T., and Alice and its region, that creates a special politics of originality. At least to some original degree, since as all settlements reside within the web of 'Australian' society, some common aspects for all will be present. One final 'special spatial perspective' is the Alice Springs local council flexible positionality on local service provision and how it is a negotiated process.

Some people impose themselves on the community. A classic of that is the Intervention, then the hangover after the Intervention. The Intervention was done here because it couldn't be done anywhere else. We didn't have our own state laws, so they didn't do an Intervention in any other part of Australia. Look at an example of it's been 40 years on a journey of self-government and still hasn't arrived, because Federal government still haven't made all those decisions. That really affects our community as a whole. We talk more about referendums today than we have in a long time. There is a very small number of referendums that ever got up in this country. For a referendum to get up... and the discussion currently around Indigenous recognition in the Constitution, or local government recognition in the Constitution...when you have a referendum, you have to have more than 50% of the population where we get a vote in that, more than 50% of the states, so we don't get a second vote. It's a bit one sided.

We're preached to, a lot. We're preached at, a lot. We have a lot of people who come in and try and do that. I think you got to come in and experience the place. We are a very progressive society in Alice Springs. Inventiveness is the genius created originally by the Tyranny of Distance. The distance is not so much there now, but the isolation is. As a community, always surprised when people think it's a divided community. Because you've only got to look at the array of events that this community runs year in year out. I defy any other community in Australia, even a capital city, runs as many events as what we do. Lots of other communities outside, may run two or three events a year...today it probably takes 365 days of living here before you know what the town's got to offer. It's a massive array of the arts through to sports...the organic through to the quirky...original to the unoriginal, so many things happen here. That's the nexus that makes the community.

Community is not just defined by the little boundaries here...yesterday there was a service to remember the Albert Namatjira Memorial, which was built 56 years ago on the outskirts of Hermannsburg, and new people to the community, under tourism about 18 months ago, talked about turbocharging tourism. What they were going to do was knock over that memorial and build a bigger and better memorial, without any understanding of what that first memorial stood for. Some long serving people went, hang on, let's look into this. There's a story alone with that memorial...why do others that have just arrived decide we need a bigger and better one....what about telling the story existing there. So, we face that fairly regularly.

As a town we have so many opportunities. Other communities that have a limited number of economic streams to what they can do...if you look at a community in the Top End like Nhulunbuy, when that one line of working, mining, disappeared, the town imploded. Today, it's very small. Here, we have defence. Which a lot of people don't really recognised as a huge business in central Australia...whether it be the joint-defence facility or over the horizon radar...it's a very big business. We have tourism. We have pastoralists. We have mining. We have health services. In central Australia, the hospital here is a training hospital. It's servicing a population across the centre of Australia around 48,000 people.

Alice Springs has got a lot of levels of economic viability. If one goes down, the others carry it. Some of those industries have peaks and troughs. Currently, there is a discussion of five mines in the area. One of those completes all of its requirements, will have a huge impact upon the town, but there are five of them out there. Only in the last week or so the community put in a bid for the Qantas Pilot Academy. The prospects of that are massive. You read, even in today's media, how many aircraft are not flying each day because of lack of pilots. Amazing number of flights that don't get off the ground anymore. Read an article today that they need over 200,000 pilots over the next ten years, a massive number. We need to grow them somewhere...a logical place here.

(Galaxies land at Alice Springs airport) The Americans have been here for 51 years. We've had just about everything out of their fleet land here. The Alice Springs strip is also an emergency strip for international flights from here (Australia) to Europe. The airport operates 24 hours a day on the basis that its somewhere for people to land. In recent times there was a Malaysian aircraft that turned back somewhere over western Australia. Didn't go to Darwin, it came back to here to land. Sat on the ground for quite a while too. Had to bring a lot of pilots out from Malaysian Airlines to fix it.

We're an important cog in the whole operations of Australia. If you took Alice Springs out, it would even be more coastal centric. Even within Aboriginal terminology, all the song lines of Australia come through the centre of Australia...Alice Springs is very important. So, it is important to understand what has come before, before you go imposing changes on it without understanding what is underneath.

(Indigenous) I don't divide them up like some people do. If you live here, you live here. Whether you're an African Australian, whether you're Indigenous or whether you're non-Indigenous Australian, you're all part of this community. So, I've never had a real thing around dividing them into services...(Indigenous welfare) but it's welfare, full stop. That's a real issue. There are some very good Indigenous operations, but they're not just their own people, all sorts of people work in them...only look at the concept of CentreCorp...it's the biggest investor in our town. Owned by Aboriginal people, but all sorts of people work within it.

I see some really strong things going forward. Health will continue to grow, sadly. There are diseases out here that have not been capped, so to speak, and there's always going to be a growth of the supply of health services across central Australia. Some of the demographer's stats...there is a figure of 250 communities across central Australia that use Alice Springs as a service centre. Those communities can be as small as an outstation of ten to twenty people. They can be large, like a Yuendumu or a Ntari, may have 300 to 900 people. So, Aboriginal outstations are not really defined by Territory/Western Australia/ Queensland borders...APY Lands (Anangu Pitjantjatjara Yankunytjatjara), those people have connections to Alice Springs. They are a long way from the next place. Port Augusta doesn't have anywhere near the facilities that Alice Springs does. So, the top of South Australia, it's Adelaide that provides. So, Alice Springs being five hours away...it's a lot easier to access than Adelaide, which is nine to eleven hours away. The outskirts of western Australia, totally unrealistic to think they will all go to Perth. Health, right across to the western Australia area, come here to Alice Springs. We've got our own communities across the Territory, whether it's Ti-Tree or Leramba, it doesn't matter.

So, we do service a lot here, out of this place. If you look at the hospital in our community, it's a 183-bed hospital, which rather is a large hospital in any regional area of Australia. Tennant Creek has a 20-bed hospital, but it's governed by this one here. All of those things make to an interesting community. All of our health funding comes from the Federal government. It's a hard process around that, because you get given targets you have to reach, which seems odd. I grew up thinking health, you've got to fix it, not, you've got to fix so many this year. Health is in need of a new facility in the next 20 years. There'll be big investment to Alice Springs. Some things health has done in recent years have been exceptionally good...the Start of Telehealth (use of tele communications techniques for the purpose of providing tele medicine, medical education, and health education over a distance (Australian Government, Department of Health)). If you think about it, if you're a patient in Tennant Creek most of your life you've got on a bus, travelled to Alice Springs to see a specialist, and a specialist who's come in from another area then tells you to have your bloods taken and yeah, what do I do now...I'll see you next visit...the specialist doesn't realise you've lost three days of work, you've sat on a bus for ten hours total, there and back...so, Telehealth became a big thing in Tennant Creek. A massive number of patients now go to the hospital, go to the back, there is a room and there is a nurse on hand, and they talk to the specialist anywhere in the world. Not necessarily just with Alice Springs...the specialist can, through a Skype process, assess you with the help of the nurse on the ground and say, I'll get you to have your bloods taken in Tennant Creek, I'll be in Alice Springs on the 29th, and like to see you then. But instead of in the past they would have travelled down on the 29th just to be told...I'm being very simplistic...but a specialist sees people coming through the door and adjudicates accordingly, doesn't ask how far you've come.

Doesn't say, I'll put off that other Alice Springs person to fix you because you've got to go home to Tennant Creek. (doctor) flew in, go to their accommodation, go to the hospital...whether they've come out of Salisbury or Sydney they're not inclined to say, so how far have you travelled today, because in affect they felt they have travelled along way because they flew here to service you. E-Health is a way of ingenuity that happens in a remote area. It's not necessarily going to happen on the eastern seaboard, because you have better connectivity, more services. If you look at a map of Australia, and just take out the area that doesn't really have people, just end up with a little 'c' on the east coast of Australia and another blob in the west, very small. In the overall scheme Darwin doesn't really rate with 140,000 people. Very similar to the Chinese map, take a map of China and take out all the desert country, their population is very much in a 'c' also.

People complain about air travel prices...never take into account that we've got 30,000 people max, a plane is not going to fly here everyday and fly out with $120 flights...there is not enough people here to fly out for starters, but we've got all these other benefits, but we feel we're being hard done by because we have to pay extra for an air fare....isn't there a balance! I post a picture of Sunrise here in Alice Springs and I get hits from all over Sydney and Melbourne and people are going, well, you're lucky. Yet, an hour later somebody will say to me in the street, oh, I can't get a cheap airfare to Sydney...you can go back to live there if you want to, why do you live here...because I love it...but you can't assume you get the same benefits of flights between Sydney and Melbourne, $59 seats, you just can't do it out here.

(commuting) people sit on a train for an hour and think they are lucky because their mate's on an hour and a half bus ride for a job. This is the thing about we accept all this, or we expect it. It's like our community doesn't want any change...don't build the gallery in town, don't build any high-rise, but I want cheap air fares and I want the best NBN (National Broadband Network) in the world, and I want...and I want...and I want. Sustainably, we have to build up in the end. Can't just keep spreading out over the land. Cost us 'X' amount in bitumen to service this place and as we keep going out it costs more and more, laying the bitumen...so, if I put two people on top of each other here, I'm doing some savings in the sustainability stuff. There is a whole lot of things. It's the old Australian, not in my back yard. Give it to me all, but don't change what I've got.

In this role here, I see a fair bit of that. You have to have a bit of give and take. Personal responsibility as a society, seems to be disappearing. Kids want to start at the top job, but don't want to do the apprenticeship. Going to your job every day is an apprenticeship, you're learning all the time. It's not just a matter of...I've done well in secondary school, now I've got a university degree, I'm due the top job...there is a hierarchy out there...what experience have you had of handling people...oh none, that will be easy, you just move them around...doesn't really work like that. The Now generation are putting a lot of stress on the whole system.

The community expects the council to provide services, and the council does provide services. The council, it's an old cliché, but still pretty true, is still the closest level of government to the people. If a pothole appears in the road, they ring the council. There is a hierarchy of roads. Some roads, the council is responsible for in this town, some roads, the Northern Territory government, some, the Australian government. Always been that way across the nation, so the Territory government won't hand over ownership to one part of the road to the town because they want to cart stuff on that road, and they don't want a weight limitation. There are different reasons for different whys, but that's how roads are. Of course, if there is a pot hole on the road and they ring us and it's not ours, we're work with the others, but no one would even think to call them. If there is a light bulb gone out, they don't ring Power and Water, they ring council. It's not our responsibility, its Power and Water's. So, people perceive the council as the first point of call to complain.

So, in the same breath, the council prepares all the sporting grounds in this town every week. We're probably one of the few councils in Australia that provides cricket wickets for cricket in the cricket season. So, we fix all sports grounds, prepare them. We also look after 84 parks in town. Now, some of those are interesting because they're sacred sites and we can't do anything with them, but when a developer comes in and cuts up this piece of dirt and there is a sacred site there and there, he builds his blocks and leaves this little odd shaped piece there and says, I'll give it to the council. So, washed his hands of it and the council go, it's called a park. An obvious one would be next to Araluen. There is a hill there that always looks messy, and then there is beautiful green grass where people sit and leave mess. Well, workers are not allowed on that hill, because it is a sacred site, but the itinerant people don't respect that. It's a real contradiction in terms. Or they leave rubbish in the park. One puff of wind blows it up on the hill then residents say, why don't you fix it up council? So that's a recognised sacred site. It's got some bollards around the bottom and basically when we cut grass down there, we're not allowed to cut anything on there. Another little one would be over on the east side, not far down from the university, where the little petrol station is. There is a park across the road, but on the western side of that there is a hilly part that's a bit messy. So, we got grass here, some play equipment there and we've put trees in, but that other piece in the corner, that's a sacred site that runs right down the front. Some people have driven up the side to get into a cul-de-sac out the back, and we've had to put rocks there because they're knocking down the sacred site.

Sacred sites are a funny thing that councils have to find a way around. We have a lot of abuse, although the Territory government did it, building the boardwalk past Olive Pink (Olive Pink Botanic Gardens). That little thing out over the river, halfway along there is a sacred site, and people walked around the base of that hill for fifty years. So, they disregarded the sacred site, and the track used to get deeper and deeper. Right on the point of that Hill is a gum tree that's sacred. So, Territory government said, we are going to build that there (the pedestrian/cyclist gantry). We got all the abuse in the world from Aboriginal people encouraging people to use it, but we're going, but they were using it before and they were wreaking your sacred site because you used to come and see us monthly. A bit further down there are some rocks there in the river, they are sacred. That's why that is there (gantry). So, it's a very interesting world to balance in.

You do find more noise from people who are agitated by people who aren't Aboriginal, but who work in organisations. That's an interesting part of this job. I've lived here all my life, so I have good relations with all the people who have lived here a long time. But you get a lot who come in on a short stay and become very much experts. All those balances. So, as a councillor you've got to try and find the best for everybody.

Council gets asked to do a lot of things which are not really in their paddock and they have to explain that. Council's responsibility is the rubbish. We spend a million dollars a year picking up rubbish here, because of people who won't use bins or who abuse it. It was a lot worse before this council created the container deposit legislation for the territory. South Australia have been doing it for forty years. About eight years ago we started collecting cans and bottles and paying a five-cent reward for it, and by the time we got to 17 million containers we collected, the Territory government finally accepted their responsibilities and brought in container deposit legislation. So that's made a big difference to our rubbish...that's all your soft drink cans, your alcohol cans, and so forth. So, that is something this council did do. Still got to pick up the other rubbish, people would leave a lot of rubbish around their town. We have a responsibility to run the library. We have responsibility to run the Aquatic and Leisure centre. They both are paid for out of ratepayers' money, and to manage the landfill is a very big expense. So, they're the main things council are responsible for.

Sometimes people run for elections in town promising law and order issues, which we don't have the power for. That's a Territory government responsibility. People do it every time...they go on and on about law and order, then the community don't hold them accountable once they get elected...sad state of affairs. Easy way to get elected in the Territory.

Other things the council do in the Territory. We don't have responsibility for planning, which is an issue controlled by the Territory government, but we have a voice at the table. We are an advocate for everything within the community. Lot of people see that the parliament (located in Darwin) is 1000 miles away, so we get asked to do so many different things here. So, there are all sorts of different facets of what council does...within councils now...ten years ago, 80% or even 85% of our work was roads and rubbish. Today, there is a lot more community involvement. Probably 35% today of what we do is community, whether that be a seniors co-ordinated committee, whether it be youth action group, whether it be grants to the community, whether it be markets that we run, whether it be functions we run throughout the year, it's all community based...there's so much more. The infrastructure stuff takes care of itself. We have a small rates base. We only have 10,000 people who have property who pay rates. So, we're very reliant on the ability to attract grant money outside that.

We're very dependent on our population, which the last census was disgraceful, and even with talking with Northern Institute (University research hub) recently, they're convinced the number are right...they say we've lost over a 1000 people, up to 2016. Well...I've argued with them, their numbers on other nationalities who have become Australians are very, very low. Those numbers, and the Northern Institute support them, affect our grants this year, and for the next four years. They're out there supporting it. Our Federal Assistance grants...the Federal government gives Federal Assistance grants to all 537 councils across Australia. They're based on the population. So, we're going to go backwards this year, for the next four years, until the next census. A lot of the community from overseas said when they did it the first time on the computer it failed, they didn't think it their responsibility to do a paper one. I think it was disgraceful that the Bureau of Stats just covered up their inability to do the job and just threw it back out there. So, the Territory and the Federal government, when we asked for assistance for things, they go, oh, your population shrinking...easy for them to take that road.

There's lots of things that happen through here. We have representations through economic development. We're always out there fighting for that. Example of that was last week with the pilot's academy. That was very important. We're always being addressed with different businesses who are looking to start things or do things here in the centre of Australia. Most people at some stage have interaction with council, because everything they do...when you left home this morning, you would have walked on a council asset or rode on a council asset at some stage, and most of the day as you go through, it would be a council asset that you are using, which is a community asset, which we all pay for through our rates on our properties.

(over 50's) the building is owned by the council and we work closely with the seniors. There are three clubs that use that...the U3A (University of the Third Age), the National Seniors, and the Seniors. So, three different groups there. Council looks after three childcare facilities in town. We own the asset. A peppercorn rent. Governments make decisions and hand them over to councils, and they cost well in excess to run than what the rent is. That's another responsibility for council. So, have three pre-schools, kindergartens.

So, local government is governed by the Local Government Act. We can't budget for a deficit. Whereas the Territory government can budget for a deficit to whatever size. The Federal government can budget to a deficit. Last year wasn't the Territory budget 1.6 billion in deficit...their entire budget is 6.6, and they spent 1.6 more than that. We can't. We have to have a balanced budget. So, when we work out a budget, we work out what is required to provide this coming year what the community expects...say that's 100 dollars. Then we've got to say, that's 100 dollars we need to get from the community. All the people in the community are divided into that, basically. Whereas a business might set its budget up at the beginning of the year for four staff, and it goes gangbusters, and they got to put on eight staff for the year, that doesn't really affect their budget because they are now making more income, they can afford more staff. So, we have to sit down and say at the beginning of the year, how many staff do we need to do that. If four is the number, that's all we can do. The officers can't come back half-way through the year and say, we need two more. We should have budgeted for six, if that was the case. We do budget to fill every position. If we don't fill every position, which can happen, we may have ten librarians and half-way through the year, one and half of those positions are empty, because of retirements or somebody's moved on. You just can't pluck another person to be a librarian. At the end of the year, we'll have excess that wasn't spent, but we'll make a decision as a council to either commit that to be reserved or commit that to a project.

People ask why the council runs reserves...well if we have a disaster, like the two extreme weather events we've had in the last two years...if we didn't have reserves, because National Disaster Fund will pay so much...doesn't pay all the wages, doesn't pay the overtime. Like if the trees are knocked over, we got to put people out on the street now to go and cut them down, even if they are not working now. So, we have to have reserves. We have to have reserves for the simple facet of the one in one hundred years flood. So, some councils in Australia value the lands under roads. I find that a real falsehood myself. If you're on the waterfront and you have a magnificent hotel and there was a road in front of that. In that situation, the owners of the property might come to you as a councillor...if we could buy that road and turn it into gardens, our guests could have this wonderful run down to the water...so it's got a value. But the road out the front of here right now doesn't have that sort of value. So, if my assets reflected the dirt underneath it, I can't cut 100 metres out of it and sell it to pay the bills or wages next week. It is a real falsehood that some councils are becoming massively asset rich in other parts of Australia, because their local government allows them to do that. I'll never be supportive of that here. The value out the front is the value of the road, not the land under it. That's a falsehood. Only in very small occasions would that road return money to you by selling it like the one in the front of the hotel, in the example I've given you. But if you didn't have the value of land under the road, you'll never been able to sell it. If you sold it, it would have been for tuppence.

We have to be responsible for the budget of the town. Now there are people touting that councils should disinvest any of their money from the big four banks because they support fossil fuel, and we should put all our money into these smaller organisations who don't support fossil fuel. A beautiful ecological utopia, but our role is invest our money with Triple A banks. Any institution can get to Triple A...it's just got to do what it has to do. Right at this stage the only Triple A organisations in the country are those big four banks that people are so offended by. But we've got not our money, its other people's money we got. We have to get the best return we can, for the money we hold when we do a project.

Footpaths another thing we are responsible for as a council. Alongside our road, guttering on the road, the drains underneath. We spend upwards of 600,000 dollars every two years of drilling out those underground pipes, because of where we live we fill up with sand. We haven't had any rain here for a long time. The soil is all loose. The next rain we get half my garden will go down the gutter, down the drain. Lots of other run-off will, and that silt just builds up in those pipes. So, I've got a pipe this big, and only got this much for water to flow through...got to go and mine it. So, it's a suction pump that does it and I mine it all out. Last time we took 800 ton of dirt out of the pipes. So, we stockpile that at the landfill and use that to cap our waste. All of our waste has got to be built into honeycomb cavities. Lots of fascinating things happen with councils.

When we started collecting wine bottles years ago...wine industry has always been left out of container deposit legislation...we crushed that glass, so that's just bottles. That's what we were using in the making of concrete. When we make a footpath, we use this instead of creek sand. It's not cheaper, but 5,500 stubbies or 375 millilitre bottles makes one ton of crushed sand. You've 5,500 bottles sitting in the landfill doing nothing and just filling it up. We use 385,000 stubbies in underneath, when we did the northern end of the Mall (Todd Mall),...all the trenches. That 385,000 bottles would still be sitting in our landfill, if we hadn't done that. Big numbers. So, we grind the glass up into four different levels.

You've got to be a bit creative in what you try and do because you live a long way away from anywhere else. Inner city councils just transfer their waste to somebody else...somebody else's responsibility. We're a little bit isolated, so we have to be creative here. It costs you a lot of green miles to cart it away...1000 miles from here to market. That's the biggest problem we have this year with the discussion around kerbside recycling. To take all the paper and cardboard out of here would have cost the community 136,000 dollars in freight, on top of what we would have got back from the paper. That was the decision made by the Chinese that changed recycling so much. So, a lot of work to be done on that. Tonight, there's an interesting show on Q and A

(ABC current affairs talk show) Tuesday night around waste, and my counterpart David O'loughlin who's the president of the Australian local government association, he'll be on that speaking.

(parks) They're all there and we have to go and cut grass. We are working on a system at the moment, with another researcher in CDU to try and create something to help us going forward. Gillen Park on the east side...we've pulled up half the grass...so we've talked with the residents there, want to cut back on the water that's spent on that...plant some trees next Sunday for National Tree Planting Day, and work through it. It was just one big expansive grass.

The 18 councils in the Northern Territory, we have a local government association...Local Government Association of the Northern Territory...It represents all 18 councils. Currently I am the president of that, and then what happens from there is every State and Territory has two board members on the Australian Local Government Association. I'm the vice-president of the Australian Local Government Association. They're two jobs I hold at the moment. Have one other one which enables me to travel to most of the remotes. So, the Federal Assistance Grants (FAGs) money gets given to every grants commission each year. Every State and Territory has to have a four person grants commission, and I sit on that as the municipal representative. A gentlemen from Timber Creek sits on there as the regional representative. There is an independent chair and there is a delegate from the department. We travel to every community, every three years, to break up the FAGS money.

The layered politics at the town council level, central Australia, N.T., and beyond, and the associated saturation politics, has, through the lives of all who dwell within these spatial locations, profoundly influence the quality of the dwelling process and accompanying society being serviced, and the quality of the arrayed services. The political field as well as the fields of religion, education, government, welfare, Indigenous and tourism, contribute to the process of servicing this dwelling performance. The next chapter offers a self-assessment by those that dwell in the Alice and its environs, drawing upon these fields, of their quality of service. The purpose being to empower/disempower the wellbeing of Alice Springs and environs, and in its micro societal way and presence, empower and disempower the wellbeing of society, as it is serviced.

Chapter Ten

Dwelling Reactions to Alice Springs

Utilising voices of those who have immersed themselves in the Alice and environs, and 'expected' introductory paragraph to 'introduce' them was the original intention at this narrative juncture. This paragraph was going to set some sort of service scene, an infrastructural service space, to prepare the reader for the following array of sounds, tones, inflections, articulations, and sounds of not so silence. However, doing such a thing, it was realised, would put the author's voice in the way of 'pure' place expressions of what this central Australian dwelling means to people. So, filtered expressionism at this stage is not the way to proceed. Therefore, what is offered here is an uncontaminated, untainted, unpolluted, clean vignette of voices of Alice Springs. There is no particular, purposeful order of engagement in content and context when giving these opinions, of creating individual ideas that serve the place, but within that 'individualism' there is a sense of bringing together wholeness of expression, a wholeness of Alice expression. Let these voices gauge the service capacity of the Alice:

> *I was born here in Alice Springs. We got people from Pit land tribe, Pitjantjara, we got Aranda, we got Warlpiri, Luritja, Amoonguna, Kaltjiti, there about in our region, we got about nine regions within the Central Land Council organisation. All got different languages. All that language, all connects here, when we get together here in Alice. Either talking to people in the meeting or getting to know each other or inter-marriage. Being with and exchanging cultural activities like the corroboree, the laws, interact, exchanging weapons, cultural artefacts, sacred ones, non-sacred, talk to each other...this is what it means, connections.*

> *Very important getting together in place, congregate, sacred site place like Anmatjere, here in Alice Springs. It is Aranda country, but you've got these other tribes coming in and getting to know each other, interacting, inter-marriage. As we speak, we've got Africans. New people from internationally. They just want to live in a peaceful place like here in Australia. Never met up with Aboriginal people. They're married to Aboriginal people, and they've got this African/Indigenous child. We've got a boy who can speak his father's language, his mother's language, Warlpiri. That's life. It's got to be life. It starts*

from that little meeting. That little meeting one day can become a very huge family. Connect African, in Zimbabwe to a Warlpiri here in Yuendumu, in northern central Australia. It's all connections, from that one new connection.

That IAD (Institute of Aboriginal Development) is where they do the language courses. I used to teach there, Warlpiri. Other nights the tapes and the books. Used to have them tapes, language.

(changing family name) In our ways, if I was born a John and there is a death in the family, and in the community when John passed away, got to call the name John to someone else, or call him Kumanjayi which means a name, taboo. Can't call his name because the name of the dead person can't be called again. When he's passed away, the person alive whose name is John, he'd be called someone else. He can change his name. His real name will be John. Find his name on chequebooks, signatures, and all that, but it can't be used. He can't be called a name, John. It's not really complicated. It's easy when you understand...put in on a blackboard...it will explain it to you really clearly. The thing is, if that John's, probably about five years later, he changes his name to Fred. Fred might pass away. That man Fred, whose first name is John, would be changed again. So they call him someone else. Or otherwise, we call him by skin name.

We used to have names for old people like the elders, we had Jack, Bob, Banjo. All those names, Jack, Whiskey, Jumbo. Nowadays you come to the hospital, there are new names that come from the Bible. Names from the Holy Book. Obama, the American president. One day you will find someone calling themselves Obama. Might have Nelson Mandela. Singer called Michael Jackson.

Most of the street names were from the early explorers.

--

Impressions of Alice Springs: Only been here 13 (now 14) years, not a long long time. It's amazing how much it has changed since the intervention in 2007. When I first got here you could walk around into a job you wanted, pretty much. It was then, at one stage, not long after the intervention, there were lots that needed to catch up with rest of Australia in terms of regulation around some stuff...how they went about things. Now I know, even within the youth sector, there are far more people around who have at least a basic qualification. Use to get people walking in saying, I think I might try this...and off you go. I was amazed when I first came to the Alice, if you've got an interest, there is a club. Whether its sports, whether its arts. Like if there is two people who like the same thing, there is a club you can join, and meet up regularly with. Sports fields, it's absolutely phenomenal the amount of sports and the range of sports. Arts and culture took a fair dip over the last five years or so and is starting to become more in favour again, I guess in some ways.

I'm still here, I come to work every day, I like Alice. Freezing cold, still has beautiful blue skies, by mid-day, even if it's only a short window, you are quite warm.

It is always interesting around the moral panic of young people and how regularly that pops up. Everywhere else in the country, and the world, seem to run on about ten-year cycles of youth issues. Here it is a period of about five years. If you look at some of those crime and justice statistics, actual crime has fallen in terms of Alice Springs and the Territory. The calls of people, of how bad young people are, how unsafe it is in town, become far more invasive, pervasive. With social media people find out things about what's happened around the corner, that's always happened around the corner, but they only knew about that from their circle of friends who went around that corner. But now there is all this confected outrage of how bad it is in town. Because I have worked in the youth sector for as long as I can remember, and we missed the boat with young people ten years ago, when talking about after hours drop in centres, the increase in community based programs is really around a Justice Reinvestment framework. What we have is a revolving door around the punitive framework we have, which is about the psyche of the Law and Order response that seems to dominate in the Territory. If you listen to the hoi poloi... young people are mad and out of control, disrespectful, and people fearing for their lives, prices going down, tourists not coming...really, young people are always a product of their environment and these attitudes/comments about young people are common fodder since the inception of the idea of 'youth'.

So, for those who have struggles at home, because of whatever the reason may be, and then we have an overarching....whether it's the laws of the town's council or the way policing is done, or what programs are available, the Territory is fairly fixed in what consequences there are, lock you up if you do the wrong thing more than twice. Whereas, if you look through a justice reinvestment prism or lens, you look at bolstering what community programs you have out there around social support, alcohol and drug support, education, legal services, community corrections and general community services. The general sense for a lot of young people in town, apart from being a general adolescent, marching together, causing mayhem and destruction, because that is what they do, because of their own mental development, their brain is not formed enough to make good, rational decisions, it operates off instinct. Or basically, that seems like a good idea, I'll go and do it without any thought of consequences. I'm just going to jump off this building and hold this sheet with me thinking I can fly, or I'm going to run down the Mall screaming blue murder, just for the fun of it, because it's a good laugh, but not realise that there are unintended consequences. So, you get a group of people together, and collectively they bounce or feed off each other's exuberance and there is not a lot of thinking involved.

So, it's a battle always pushing forward that socially and evidence engagement strategy. Inclusiveness, rather than exclusiveness. Everyone is scrambling around now trying to do that sort of thing, in a way. We have been telling you for years this is what we want, and now you expect it's going to do the job of that. Can be very frustrating. Governments of extremes. When I first came here, Labour got in. They proceeded to do a lot of good things, but a lot of wrong things. Got themselves out again. We then had the CLP (Country Liberal Party). They really went from bad to worse. Back to Labour. They look similar to the CLP, but with different faces, but with more money going to social stuff. They had the Royal Commission, which generates a lot of angst and a lot of flurry of activity around stuff that needed to be done, and still needs to be done. Finding the money for it is difficult for politicians making all these promises, people object, saying you shouldn't put money into that. General consensus seems to be let's build more prison space rather than going to the opposite end where you are doing stuff that negates the need for prisons.

Justice Reinvestment started in the United States about 15 years ago. It actually started in Texas when they were contemplating about building a prison of eight billion dollars. So, instead of building a prison, they started down this re-investment line. So for them, parole services, alcohol and drug services, counselling services, other social services in communities that have had high rates of criminality or criminal things occurring in run down neighbourhoods, did not have education systems, so putting that money into those sorts of programs. Ten to fifteen years on now, what they found within the first three years, they didn't need to build a new prison. That their overfull prisons were starting to empty or starting to be less overfull. In the last five or ten years they have shut another prison, so these sorts of things have expanded out across America. Certainly through Europe and England there are different areas of youth justice that go down the justice re-investment principles. There are a couple of projects in Australia, one in Bourke NSW, addressing what's happening in the community, and bolstering those community social service stuff, which has had a dramatic affect.

Google Tom Calma, he was the anti-discrimination commissioner for ten years or so. He started talking about justice re-investment program, but there are a whole range of stuff, even in Australia with people pushing that sort of approach. Makes sense in the Territory, where we have a phenomenal rate of incarceration rates for Aboriginal people around mostly fairly minor crime. It's been interesting that in other jurisdictions like NSW, they are having a decline, especially within Aboriginal people, of crime related stuff, violent crime and all that, and yet incarceration rates are still going up. It just doesn't make sense. It is about a couple of centuries messing around with people, paying lip service, listening to what they think communities need, to do the right thing. The intervention really compounded all those sorts of things. It came in, and yes they did want police on their communities, but didn't quite like the way they had done it. Yes, they did want to look how grog (alcohol) was handled on the communities, but not quite like the way they had done it. So, there are lots of anomalies. The justice re-investment framework makes perfect sense. It's not anything I haven't been talking about for 20 years in terms of the principals of it. It's always been the issue with early intervention or prevention stuff, that you don't see any immediate or discernible result that a politician can hang their hat on and say, hey aren't we doing a great job. It is a cost that because we have the system that we have, you need to continue the ambulance end of it, and pick up the bodies as they fall over the end of the cliff. The metaphor is you should be able to build a fence at the top of the cliff and stop people from going over. So, you got to continue to fund the ambulance end for a period of five or six years, while fencing, and double the money you are spending almost into the prevention or intervention programs. So, after three to five years, all of a sudden that's when you can start reducing your costs at the crisis/ambulance end. The formula's been around for quite a few years now...for every dollar you spend for prevention or intervention, you save ten for appointing courts, judges, jails, your police...better to stop it, than respond to it.

Still enjoy Alice. There is opportunity there, it is a friendly town despite the social media outcry or the headlines in the Advocate (local

Alice newspaper) at times. You can walk through town and people smile and acknowledge. You can walk everywhere in town when going to meetings. Can go bush and camp out. If you are interested (in activities) you can do it. When you look at the festivals that come through, the range of different stuff that is available at different times of the year, something for everyone. The dearth of good fine dining. There is a whole heap of stuff that flicks and changes, but the town still carries on. Despair at the lack of engagement with Aboriginal people other than through exclusive things, rather than being inclusive in looking at what's happening and how you might address that. The Todd River and the whole events happening around the river and people camping in it, and how they do it and how they treat it, and what happens of course is that rather than work with Lhere Artepe (Traditional Owners for Mparntwe/Alice Springs) and work with the people in there of how we might manage that better, we send council rangers in to move people along, kick fires out, confiscate bedding and get rid of it. Whereas, if we had a more inclusive practice it might be that council opens up an area...if you camped out, here is where you can store your stuff until tomorrow night, or tonight again when you need to sleep. Not breaking down trees, there are different ways you can do stuff that are about inclusion, rather than exclusion. All these by-laws that are about punishing people. Engaging with young people in the Yeperenye Centre (shopping mall), *rather than putting security guards onto them because they are a bit raucous and rowdy, depending upon which security firm is on. Creating a relationship with these people which is around respect, rather than kicking them out of somewhere.*

--

On Alice: Pretty good place, vibrant, cosmopolitan, multi-racial, tolerant, Aboriginal, African, white and in-between. Not seen any racial stuff. Frontier service town. People making it home are migrants, 26% of the demographic, and a big percentage of refugees who fit in well. A staging point for outback travel to the Rock (Ul<u>u</u>ru), West McDonald Ranges and Tanami. Adventurers come here, travellers, nature lovers, so the service industry is based around tourism. Backpackers working in cafes for six months, finding employment through internal networks.

--

Alice: I like living here. Been here for five years. People stay for one or two years or live here longer. I like it's close to nature, and I can jump my back fence, be in the bush. It's kind of a small town but has lots of things. There are a lot of other towns this size who do not have as many things, so it's kind of good that way. Awful to commute for an hour...to go back travelling for an hour to get to work and back. Miss the surf. There are obviously social issues in Alice Springs you don't get anywhere else, which sometimes gets annoying, but it's all good. That's what's good about it too, it's quite multicultural, and also the people are a bit more...lot more educated people for a small town. I've been to other small towns and there's not that many professional people...they're like tradesmen, farmers. Here it's mostly civil servants, educated people. When you've got a degree, kind of hang out with the people with a degree. So, there's more people in town like that, than doesn't have.

--

Over the amount of time that I've been here, we've gone from being a couple to having a young family, to having teenagers, to having uni students, kids leaving home and coming back again, and now we are just a couple again, and getting toward the end of our working life...we don't have the same community involvement that we used to, because when you've got a family you're doing all the time your children's interests and then volunteering, because of the activity they are involved in, people need volunteers. Your life is full. I suppose you've got the time and, not the time so much, but energy to do a bit more study...I found myself studying again when our youngest was finishing high school. It's interesting from that perspective because yes, I think the community's changed, and a lot of that's because the visa expectation on immigrants. A lot of people have come to regions because of visa restrictions. That's a great thing. That's a fantastic thing, because we are one world. It's nice to be part of that, not just segregated from what's going on in the world....I don't think that would be different really from any other place.

The fact is that our children are having children. We are at soccer. We are at ballet. We are at all the things that our kids did when they were little, and now we're going through it as a grandparent. So, that sort of opportunity is still there to be part of your family and see what's happening in the community. It's interesting because you are reconnecting with people that know your children who now are adults with children. It's just life. It's a cycle.

You have that phase where you've got the earning potential or you've got the entrepreneurial approach, you can do things. There is a real phase, it's usually when you've got young children. It's that responsibility for family...security...financial security...provide...how is that going to look. That's one fantastic thing about Alice still, is opportunity, but people are generous with providing those opportunities...I can pick up the phone and call people about work experience for our students. In all the years I've been doing it, ten years last February, had one person that said no thanks. Our community is very generous about young people. Alice has always had that reputation. We've always assumed it was because most of us had come from somewhere else, and so your friends became your family. People are generally friendly and trusting.

Some of those things have changed. We've been very fortunate in that we've not had a bad experience, but often think for people that have, whether it's a break in or a theft or assault, that must change your opinion of the town. But again, that's no different to any community, that's human nature. So, we're just a little part of the whole.

--

(Alice Springs as a place to live in) It's a fantastic place to live in. It's got so many opportunities. It's a service town. It punches above its weight in terms of services and amenities and events and festivals. All sorts of things that if you look at a town of 26,000 outside of Melbourne, it hasn't got the range of things that we see here with the hospital, and the facilities that's got. I guess like many people I came for a year, now I'm 13 years on. The lifestyle suits a lot of people who come here. If you're prepared to give to the town, the town gives back. (commuting time) everyone thinks I live along way out because I live near the airport, but I'll have 15 minutes commute. That amount of time that you can then spend doing things you want to do, or with your family...we've had a couple of boys born here, they are now at school, they are enjoying life.

You read all the horror stories all the time. In the papers sometimes. In the media, but most of the time it's pretty peaceful. Obviously it's a town which's got its issues, and that makes it different from many other places as well. Even with the issues with the progress that is being made in areas, it's going to be slow. There is no overnight answers, but as long as people are prepared to try and keep on trying, the progress will be made, but it's going to be slow. Some of the kids you deal with, they've had a rough childhood, backgrounds, but they're still there, and there is still hope. Where there is hope then you've got a responsibility to foster that, and try to be part of the change that happens. There are lots of people with passion in the town that try to do that. Sometimes you feel like you're not winning.

You do see people progressing really quickly through. That's part of it. It is a transient town and people do leave. If people stay, then they do keep their position. You do see that with the number that go interstate and do come back, that it's not always greener. There is always issues about isolation...people with family in other states, you do feel far away from them at times. It's not always easy to get a flight last minute. That's a real barrier in some respects. If you've got a friend who's getting married interstate, to get the flight to get there and get back, often having to take a day off work. That's not always as easy to maintain those networks elsewhere, when you're here. You make your own friends here as well. Sports, leisure, bush walking is amazing. All the camping on your doorstep.

--

(Alice Springs, place to live) Yes, but it has some problems. I like the space. I like that many people don't have extended families so become family to other people. I think the crime has changed in the 17 years I have lived here. My measure of that is I would previously ride my bike at night. I stopped doing that about ten years ago. I enjoy the town. I like the town. There is everything I need here. I like to visit the city. I like to visit the coast, but I don't need to live anywhere else. The word dichotomy comes to mind. There is a lot of extremes...there is a lot of people in professional jobs, that there seems to be like a big gap...there is a lot of people in poverty. The remoteness has advantages and disadvantages as well. It's a beautiful place to live and the weather's fantastic, blue skies and everything, but if you can't afford to get out, it could feel very isolated as well.

--

On Alice: Love living in Alice Springs. An opportunistic town. Lots of money thrown around, and the challenges of retaining staff. Flexibility to acquire knowledge when working and chances to get work. There is no denying of troubles.

--

(Alice Springs) Adelaide born, so I came up, school teacher trained as well, in South Australia they weren't offering too many teacher positions. That was 25 years ago and there wasn't much of an

opportunity, unless you were prepared to go remote. Those days they used to rate you as a teacher. If you were a Level Three rated teacher, then you got a job. If you were a Level Two or Level One, not sure if there was a Level Zero...I was rated a two in physical education and two in English. Hadn't even stepped into a classroom, other than doing practicals at university...bit unfair looking back at it now, glad I saw a Northern Territory education department advertisement....come to the Northern Territory, and I applied. Within about two to three weeks I was here in Alice Springs and started off at Hermannsburg (125km east of Alice Springs). Taught there for four years and that gave me the credit. I was English as a Second Language (ESL) teacher. Definitely had the support of Alice Springs student support services. Help you with the ESL side of things. Then came to Alice Springs and taught in schools ever since.

I love Alice Springs. Couldn't think of living anywhere else. Just been over to head office last week having an induction into the job here...sitting in traffic jams, going from Brisbane to the Sunshine Coast, and Sunshine Coast, back. How can people do this! I couldn't do this. It's an easy lifestyle in Alice Springs. Leave the interstate stuff...nice to visit...don't think I could ever return to Adelaide. Adelaide is not so bad, but definitely Brisbane...how do people do this!...not for me. Came to Alice Springs for opportunity. It goes through a few troughs, a few highs. Bit of an issue around town with a bit of crime. Alice tends to work its way out of these sorts of things, and everything goes back to normal. Then we'll go through another spicier period later on down the track. It just goes through periods which are not that good, and then returns and restores itself, and then go through it again. Youth crime. We're a target at the moment. Downstairs, there's that roller door. Not working so well at the moment because I think that there's some young fellows, or young people out there, who are trying to manually raise the chain, raise the roller door on the chain, because it's been tampered with. The roller door is not working so well each morning. We're a bit of a target, breaking into some of the fleet vehicles. We might be a bit of interest to some people around town, a lot of youth who are stealing cars. They know that there's some vehicles down here which under the cover of darkness maybe steal a vehicle or two, who knows.

Alice is fine. Got everything we need. Nice community

--

On Alice: good size, all conveniences I require, weather great, seasons, and central to everything.

--

On Alice: The Alice provides a lot. Raised three children, good employment and good friends. Masters Games, Finke Desert Race, Rotary, Community, Henley-On-Todd. Good community spirit rallies behind causes. Community service groups are struggling, but not diminished in terms of support. Magnificent facilities (sporting and social aspects). Social problems not insurmountable. For example, alcohol causes social ills and to reduce demand in a group, address the driver of the problem such as intervention of some prescription. A sparse population of 27,000, so problems are more visible. A question of retire and leave or retire and stay. Alice is a positive experience.

--

(Alice Springs) I love Alice. My partner and I have been coming back here for 18 years, on and off. Was a tour guide for 20 years before I went to my previous job and then this job. Worked for AAT Kings, Tailor Made Tours, Flying Doctors service, School of the Air, Brits Camper vans, all around this area. Worked for Outback Ballooning as well. We first came here 2001, round there. We stayed for the tourism season as such and went away and travelled in a motor home for 13/14 years. Came back for the tourist season on a regular basis. At the end of the travelling heading to Queensland, where my parents are, but no, we headed back to Alice. There is always work here. The schools are great. The community is great. The weather is great. The commuting time is great. It's an easy lifestyle in Alice. If I do have to pick up the kids from school, I'm five minutes away. If someone gets hurt in an accident, I'm five minutes away. It's that kind of ease.

(hospital) You see on Facebook people complain about the hospital. I have not once had a long wait at the hospital. I don't know what it is. I've got two kids. I've had my fair share of broken bones and gastro, all sorts of things. Every time I've gone in, I've been well looked after. I've had to wait, but it's been minimal waiting. Been less than a few hours every single time. I've had great care. The nurses are great. The doctors are great. I've never had an issue.

Very happy with the schools. Extra-curricular activity. I think every single sport in the entire world is played in this little town. My daughter's been in guides, she is now in army cadets. My son is in the scouts. He's looking at joining the air force cadets. There's no reason to say, 'there's nothing to do in this town'. There's events. There's sports. There's organisations. There's volunteering. I'm on several committees. Just volunteered at the show (Alice Springs Show) turning sausages for the RFDS (Royal Flying Doctors Service). I volunteered at the Govies Muster (the colloquial name for Governesses of Alice Springs School of the Air who organise a Muster to raise money for outback children). I always volunteer at Old Timers (Old Timer fete), Red Centre Nats (a rev head's paradise, showcasing the very best in street machines, elite show cars, hot rods, classics, exotics and supercars (Alice Springs Town Council, 2019)). It's an awesome town. I love it.

--

With the International education stuff, if people can be working, there are migration pathways, which leads to population growth.

International students can work up to 20 hours a week during the semester, and up to 40 hours a week in the uni breaks. There is a lot of International students around Australia that can be studying, but the market is saturated with International students, they can't get casual work. Whereas here, they can get employment the first day they come here. You know, they seriously could, mainly in hospitality work, but places are crying out for staff. So many places that can't get staff in the hospitality sector. Also, in Australia, we really view hospitality in general terms…we view work like house maiding in a hotel or working behind a bar or coffee machine, as a means to an end. Only doing it while you are studying, or only doing it as extra work to save for your overseas trip or a house deposit. It's really undervalued work in Australia. A lot of Australians don't want to work in that environment. A lot of International people are willing to, and it is so easy to get a job in Alice Springs, since the last place that people go and get work is hospitality, because it doesn't pay well. There is a massive opportunity for those gaps to be filled by International students here.

The Indian population in the town of Alice Springs now rivals the Aboriginal population. They are comparable now. Aboriginal community in the town, it's around 18%. That's what the Indian population is. Look at the big migrant population we've got, and if you drive past the Sikh temple on a Sunday afternoon, all the taxis are there. All the Indian men are driving taxis. So many African people work in the supermarket. We've probably got a whole lot of people here in town that could potential fill some of those gaps that you guys are talking about. But their qualifications aren't recognised. There'd be heaps of people in Alice who are highly qualified but are not recognised. At least they are working...That's right, but if all those people with professional qualifications who are driving taxis and working at Woollies suddenly start to do what they're trained to do, we'd have no taxis.

We went out to Rocky Hill, where the grape farm is, Ritchie has a grape farm. It's out past the airport. Been on a pastoral property for generations and generations. One of the current members of the family about maybe ten or fifteen years ago diversified into table grapes...one of the biggest suppliers in Australia of table grapes now...but all his workers that he gets, they're not even generally uni students, they come from overseas and pick something else in Mildura (farms down south) and they come up here and pick the grapes. Their picking season...they've got a really short period that they can pick...they were saying the overseas workers are prepared to pick for 15 hours a day and earn a lot of money. They get paid per box, ten kilo box. A lot of the Australian workers can earn $500 a day. They are not doing as many. The overseas workers earn way, way more, because of the work ethic and they don't mind working ridiculous hours...that's a cultural thing too. Travel overseas to see that places are open all the time.

We've got one child in childcare at the moment. The other one been on a waiting list before he was even born, he is nine months now. When you break it down, they're getting so much out of childcare. Full of activities. Social stimulation. (childcare expense) Once you get the rebate and everything like that...(is it like $155 dollars for each child after the rebate?) I think it's $300 and something per week, after the rebate, we pay just $190. I think after the 1ˢᵗ July, it's means tested. It's not a flat fee for everyone. For us its (rebate) is capped at $7000 per year. Once you go over that you pay full fee. Thing is, if you've got multiple kids, it's difficult.

(Alice Springs) I think all of us would preach a similar story. Myself, I came here for a short stint to do a work contract, then my wife fell pregnant. We decided there was so much opportunity here. We fell in love with the community. The people. Everyone wants to help and work together. Now, two kids, four years later. Not going anywhere else. There's a lot to offer here. The jobs, education, excellent hospitals. The lifestyle great. Takes six minutes to get to work.

Great opportunity for kids. As they get older there's sports, camps, and state trips, things like that. Opportunities for kids. But, lots of employment opportunities too. My kids left in their 20s at various times, gradually disappeared and then came back one by one in quite close succession for work opportunities. There're heaps of work opportunities, and the lifestyle. They like the lifestyle.

Had a stint at Hermannsburg for a couple of years, but other than that. With our kids as they were getting older, we contemplated moving on, we thought...my wife was also born here...great opportunity for us growing up, great lifestyle. We wanted to give them the same, so we haven't moved. It's still in the plan. Maybe time to move on soon, but I wouldn't know where. Wouldn't want to move for the sake of moving. It ticks all the boxes.

I've been here now seven years. At the end of the day Alice Springs attracts people. If you are not born and bred here, sort of tends to attract people who are quite open minded, that are quite adaptable, that are quite resilient. You come here and have no family. You just make your own family. I don't have nieces and nephews, but I'm fortunate to have someone that I work in the same office with who has, that I consider to be my family. We're not related, but I love his kids to death. We have dinners. Maybe it's just me. I like to connect with people. I think Alice Springs does that. People in Alice Springs are really open and embracing. I think people in Alice Springs tend to be like minded like that. There is a set of Alice Springs that are born and bred. East side. Living here forever. We live on this street. Our family has always lived on this street. There is a social circle that is kind of a bit close. Whether it's there. Whether it's the Golf Course estate. Know a lot of families who have moved away, after living here for decades all their lives, end up coming back.

I think another opportunity for here is for the over 50s sector of people...can we say over 60s...or seniors that are semi-retired, not everyone is going to work until 60 or 65. Some people want to start kicking back at 50/55, but I just wonder whether there is...we talk about the over 50s lifestyle village, and stuff like that...there is a whole bunch of people that sit in that gap between full-time employment and the Old Timers, that are probably not really well catered for in Alice Springs. So, if there was some more of that Old Timers village, with adequate caravan parking...let's be honest, a lot of people in that sector still have their caravans, still want to get out of here every winter. They come back here every...my parents have just moved into a retirement village on the coast. They got two vehicles still, they're very active, and a caravan. So, if they didn't have their farm, they just would have nowhere to still live that lifestyle. But they are in a village

now where they have, even though they're both very active and very very fit and healthy, they have...if they don't want to cook, they can just go up to the hostel. There's craft days. There's bowls days. There's snooker. It's all happening around us.
Every block has a big, massive supersized shed, so they can put their caravans in it. That's what mum and dad are lobbying for, but again, 70 and 73 my parents, they are the youngest kids by far. Everybody waits so long to move into that kind of care. I think people are now recognising we have got to do that stuff earlier. We could be on the front foot here in Alice Springs, by having it here.

Bunnings in Brisbane, I always used to go to the guy with the greyest hair, because when I had questions of what I wanted to do, chances are, he's done what I wanted to do. Imagine how many of those people could be doing 20 hours a week at Bunnings (Hardware Store) or at the Servos (petrol stations).

More people are staying now compared to 30 years ago when I moved here. Get to retirement age and then move away, straightaway. So, we're losing those people who volunteer. There is a lot of people who retire who can contribute to society. One of the other things that are keeping people in the Alice is everyone grimes about the cost of airfares here, but when I went to Darwin in 1982, a return airfare from Darwin to Canberra was $930...so what's a return airfare from Canberra to Darwin now...probably $930. So, it's way, way, way cheaper. When we first moved to Darwin and we first came to Alice, we probably only did it once a year, but could do it once a month now. We're close to every single city

I think the other thing, we're talking a lot about people, the other beauty of Alice Springs is the lack of people. The fact that you can get in the car and drive an hour out of town, sit in the river at Simpsons Gap and watch the sunset, and there is so few people out there...you can sit in the river bed at Honeymoon Gap and there's just nobody else there. Literally only about 10 to 15 kms out of town you can go and hike up Mount Gillen in the morning. May pass 12 or 15 people, up or down. There's not a stack of people. Even if there is ten people up the top of Mount Gillen at sunrise or sunset, there is still enough space up there that all of you can have your own little bit of peace. When you go bush camping, when you go to your favourite campsite and there is somebody there...you just go a bit further down the riverbank. It's a bit different when you go to Ormiston and those places where the camp sites are controlled...but the fact that you can get away from the people, and the landscape is so grounding.

One other thing about Alice that I like is pretty well when you go to something, a function, event, market or supermarket, or wherever you go, you see someone you know. Have a chat. There is always a sense of familiarity with whatever you do in the Alice.

We go to the Show (Alice Springs Show) on Fridays (first Friday in July) to catch up with everyone we haven't seen since the last show.

Mentioned that all of the kids left, and then came back. That there is an age bracket, particularly in the education space, where they feel they need to leave because they may not be able to get the education which they require. They need to experience other things.

--

Place is so progressive. If you jumped on Facebook you could think the worse, but if you're actually involved in the community and deal with people day in and day out, the vast majority of people love the place, are keen to see what's happening. We service so much around the country, all the other states and their regional areas as well. Surprised to see how much stuff we do outside of the Territory from Alice Springs.

The head of Austrade, the CEO Dr Stephanie Fey, came to Alice Springs Developing Northern Australia Conference and at the beginning of her address she'd been to visit the Telegraph Station. She was saying 3000km of telegraph line from Darwin to Adelaide was laid in 18 months, and she was talking about how many poles were put into it. Imagine doing a project like that...how many years we'd be saying that it would take now. Imagine building a new line like that, we'd be talking years now. How innovative we were then...when it comes to innovation of what we want to achieve now, particularly with Developing the North agenda. There is no reason why we can't accomplish it, quite inspiring.

--

On the Alice: Moved to Alice Springs about four and a half years ago, did not intend to stay, just bought a house. Go to Yulara for work. Same with Tennant Creek. Go there every three months. Spend a week there. Work with eight others here. They are active around town. I go to Araluen (theatre for plays, singers, and other performances) occasionally, that's a great place (art and shows). My concern, I think it is the concern of most people here, by not going out, is my soft top jeep. I don't want to go out and leave my car in town. I read, on Facebook, what happens. I read about cars that have got hardtops that get wrecked. But it is a beautiful place, otherwise would I have bought a house here, absolutely not. Am I in fear here constantly, am I terrified, absolutely not. I love the place. I think it's got its faults, foibles, idiosyncrasies, things that need to be improved, but it's also got its beautiful parts. Like everywhere in the world, it's got balance. For me, the goods outweigh the bads...hence I live here and intend to stay here.

--

Alice Springs is wonderful for opportunity. I don't think I would have a job like this if I was working in an urban area. I'll be competing with so many other people with probably industrial relations background degree. I wouldn't get a job like this...but because it's Alice Springs, and there is such a skills shortage and a demand for employees...so that's why Alice Springs is really great. You're here for three weeks, probably got yourself a job...just becomes a foundation. Plant your roots here and stay. Heaps of opportunities and room to grow.

We really are like a social services hub here in Alice Springs. I think that's what our entire town is really founded upon now. Tourism is reducing for the centre. Alice Springs is really about public service, social service, and that's why we are all here. It's quite sad that tourism has gone down. I remember teaching tourism three years ago at the high school, we were looking at statistics published by Tourism N.T. and it showed that there had been a 70% drop in tourism since 2006/7. So, we lost heaps of backpackers, lots of backpackers have closed down, and we also lost our cheap flights when Tiger (airline) stopped flying here. We have not got Jetstar (airline). Virgin (airline) has just come back. So, cheap flights to and from Alice Springs stopping ten years ago, really affected the tourism industry, and now that we got Qantas (airline) flying much cheaper to Ayers Rock, people are now diverting. The drive from West MacDonnell Range to Ayers Rock or Uluru is amazing...West Max, Mereenie Loop and then onto Uluru. Kings Canyon, if you enjoy fitness and being outdoors, the Rim Walk is so good, incredible, really steep to begin with. Start from the bottom. Huge climb that's quite steep to begin with, then you walk around the rim...spectacular.

--

(Alice Springs) I've been here all my life...out west...been for two years at Standley Chasm on a block (certain size of land). Nothing changes out there. Peaceful. But it has changed, since I've been here. Still remember the 80s. Changed social behaviour. Generation has changed, of people. I don't stay in town during the evening. Don't really go out that much. Just here and back from work and straight home. In the winter months, rather be at home. Do my shopping at Coles (supermarket), go here and there, straight back home, it's about a 40-minute drive. Don't want to get back too late. Don't like driving in the night. Cows and horses. Horses, no cows that way. If I see a stump, is that someone there...it's just a tree stump.... who's this person walking round at night. Especially the turn off, the Standley Chasm turnoff. Walking dead.

(Alice Springs) Good town. It has multicultural. I love the drives out of Alice Springs and the camping out spots are just unique. It's hard to explain. It's just beautiful. It's the same as back home. I get to see the stars. Whereas interstate, hardly see any. All the high-rise buildings. I get to see the Milky Way, awesome, because got no lights out there. Town houses has advantages and disadvantages, like every other area does. Otherwise it's a good town. Everyone knows everyone and there's politeness too in this town. When I go to a shop, they're calling me sir...thankyou sir...actually on the registers...different tellers, might be a Maori fella and he calls me bro...see you later bro.

--

Alice Springs: two born and bred, and one blow in. Changed a lot when we were little kids to now. That's from a whole lot of different reasons, progression. I moved away for 17 years so coming back here this is where our families are, it's a funny little place. I was thinking about this the other week...what makes Alice Springs unique is not just that it is the centre of Australia, but it's isolated. Drive anywhere, it's two days to Darwin, two days to Adelaide...yeah you can go to Glen Helen or Ross River in an hour, go camping, but we are an isolated community, and I think whenever you have a bit of isolation a culture gets developed...it's a bit more accelerated. Look at Japan when it was cut off for 400 years, all their culture got really defined...an identity...Alice Springs does have an identity. It is really diverse though. We've got an Aboriginal community. We're surrounded by Aboriginal land, we know it's ancient. People come here for different reasons, it makes it quite unique.

I think the people here are very passionate about whatever space they are in. It doesn't matter who you are, what colour you are...you're here because you are passionate about something, and that isolation draws that out of people. Isolation is a big part of it. Going to be contradictory here. There is a certain amount of tolerance in the town. There is a lot of diversity...Finke race to the thriving arts community, but there is a lot of intolerance too. A double-edged sword...argue both sides there.

Family. Born here. Raised here. Whole life is here. My family is still here, partner's family is still here, one of the major reasons that people stick around. Commuting, five minutes to get anywhere, it's great. It's really relaxed too. Just chill out. Everyone takes the time...go to the cities, no one's got time for each other, you are in everyone's way.

Maybe it's the size of the population too because you are not in each other's faces, you can have a network around you. Although you see the same people around you and it gets boring, there is enough diversity to have your family groups, your friendship groups, but also influx of a lot of people. This busy time of year (cooler months) I've had people staying over the last month. A bit of diversity. There is great diversity in this town. That's a Northern Territory thing too, Northern Territory attitude.

When I lived in Perth I travelled an hour and ten minutes every morning to get to work. Just appreciate so much more. There's things you don't like about it. You miss the bigger things, but the little things...just appreciate it. There's still a lot of things around town when I was a kid, so it's good to see that. Your familiar with things...drive past something. Opened half the Mall, to my generation that was the best thing that ever happened because when we were kids, they had a mall. That was our life, we lived in that mall. So, when they opened the first half, it was a huge thing for us. It used to be a drive through all the way and they closed completely to walking only, and when they re-opened that end bit it was a huge thing for us. All kids at that age at that time. People talk about it all the time. People have been away, come back and catch up...jeez, good to see the Mall open again. So, it's just a little small town.

I think it doesn't change a lot, but then things pop up all the time. Places close, been a lot of grizzling about the Mall and businesses closing because of crime...some of those businesses needed to close.

That's the nature of businesses. There's more and more food outlets. More cafes...very trendy, trendy cafes.

In the 80's and 90's in the Mall itself couldn't put a number on how many Aboriginal art shops there were. Everything else was gone but art stores, and it just killed the town. The town centre was vacated for the tourists and not the locals, but now that's changing. It's going back now, going back the other way. I think in that time is when a lot of people left, because there was just nothing here for the locals.

(Alice Springs) I like Alice Springs. I consider myself a Territorian. Born in Melbourne. I like the lifestyle. As a resident, private resident, you do get frustrated sometimes with the amount of vandalism perhaps. I've had my windscreen broken, my side windows broken once in the car park down there, but that was about four years ago. We've just about every window broken or cracked (place of work) and that's disappointing. So's everybody else, so we are not unique. But on the scale of things we never had anybody smash in and steal anything,. whereas some people have. Some businesses have been badly hit, that's disappointing, but it is not unique to Alice Springs. You only have to read the news, only have to see the situation. You hear things in Melbourne or Sydney...my God I wouldn't want to live down there. I kind of feel sorry for those kids (local Indigenous children), because once it's five o'clock, kids come in here, and these kids are about this big (i.e. not very tall, very young) and I think to myself...what...then you look at the parents, then you look at the grandparents and you see these people are drunk...safer for kids to be here...then they are bored...then there is no control...I think the families have to take responsibility. Only way it's ever going to change is education...get them into school, give them things to do. They don't go to school, they hang around. Half of them their English is so bad, and I just find it really hard.

You've got these little kids who don't even speak English, and you've got these teenagers to early 20s angry with the world, angry, calling you names and everything. I find that disheartening as well, kid on the block. My husband's Aboriginal. He's Tasmanian Aboriginal. He says the same...You can't rule your life by the past, have to move on. Don't blame us for what happened. Go to every country in the world and see what's happened. We're not unique, Australia! Go to New Zealand. Go to South America. England. But I like living here. I like the smallness. Takes five minutes to get to work. I like the fact you can walk down the street.

A lot of our older people don't stay in Alice Springs. Very much a transient population. A lot of people when they retire, they move interstate. So, it's hard to get those volunteers. I think a lot of people have children and grandchildren that live interstate, and you really want to build a bond up with family, especially with your grandchildren, and you are only skyping them and you see them once or twice a year. Airfares are so expensive and that can be an issue.

--

(Alice Spring) I love it. I was born here. My parents are immigrants, they came over in the boat from Italy. My dad had his brother here in Alice Springs already working. I met my wife here, she was six when she moved to Alice Springs. Her family were passing through as well. They had a relative that ran the local caravan park here...why don't you stop and work for a few months. We had two kids. It's a beautiful place to grow two kids up in. It is a town you have to go on holiday once or twice a year, you got to get out. It's not so much I don't see it as a prison, it's around experiencing new areas out there and grounding yourself that there is a bigger world out there. If you do that, you are fine. It's becoming a little harder with the cost of airfares to do it as often as you would like to, but you always find a way around. Save your pennies a little bit more and do it anyway. The people I met, the network of people I know around town, even the American population...we've had plenty of American friends that work out the base (Pine Gap)...two or three year turnarounds when they come in, you create strong friendships. They leave, you get all sad, but you are still in contact with them five years later, especially with Facebook and Social Media. The amount of people that you meet and the social element that exists in this town is phenomenal. If you want to embed yourself in it, so easy to do. That to me is a massive selling point of trying to get more people here. Five-minute drive to work. Got a weekend full of things to do. You got that Outback element. You want to go and camp for a night, ten-minute drive out of town. Roll your swag (mattress rolled up in a tarp) in the middle of nowhere. If you're into that soft adventure stuff, mountain biking, bush walking, whatever it is, too easy. Can be easy to do.

So, the town itself and the services that we got are incredible. For a town this small the level of facilities we've got in this town for a population of 28,000 people is ridiculous. You compare us to a regional town anywhere else in Australia, they would be jealous of what we've got in regard to facilities and services, especially in that sporting arena, also the Masters Games. I take it for granted. Find half the stuff we got anywhere else. It's a massive selling point. So, the town offers a lot. It really does. How do you pull the emotional strings of people you want to try and drag here or bring into town around...are you into bush walking...yeah...you like mountain biking...well, have a look at this video, there's a drone following someone mountain biking, incredible scene.

So much to do. People are so friendly. We sponsor travel agents to come in, international, domestic. They love it. They love how everyone says hello to them. Freak out. You putting us on...no, this is normal. This is how the town operates. Kind of regional-local connectivity that's lost in the city, doesn't exist, not lost.

There's a great history story up and down the track (Stuart Highway). There's World War Two history. There's cultural history. There's plenty there. Always plenty of work to do.
There is a small population that live in the N.T. In Alice Springs when I came here, there is more jobs than people. It's like the Middle East, it's like a divide, the desert, you go there and earn really good money...not exactly the same terms, similar, because not so many people come here, but there is a lot of jobs here that pay quite well. At the same time the population is small, so the challenges would be, how do you fill those jobs, and if it's such a transient region, as Alice Springs is, so you get backpackers coming in doing a job and they have to move on. They work the holiday visa. We're not getting permanent employees for ten years. Not a lot of pathways to get permanent residency in Australia, like that changes every now and then. The rules become stricter and stricter. In terms of youth that would be a challenge. Getting people here on work permits. I don't think it's straight forward for that to happen to people.
Alice Springs a really amazing place. It's like a well headed secret. People don't know about it. When I tell my friends from other parts of Australia how amazing it is, how progressive it is, they are very surprised to hear that. There is so much arts and cultural type activities in Alice Springs. There is always something happening. I feel the community itself is very strong. You can make friends really quickly. It's really great. You have a lot of those great attributes you do want for a good quality of life. In Alice Springs, it is possible. Except the rent is quite high. Housing is expensive. It's the same as Melbourne, very surprising.

Go, Alice Springs!. It's a fantastic community, hope it does well and keeps thriving.

--

Alice Springs is a great place. It's full of opportunity. People say that time and time again. Invariably you can find some sort of work. You can make a real go of it here. It's a good place to rear children and give them a good lifestyle. Beautiful, clean air. Limited traffic. So many things to be absolutely thankful for here. My husband and I are still here because we've enjoyed great opportunities workwise...got a nice home...we just enjoy the country's laidback lifestyle and the fact that we've done o.k. It's a land of opportunities. It's good to be aware of that, just how lucky we are.

I think a lot of people choose to leave because it does have that hard edge. People want to go back to something that is physically and psychologically a bit softer. They want to go back to the beach or the rainforest...just that coastal strip that seems to be better, or softer, or amenable to an easier lifestyle. Whether they find that anywhere else, I don't know. There is a perception that life is a bit easier somewhere else, in some respects. We are used to living in a small community here. It is very personable. You can walk down the street and know a reasonable number of people. We're connected. We have a great sense of community here. People can come here and fairly quickly find themselves friends, be part of a network. You can do that really easily here. Not sure you can do that as easily elsewhere. It's still a bit transient. In our community, everyone counts, because we are all connected. We all count more so here than in a larger place that's got towns very close to it.

The other thing people can't believe when they get to Alice Springs is how strong our alternate community is here. The fact that you've got the Beanie festival, don't know if you would call it alternate these days. That alternate side of life is quite vibrant. We've always had, for many, many years, a big gay community. There is lots of alternate things happening, which is very appealing to a lot of people. It's sort of like an inland Nimbin...not as much as Nimbin probably. People associate Nimbin with drugs, but I'm thinking more of the alternate lifestyle that's very strong here.

You can do things here that you wouldn't do anyway else, that's for sure.

The other thing is we've got the Steiner School out on Ragonesi Road, which has gone from a couple of dozen kids when it was at the back of Araluen, to hundreds of kids out there. It's a sizable school. Don't know what the attendance rate is. Who would have thought 30 years ago that Alice Springs would have a Steiner School, a large size Steiner School. We've got all sorts in our community, but it's a vibrant, strong community. We don't go through the economic boom and bust periods that Darwin does, we are a very economically stable community. That doesn't mean to say that we're always doing well, but it is stable. We just keep going. Our expectations here are much lower than Darwin. From my perspective I go up to Darwin and people expect far more generally than what they do down here. People are used to just getting by down here with minimal government attention or intervention. Whereas up there they really are spoiled rotten. Everything is laid on in Darwin. It's a beautiful city, because it is a capital city it gets very well looked after by all levels of government...Local government, State, Northern Territory and Federal.

Down here we realise we are not particularly special in the scheme of things. It annoys us, but we deal with it and get on with it. We make our own fun and make the most of what we've got here, which is a lot. It is a hell of a lot. Look, last weekend, Finke weekend, the town was just booming. It's probable the busiest week of the year. People came from all over Australia, indeed the world, to engage in something uniquely Central Australian, the Finke Desert Race. We've got other festivals like that, that attract people from all over the place...the Red Centre Nats (fast cars and drag racing)...that's incredible how successful that has become. We've got our own style of entertainment. Our own style of hospitality. We have got our own persona as a community and it's very rich. It's based on a strong history of settlers and Aboriginal people. So, we're travelling well, really well as a town. It can only get better.

If you want to talk about the negative side of Alice Springs...youth crime, it has got worse over the last couple of years. It is something we have to constantly address. You can't take your eye off the ball for a second, and you can't take a 'namby pamby' soft approach either. You've got to be quite strict and clear about the boundaries and the consequences. This Royal Commission that we've had into child protection in juvenile detention, that's sort of inadvertently took the pressure off the kids for a while. The police and the authorities were generally spooked by the fact that this Royal Commission was at play. That has led to this sort of resurgence of quite significant youth crime across the town, but it's time to put the pedal back down again and say we're not putting up with this. Kids hanging out, there is nothing wrong with that, its kids getting up to mischief. Invariable there is a couple that urge the others...police say that...you take out the one or two instigators and things just improve automatically.

--

Alice Springs: been here since 2003 off and on. Had two years in Aboriginal health down in south Australia,, retired in 2014 but drove me mad. Alice Springs is where older people can find work. I still had family here. I came back here and have been working since coming back. Alice Springs, a fascinating place to live, I love the diversity here, don't like the weather. I don't like the heat. As I am getting older I just find come February I'm over it. This last year was just awful, and then a change within a fortnight of forty-degree heat down to frost...bang like that! I don't mind the frosty weather, because normally we get good days after it. I lived in New Zealand down south where a frost is a frost, and snow. Here, at least, you can have a reasonable day. Apart from that, I love the diversity around the place. My experiences here have just been amazing. I am a social worker by trade, and I've got education in my background. Used to teach social services in New Zealand. Worked with CAT (Centre for Appropriate technology) as an educator. Worked with Youth Justice. I was a domestic violence specialist in the Emergency Department for a year until they de-funded it, because they thought we didn't have enough domestic violence to fund it. Worked in women's health. Worked in Stolen Generations people, which was pretty amazing. That's how I got to know the big families in Alice and how they got to be in Alice, who they all were related to and the community connections. For example, family coming from Yamba down to Old Timers, and through the Catholic Church, sent to Santa Teresa and Amoonguna and some of them having connections over to Hermannsburg. You can track some of the families to where they have been, why there are still family in different places.

--

At the core Alice is a wonderful town. Like it really is a town full of people who...it's a town full of workers, it's not a town where people come and sit around and do nothing. People work hard. I think people who aren't working often having to work very hard to survive. It's quite a harsh town in some ways but it's also worth the work. It can be really challenging, but it exposes who you are in so many ways because you often have to respond to situations you wouldn't normally have to...someone fighting outside your house...Working in the work I did I heard lots of awful stories about high levels of violence, but then how do you integrate that into how you interact day-to-day. So how do you deal with people who are visibly drunk, how do you deal with people being openly racist. It's a challenge on how to live in this town sometimes, and how to be non-Indigenous and be respectful and acknowledge where you live. To raise a son who witnesses a whole lot of things that you would never witness if he lived in middle-class Melbourne, the suburbs of Melbourne, but it's still a challenge to parent. It's a challenge to explain why there are people living in poverty within 200 metres of our house and why we're not, and why that's not o.k. Yeah, we keep living it.

Those are the challenges that I really love about this town, and I'm very fortunate to be in a position to try and work through some of those issues. But it's a wonderful place to be, and for me it's all about that community...and when the community works well here, it works really, really well, and we need to keep aiming for that...Alice's best, not its worse...we've got to keep aiming for that best. Aim for our best day all the time.

This wholeness of Alice expression, drawn from individual dwellers, allows entry to the thoughts, imaginations, and inhabited considerations of those at the coalface of the Alice. The authenticity of opinion demonstrated, free from set questions or set agenda, hidden and otherwise, serves to create an environment that lives the services offered. This, in turn, allows the services offered, to live! The service lives may be varied within a feeling of sameness, as all contributors to the vignette are subjected to the societal space of the Alice, but it is the individuality of detail of perspective that is priceless in gauging how well the services of the Alice are doing. Accordingly, all in Australian society, and in all societies, are unique to a degree, but still regulated by whoever their society is, to conform. Hence there is a 'filing' down of individuality, but not its eradication.

Conclusion

Concluding the Service

Singular and multiple agents make up and construct the membership of society, creating a hierarchy of differentiation as to who influences the greater and lesser spaces of societal production, sustainability, and waste products. These three effects of societies causes do not only represent material production (goods and services), material sustainability (urban and rural made environments and services), and material waste (environmental degradation, disposal or lack of disposal, of discarded products and wasted services), but also human production, sustainability and waste. Humans are vulnerable and subjected to the causes and effects of the processes dictating the relations within and between singular and multiple agents, and are or eventually become and succumb to states of being 'produced', 'sustained' and 'wasted'. Wasted implies marginalisation from society and not having a voice, or much of one, to finally the fatal conclusion that awaits all living species. Sustainability infers going along with and maintaining the status quo of what is regarded as 'expected' societal behaviour, thus 'sustaining' and maintaining the hierarchy of differentiation. Produced indicates shaping or fabricating the societal framework, and as part of that, forming the 'initial' societal framework to become and evolve into the current framework, to encourage sustainability of hierarchical purpose. An unavoidable, or purposeful product, of the produced is material and human waste. It is simply part of the life cycle of differentiation and endings. Purposeful in terms of reminding those that difference exists, and how that purpose knowledge is used for good and bad for societal wellbeing.

Based upon the purpose of economic performance to seek profit and advantage over the competition, it is the human performance that drives the economic performance. The latter would not exist without the former, and consequently the human former would not be 'formed' and moulded into its present character without the economic latter. Essentially the human performance can exist without economic performance, it would just have created an alternate functional platform and networked structure to dwell within and through time and space. However, due to the 'hardwiring' of humanity in relational aspiration to survive and thrive, the capitalist economic system has emerged through the many winding courses of human history as the convergent current dominating blueprint of how life is and 'should be'. Should be is an aspect of coercion and in a way a sense of belonging, belonging to the societal 'family'. Singulars and multiples like to enjoy a sense of belonging, and the sense of identity that this brings, a sense of security and comfort. People in general are social beings, hence the creation of this thing called society. Without the drive of sociality, humanity may be a mass of individuals, lacking cohesion and lacking society. But humans do have sociality and to 'sustain' and 'produce' it, a touch of coercion catalysts the singular and multiple agents.

Paradoxically it is the mass of individuals that 'mass' together within varying degrees of commonality that sculpt into a 'grouped' society. This forms the shape and shapeless of society. Or a shape and shapeless form reflecting human input into the singular and multiple, characteristic of their time, place, and space, *a* particular shape/shapeless that becomes *the* shape/shapeless of its moments in time, a momentary state of affairs. It is the vibrancy of the ephemeral (shapeless) that keeps mixing with the permanent (shape), which produces the bubbling surface of society and the hidden swirling currents of performance enhanced actions and reactions, shown through these resultant metaphoric bubbles. Each bubble is an event, a repetition, an action, a reaction, an encounter of coming together, and departing as the bubble(s) bursts, to be replaced by newly formed and forming bubbles. Consequently, the constant moving and movement that society's individuals experience and are steered along from the felt, but unseen depths of the coercive shape beneath.

It is from these coercive and shape shifting performances that the place sovereignty of society is fashioned. That precise 'place' is society as a wholesome entity of the familiar production, sustainability, and waste. Although, wholesome for some, and not so much for others. Within that 'whole' of place, there are many sovereign spaces competing and compromising for position and juxtaposition. The singular and multiples create and occupy these spaces and can belong to one or more of them. Belong is a loose term ranging from temporary membership of literally moments/minutes, to days and years, and onwards to indefinitely, until wastage finally arrives. It is those who utilise and use spaces on a fleeting basis that enjoy moments. Others may repeat the spatial encounter on a regular basis, and would incorporate those who require regular contact with certain chosen, or chosen for them, spaces of sovereignty, or those who actually work in those spaces. The contact can be for years. Chosen for them implies a coercive ingredient, decided by unavoidable necessity or lack of choice to the contrary. As to indefinitely, until wastage, are those who own these sovereign spaces. It is normally the singulars that possess sovereign spaces and the multiples that 'work' them.

Within the structured and unstructured capitalist blueprint, what is spawned is an array of services that saturate these sovereign spaces. So much so, that one becomes indistinguishable from the other to an extent that they are effectively one and the same. The individual agent contacting these services reflects the performance moments and again, similar to the singulars and multiples, onwards to days and years. Also, the individual agent develops temperaments, characteristics, dispositions, when responding to the subjectively objective service conditions encountered. It is these fostered outlooks defining behaviour in the service encountered environment that Bourdieuan theories can latch onto, by inculcation of perceived serviced objective structures being immersing within the subjective, mental experience of agents. These objective influences place or misplace requirements on those who participate in its membership. Therefore, having absorbed objective social structure into a personal set of cognitive and somatic dispositions, and the subjective structures of action of the agent then being commensurate with the objective structures and extant exigencies of the social field, a doxic relationship emerges. The six Bourdieuan theories flagged; linguistic inquiry, field, political field, powering the symbolic, culturing the capital, and habitus will be 'latched' onto, to see how each offers a serviceable theory of society to understand the service of society.

Linguistic Inquiry

Inquiring into the world of linguistic processes within the service context is a process of agenda creativity. The agenda is tailor made to suit its related service context. Tailor made is a purposeful aim at deliberate ends, since the hypothesis has been set and the subsequent service performance aspires to validate that. At best this is the idealised version, as in the space of the primacy of relations involving human interaction and communication procedures, the 'ideal' of the situation may not always be possible. For instance, layers of 'ideals' may come to the fore, or remain in the background, from the serviced, the servicers, and the service owners, and it is these multiplicity of ideals that can dilute the service projection effectiveness, as contending claims on that service are presented and misrepresented.

The presentation and misrepresentation are powered by intentional and unintentional performances 'voiced' as the end product of linguistic expression. Therefore, it is the 'sounding off' aspect of the communication between the service stakeholders that is actually the end of a complex journey of serviced considerations. These considerations are derived from the context driving them. For example, within the spaces of religion, education, government, welfare, Indigenous, tourism, politics, and dwelling place reactions in the Alice, all have their own narratives and discourses arrived at over the course of overlapping time. Overlapping in the sense of a longitudinal historical and contemporary unfolding and folding of social events and associated life processes, that all are directly and indirectly affected and influenced by, in minor and major encountered ways and means. These would be occurring in conjunction with the shorter term and immediacy of time and its present moments in time, that are blanketed by the time eternal, but arriving at the fore during the propinquity of the service situation.

These shorter time frames would have been created during the life span of an individual up to the present moment. As she or he has been moulded, manipulated, and managed to particular behavioural patterns of thoughts, deeds, and actions through the actuality of being in society as a whole. Also being in a more intimate space of family, care givers, and close friends, acquaintances, and enemies, whose spatial capacity may expand and decrease, expand and decrease, along that living and dwelling short time frame of human existence. Each of these macro and micro societal interactions with the lived space within and around the individual, would have produced a reaction in the individual. The reaction would be categorised by what the individual is.

The becoming of 'Is', is key to the whole linguistic appreciation. It is a person's 'is' that is their identity. It is what makes them feel it necessary to take part in this process of service. Part of this necessity is the limited option to opt out of the service process for to try and do so may be an unrealistic course of action, and associated inaction, to take. For instance, society and its parasitic services may just be too strong to avoid, resist too much, manoeuvre around its flanks, or unrealistically assume a position of societal denial. Parasitical implications may incorporate a number of meanings; opportunistic, dependence, biting, however within the linguistic interaction these should not be thought of as negative connotations, but as the way things are in the service environment. Essentially, it is what the service environment produces.

There is the opportunity to create a service out of 'nothingness'. This nothingness may have evolved into 'somethingness' as to the way society was travelling, and a demand for a new service was produced and grew out of necessity. This may have been due to colonialism and post-colonialism giving birth to and sustaining Indigenous related services, technological developments producing new forms of education training and innovation, and surplus leisure time and allied spending ability flowing into fresh and new tourist ventures. Alongside this, fresh service opportunities can encourage dependence upon these opportunities, as people become reliant upon these created services and experience difficulties in getting by without them. People includes service owners, service agents and service customers. Subsequently, the service itself becomes literally a living system supporting the living practices of those that support it through earning a living by it, and improving quality of life, sometimes fundamentally, from a position of survival. The NDIS is a case in point, where quality of advocacy is essential to a linguistic inquiry of matching what is needed to what is offered. Within this dependence upon service provision, one does not bite the service that 'feeds' when the dialectic process between serviced and servicer is taking place. Of course, this may depend upon who is doing the biting, the service agent or the serviced.

Additionally, the service itself can bite. Bite in the sense that the linguistic encounter already has it dialogue prepared. For instance, a service voice that is contrived, skewed to a predetermined pathway or pathways of how the conversation will pan out. Thus, a power play that tries to ensure the result is already a formality for the servicer. However, the serviced can contribute and be implicit in this loaded outcome, since the like-minded education in and of society would ensure a commonality of thinking along similar lines. This is why services exist and are accepted, they become normalised and lack criticism of their existence. For instance, no one raises an objection to why religion exists. Not in the sense of one religion competing with another or the dogmatic way that religion can sell its beliefs, but in the actual existence of this thing termed religion, e.g. Why have religion? Even asking that question raises issues of perplexity and puzzlement amongst societal members. Hence the extent of acceptance of services, and the resultant silence due to that passive acceptance. This passive silence of non-speaking may come from being comfortable with services offered, a self-realised non-powered voice marginalised by the service, or not comprehending what the service is about, perhaps truly about. The 'truth' may be residing within the hidden aspect of the service agenda so cannot be argued with, or at least without considerable difficulty.

Linguistic inquiry and its attendant expression are always limited when negotiating service quality and quantity. The limitation is served due to language being comprehended from a praxis appreciation, and not as a logos. There is an array of reasons steering the practice of praxis along certain 'limited' pathways, normally associated with keeping the service intact, and as a prominent voice in society, a service voice championing that service, to justify its place in society and in turn justifying the place of those working and possessing that service. It gives them an authority to speak, which otherwise the 'opportunity' to do so would not be there or be limited in scope. So, in turn, the service possesses them and those that use it, limiting all from their position in the creative agenda hierarchy. Indeed, linguistic inquiry, not just within service linguistics, although one overlaps the other greatly, is a product of a complex set of social, historical, and political conditions of formation, but a formation hidden behind the linguistic communism illusion.

Field

An imagery of field produces imaginations of fields to play on, a playing field. This, in turn, denotes that place and space is required to make the field available for human consumption. From this consuming process, there must be abstract and concrete spaces within the field place for it to service and be serviceable within the overarching field of society. Since society enjoys a finite space of functionality and manoeuvrability, it follows that the fields within its spatial influence in turn have limited space of movement, and expanding their field space is at a premium level of configuration and competition. Labelling fields as to what they represent and are, is at differing scales of recognition both in size and what the field actually does. In general terms society is made up of fields of religion, education, government, welfare, Indigenous, tourism, politics, amongst others. However, establishing these field characteristics as defined boundaries would be fraught with difficulty, as each would possess its mini fields, but apart from the commonality of being labelled or classified as being in that field space, there would also be competition between those in that field. Thus this turbulent space can create field instability and hence service instability.

As an example of field service instability, the tourism field is adopted, despite the fact that anyone of the other generalised fields could have been selected. Tourism requires space to be productive, though (in theory) any space can be marketed as a tourist place worth visiting to gaze upon or doing activities in. However, tourism can be a fickle field to maintain all the mini fields within its 'field of operations', since the serviced, i.e. tourists, enjoy an immense array of touristic choice and destinations, but if they do not choose a favourable tourist outcome, these tourist fields flounder. As a result, the structure of these fields begin to weaken, break down, and possible cease to be. The point is fields require a steady supply of service customers and consumers to be. If this supply reduces to a trickle, or not at all, the service stops, or reinvented. This service reduction is compounded by other tourist fields within a same locality of space competing to receive a contracting portion of the tourists serviced pie. Of course, an opposite direction of expansion can occur, if a tourist field becomes flavour of the month or years and its service capacity correspondingly grows in proportion to the serviced flow. This, in turn, can attract other tourist services to spring up, so multiplying fields within the tourist field. Thus, a healthy service environment results, which in turn contributes to the well-being of society, at least from the space(s) of prime serviced tourist 'hot spots' or 'hot spaces'. Alternatively, other tourist spaces in that society may contract as a result.

There is a set of relationships within fields and between fields that provide motion, hence giving movement for society. It is this movement that allows society its life, as a network of fields and their service connotations are the backbone of society, for the network provides structure and a sense of rigidity for society to 'stand up'. The network of fields is not necessarily a harmonist relationship, as not only do mini fields within a one field struggle with each other to survive, dominant fields, i.e. religion, education, government, etc. would struggle with each other to become more dominant. Hence, the field of society is not a harmonic state of affairs, more like a demonic state of affairs, or perhaps a bit of both, with one dominating for a time and then replaced with the other, depending upon the health of the service context and also the health of society. To illustrate, if society is going along well, that can reflect a bountiful supply of service equating to a bountiful demand of service, a happy, harmonious time. Alternatively, if society is not going along well, fields become more guarded, protective of their space of influence. Hence, suspicious of each other as anxiety sets in, and creating a demon spatial field of existence.

The demon can arise in all who are involved in fields. Essentially that involvement would generally apply to all who reside in society, since everyone would experience greater or lesser contact with a field or fields through their life course, as field interaction is unavoidable. Even when one passes on, they are still subjected to the religious field serviced customs and rituals. Indeed, before birth, the health services checking the progress of the unborn child. Consequently, when being mindful of 'demonic fields', an awareness of attitude is necessary of this field contact through one's life course, and even extending that awareness to one of prior (as an unborn baby) and beyond their life course, of being vulnerable to field(s) imposition.

The demon also rises in fields when capital accumulation is at stake. As society is a capitalist system, fields require funds to function. The tourism field is an obvious one, as its industry keeps people in work and supports regions that have nothing or very little else to sell to keep them economically afloat. Government and the political system advocate economics as a matter of course to create wealth, as well as shouting about it and encouraging the field others to do the same. When negotiating through this political economic system, non-profit organisations such as in the welfare and Indigenous fields, need to attract funds from the said governmental field system, otherwise not a lot of field activity occurs. As for education, it draws from government coffers and private fees from parents and caregivers of students to 'educate', producing a reciprocal fielded system approach. As part of this economic relationship, the education field teaches how to function in the capitalist society, reinforcing the capitalist society as the way to be, regulated by the government and associated politics. The other main fields (welfare, tourism, Indigenous) do the same, as does the religion field, although it is powerful and established enough to be self-funded to take on the threat of demons in the field machine.

These playing fields encourage agents to play the game of the field(s) and also to be game when playing the game. For instance, there must be a willingness, spirit, and inclination to treat the game as not a game in the sense of the consequences of not being successful can be life changing, or life threatening in terms of quality of life, not necessarily termination of life. To 'field' one's life does involve a tackling of it, trying to get a handle on it. It is a serious business. But, playing the field is simultaneously a game as a game, a contest and a fixture of life in society, an event, a performance, a pastime. Accordingly, playing the game of fields as structured spaces of positions and dispositions in society's finite field space.

Political Field

Politics by its very nature is biased, opinionated, perhaps to extremes of prejudice, dogmatism, and intolerance. Politics, in its field of inquiry, is also compromised based, reaching 'common' grounds of agreement, enabling things to move onwards rather than forwards. For instance, forwards may be too an optimistic pronouncement, as the imagery and practise of forwards is regarded as 'backwards' to some individuals. Alternatively, driving politics onwards is based on beliefs, although it is also acknowledged that beliefs between people can differ. Nonetheless, these beliefs would enjoy intimacy with how society is structured and planned, of course assuming that it is feasible to plan for society, at least from a comprehensive platform of engagement, amongst its layered complexity. This is because society retains its own sense of movement, direction, and momentum, and individuals, elites, and groups or singulars and multiples can attempt to steer the societal ship, but mostly just ride its social waves. This is due to society as being a product of historical performance, crafted over many generations. Technological innovation or imposition, depending on which side one is on, may alter society's surface landscape of material appearance and usage, but the undercurrent powering that 'upper' process and performance has used the same rationale for countless generations. Namely, getting control and 'ownership' over space, place, and the people occupying such geographic locations or, if not control and ownership, having influence. Preferable political influence.

Field craft or crafting the field to ensure political influence, composes the political field. This is rather like a conductor drawing together the disparate segments of the orchestra to go along in the same direction to create a pleasing melody for all listeners, and players, to relate to. Or at least react to. Similarly, the political 'players' conduct the fields of religion, education, government, welfare, Indigenous, tourism, and...politics, so it can be thought of as the political field is the performance and process field behind all the fields in society. Hence, the political field classifies how other fields 'are', in the network of society, what their agenda is, what is sold as service provision to the served consumers and sold as service provision to the servicers charged with 'selling' services. Indeed, those members of the political field may also have personal ownership of fields of service or have a voice to influence those that do own. Additionally, the political field may self-classify, of those that belong within the 'inner circle' of political power and influence, and of those that do not. The political field, by its nature, is a sustainable field of production, sustaining and limited its membership. Thus, a set of singulars and associated multiples, within a loose to tight fit, to politicise society along specific partisan compositions. Hence, creating society's 'musical score'.

Political fields are not only the domain of particular singulars and multiples, since for political fields to be effective all in society must have degrees of access to the political playing field(s). This in one sense cannot be avoided since society, as part of its complex identity, is the political field of play. Thus, all in society are already on that field of play or at the very least, part of the crowd, the audience, surrounding the playing pitch, cheering or jeering on the principal political players. In another sense the political field needs this connectivity and contact with all of society, as it is this correlation which provides the potency of politics. In consequence, the political masters cannot provide their version of service to society, without an audience. It is this audience that works this rendering of society, to clad it in the cloak of political acceptance and 'majority' justification, i.e. the majority of society acceding to this rendered political field.

Political power capacity is key to the extent of how one can 'play' in the political field. For instance, the limit that one can rally, assemble or mobilise resources of relevancy, determines one's level of immersion in the struggles that delineate a field, political field included. Resources can be thought of as capital, and how much capital one can draw upon or manipulate would equate to how much of a voice, action and reaction one has, to meaningfully play the field. Bourdieu flagged four capital types; economic, cultural, symbolic and social, and all can be drawn upon to give a field a certain taste, flavour, whose uniqueness will depend upon the field's context as a service to society. Also to be taken into account are the individual and combined constructions of capital assisting the field from the accumulated capitals of field members, both servicers and serviced, and the field owners.

Economic capital is thought of as the most potent, the most powerful capital to grease the wheels of society and attendant services. Along these lines, money and funding flows pervade all fields and all come at a cost, and this cost must be met, regardless of field credit or debit, since profit and loss indeed does create profit for some, to loss for others. The profit comes in the form of material wealth, which implies it can be seen, touched, measured, i.e. forms of land space, buildings and money, essentially economic accumulation to provide greater leverage for field play. It is the economic clout that reinforces one's clout in the political field, but it would be misleading to assume economic capital is the be and end all of 'owning' the political and other fields, since actually it can be thought of as the be and end all product of the other three capitals. For without their input into the process of becoming an economic and political player, economic opportunities would be limited.

Cultural capital traverses' cultural possessions and educational authorisation. These are the ideological representations and drivers that make society what it is, and guides people along on how to behave and what is valued. Hence, contributing to the appreciation of symbolic capital. Symbolic capital is another member of the representational society process, and offers acceptability and sincerity to all the capital types, allowing them to proceed, i.e. it gives legitimacy to economic capital. As for social capital, this brings people together within workable networks of connectivity. These networks are 'social' in nature creating membership groups, hence singulars can get together to form multiples, or 'multiples groups'. These would retain an underlying doxa of 'common' belief or 'popular' opinion, although only common and popular to the group members, but perhaps not so much for those who are not members, or are excluded. The excluded may be 'ordinary' persons, or those around the political playing field, playing at being the audience who generally are consumers of politics and consumers of fields, therefore consumers of services, not the drivers behind the fields and services.

Powering the Symbolic

Services are symbolic. They are a familiar everyday presence in society. Those in society know what they are, where they are, and how to use them, if necessary. It is this acceptance process with little or no questioning that grants normalcy, routine, the status quo. No one really questions why services are there, instead they may question the limits of service provision that services offer, especially when encountering services becomes a personal choice, or one that is 'choiced' by the societal system. 'Choiced' in the sense that one is required to access a service or services, which is due to the mechanisms and workings of society dictating one's actions towards narrowly defined preferences, i.e. one has little or no choice but to go along with such dictates. Examples are associated with welfare and dependence on welfare, political pressure, being Indigenous and the marginalisation that carries, the tourism space clashing with environmental space, government backed services, compulsory education and 'voluntary' education (still determined by what society offers or what one can offer society and be trained in, but still within society's framework), and religious teachings and exposure. Considering the latter, behavioural patterns in society are still heavily influenced by the legacy of sacred religion, within its profaned form.

The potency of service symbolism sells society, and what services evolve to service society. This evolvement is from intentional actions sometimes manipulated by a rigorously thought through plan and other times by chance, which grants opportunity to acquire spaces of control. Although, the advantage given by chance can only be realised by one's field capacity, political field knowhow and understanding, and speaking the linguistics of the language of power. Possessing these can create more vocabulary to strengthen and own controlled spaces. Once spaces of control or fields of control are legally owned, they become commodified service places. Places where the buying and selling of service goods and performances are traded, and in which the communication processes within the services are the traded commodity. These are communication processes that symbolise a layered system of operation. One layer is the symbolism through what the dialogue of service interaction represents. For instance, why those specific words, why that order of word expression, and why that emphasis on intonation along certain parts of the verbal sentence. Consequently, the language of symbolism is a powerful tool to encourage people to act and react to what is voiced. This is the symbolism of the place of the voice.

Another layer is where the voice is heard, offers more than the sum of its parts, with the symbolic authority of the placed service institution adding weight to the prearranged enunciations. Accordingly, symbolism of place cannot be underestimated, it is a wordless place, standing sentinel, but if it looks impressive enough, for example the seat of government, the cathedrals of religion, a sacred site and sight of Indigenous Dreaming, these 'wordless' symbols can be the loudest and most effective symbolic expressions. A third layer is symbolic legitimation, essential for service success, as it adds weight to the authenticity of the service process. The brand name of the service, its logo, symbolises that success. Success can take time and space to succeed, but the longer it exists, and its spatial influence expands or at the very least does not contract, its legitimation increases and hence its symbolic prowess. Eventually, it symbolises an established and accepted service pillar of society, an official service.

This disclosed and enclosed service of official revelation, its Bordieuan *nomos*, becomes an authorised, approved, formal societal principle of vision and division, a symbol of societal unification, adding weight to its strength and strength of purpose. It offers a vision of unity of all travelling along in the same direction, but the paradox is at the same time social division is concealed along society's highway of movement. Dividing the haves from the have nots, society is being purposely divisive to enable the official version of the vision to remain so. This produces the hierarchy of capital capacity, diversifying the capitals into symbolic capital, metamorphosing or transfiguring the symbolism into a pleasing public product, but nonetheless a product of concealment, suppression, disguise, or dissimulation. This camouflage helps to constantly renew the service, and simultaneously helps to constantly renew the will of the people, to its legitimation.

Misrecognition of the recognisable is a symbolism of practice that does sustain service provision. This is where symbolic violence is the most potent form of persuasion, applying thought and perceptive processes upon the social agents of the serviced and servicers. Since this type of violence is not easy to detect, but easy to accept, its allegory flows through the service offering of least resistance. However, legitimation of a service, regardless of if advertised through symbolism or the more concrete performance of every day, is not a negative thing, if the service has quality. Quality to do good, and people do benefit from what is offered. After all, service is purported to serve, to improve one's lot in life. Quality is needed to keep the service going: quality of service and symbolising the quality of service.

Culturing the Capital

Capital culturing implies a 'forming of' the social world, shaping the social world into a desired shape, or desired shapes whose amalgamation is the formation of society, its sought after silhouette of the socially formed one-shape. Shaping society can be thought of as the outline of society; the outer surface, the perceived surface, what is effortlessly seen. This 'outsideness' is not necessarily reflecting the nature of society, that of and in itself, takes effort to perceive but perhaps not too much effort to feel and experience the effects of. So, the perception of the social world requires enlightenment of understanding to what the shape conceals, opaque for some, transparent for others.

When reacting to the process of cultural capital by its concrete performance of will and will power, encourages experiencing and feeling the effects of it, which inclines towards social differentiation. When defining the 'willing' performance, society is thought of as a combination of singulars and multiples and their service consumers; those who drive the agendas of society, and those who react to that, ranging from consensus and consumption to resistance. Social differentiation comes into play depicted by the way services are interacted with. The interaction ranges from ownership of services to being 'owned' by them out of societal necessity and personal health status, both economic and embodied. This not to say that services themselves produce the social differentiation. That distinction of space may have been present prior to the existence of certain services, whose existence may only be due to the potency of differentiation, and the social disadvantage that perpetuates.

Also, what should be considered is the social advantageous distinction that society perpetuates for services. For each of the service themes in the book; religion, education, government, welfare, Indigenous, tourism, and politics, are all products of differentiation, and exist because of this distinction, which places them in expedient positions in society. However, the expedient performance suffers from inconsistency, as these service themes simultaneously try to reduce the effects of social disparity, but also sustain it. This is because the services are part of that disparity, and essentially not comprehensively addressing the root cause of differentiation, which may be too big a task and ask anyway. To clarify, the root cause itself is how society operates and how it has operated along the past to the present, and future intended agenda, and its attendant differentiation tendencies creating social disparity. As a consequence, the services cannot escape the cultural hierarchical performance that is inherent in society, since being serviced parts of that 'root cause' hierarchy.

When meaningfully addressing social differentiation, perhaps the only way is to step outside of society, to step away from its distinctions, and not be shackled by them. Thus, an 'external' service provider for the equitable health and wellbeing of society, an imagined space of existence beyond societal space. This imagined place in practise would have to consist of people not 'contaminated' by the society they wish to assist. They must not have knowledge of its workings, since there is a risk of being influenced by it and operating from that distinction position, with the probability of reproducing another version of social differentiation. That is the external service rub, in that knowledge of societal workings must be made aware of, before forms of assistance is offered. Also, the services which are 'internal' of society have the same dilemma, as their structure is based on stratification of power and access to it, just like society itself. Accordingly, services are mini versions of society. Besides, an external service may not be welcomed, since it would be seen as a threat to challenge the social order. Paradoxically, many people are comfortable with what they know compared to what is unknown or alien, even if their life chances are lower down the rungs of society's climbing ladder.

Life chances are dependent upon how much of cultural capital one possesses. The more chances one has, the greater the possibilities for life changes, life changes due to added life choices. The possession of cultural capital entails the retention of material and non-material assets and incomes, namely economic and social capital, but also the cultural capital of objectification, embodiment, and institutionalisation. Objectification is access to the art and literature of society, of what is valued both in monetary terms but also artistic appreciation. This value and appreciation are part of the cultural education of society, being educated to be an effective member of society. The level of effectiveness equates to the higher rungs of the ladder, hence the higher levers of the service performance; being the owners of services and being servicers, rather than the serviced. Embodiment is in a sense the culture of the self, of what cultural capital has developed and evolved literally over one's lifetime, one's character, nature, disposition of the spirit, mental capacity, and bodily potential. It is the product of this disposition that positions the personified person to the vulnerability of service usage. Institutionalisation is acquirement of a skills base and fluency with societal cultural speak and erudition, and the more one acquires, the more one is of society, the more one is of its services.

The more one is of its services, the more one has a superior strategic conception of the agency of services. The level of this conception depends upon one's conditions of existence, how one relates to others, what are the extents of commonality to others, and the extents of un-commonality, within the societal niche in which one finds oneself. The nature of this relationship will be influenced by one's material and non-material capacity, and ability to gain more of these and ability to lose some or all. Essentially one's position in society is one's condition of existence in society, and one's condition of existence of extent of service contact. The extent and reason of service contact can be 'conditional' on how it is voluntarily used as opposed to obliged usage, for example tourism as opposed to welfare. Consequently, one's initial reason for seeking services greatly influences how the service encounter is judged and received. Thus, the resultant service being one of freshness or one of oppression, may depend upon preliminary attitude and where one is situated along society's condition of existence continuum.

Culturing the capital reproduces society along similar or the same culturally generated environment, i.e. a purposeful sequence of events repeated over time, so the majority of capital is retained in the hands of singulars and their associated multipliers. Although all have access to capital, it can be a sparse commodity to get hold of, and one can speculate that the embodied cultural capital of the self can be unlimited in its imaginative potential, so that one's self may be regarded as not too sparse. However, it is also the 'unlimited' imaginations of those that own the capital forms in society, which can subdue the mass imaginations, or imaginations of the masses. As a result, this unseen singular and multiple imaginative streak overrides the imaginings of the many, dulling their sensibilities and correspondingly increasing the acceptance of power and control. Ultimately, the many, if not all (singulars and multiples as well) in a sense, serves the societal system, as people are also capital that cultures the capital of society.

Habitus

The habit of habitus resides within all individuals in society as an automatic response mechanism, originating from an unconsciousness reactive riposte to what is thrown up by society. It overrides the conscious act in performance, when societal stimuli demands or expects some sort of reactive action. Also or alternatively, perhaps the unconscious habitus works with or is absorbed into the individual consciousness to produce an outcome. Hence, they work together and, along the continuum of human awareness, may be one and the same. Consequently, it may be that the emphasis differs in terms of intensity of automatic response, tutored by a habit of 'non-thinking' and 'non-consideration' of successful resolution, to one of pause for thought and pause for consideration. Therefore, in certain situations, and contexts, one may be the preferred course of action over the other, although one can speculate that 'choosing' the habitus of the unconscious or the 'non'-habitus of the paused conscious, when negotiating pathways through life, comes back to the habitus. In this manner its unconscious energy may control all of what the self decides upon and consequently what performance results, and resolves, from the choice(s) on offer.

Habitus is 'thought of' as arrangements of long lasting, resilient, sturdy, compatible dispositions, of structures inclined to manoeuvre as structuring structures. 'Thought of' is an ironic inclusion, as habitus seems devoid of the thought process, as it just does, rather than think about doing. As habitus is perhaps an unconscious conscious doer of structure building, it creates and reflects social differentiation. This differentiation is a consequence of all individuals in society retaining capacity for habitus, as all have habitus as part of their decision making armoury, so in one respect all are equal. This equality is only possible if societal capital is either withheld from all, or if society has just been born since it is new and fresh without hierarchical structures in place. Hence, capital acquisition is not possible or has not taken place as yet through time and developing space of difference. However, the perspective that habitus is present for all in a mature society, does not imply that there is equality of habitus usage, as the inequality would be a result of one's disposable and reusable level of capital income. In this manner, the ability to instil one's habitus over another habitus or many habitus, is enhanced, if one's capital grants grander power plays than others in society.

From this stratification of habitus, it becomes fundamental between the singular and multiple and the rest of society, and their corresponding socially structured environment. 'Their' socially structured environment implies a singular and multiple socially structured environment as counting for the 'full' membership of society's environment; a dominating and subordinate habitus process. The created habitus environment of society would include the services of religion, education, government, welfare, Indigenous, tourism, and politics. These would carry within them their own sense of institutional symbolic habitus. The sense being that any service environment would retain a performance of automatic process and reaction, systems in the service mechanism that runs on 'unconscious' lines of decision making and retaining the inner essence of what the service essentially is. The inner essence is the service itself; its bureaucracy, its physical structure, its status, its reputation, its familiarity, its institution status, and its sense of permanence. Those individuals that own it, service it and are serviced by it are of a temporal nature. They would be at the conscious end of the habitus, the visible part of the service. They come and go, but the service place remains, as long as society remains in a form to sustain it.

Since the 'learnt' habitus stems from an unconscious space, apparently beneath consciousness, language and self-will, it is the uncontrollable aspect of it that may lead to vulnerability. For instance, members of society are most easily manipulated when young, and the habits of habitus are initially learnt during childhood, so a double vulnerability. The first vulnerability is a societal ability to form one's habitus to be of a certain quality that benefits society, and not necessarily that person. The second vulnerability is the ease of that formation due to the person being of an undeveloped, fledgling, immature biopsychosocial character. Accordingly, the uncontrolled aspect of not having a will to resist, language to think and consciously decide for oneself, and the unawareness of unconsciousness, suggests that habitus, far from being a 'free form' ability to make instantaneous judgements and decisions, may be saturated unconsciously within its unconsciousness, of societal norms, values and judgements that choose pathways already pre-determined. As a consequence, the self-will definitely could be lacking when it comes to habitus, and replaced by the will of society.

An irony for those singulars and multiples that like to believe they *are* society or at least run it, is they would also be vulnerable during their adolescent habitus construction phrase, vulnerable to the reproductive and sustainable practices of society. Also, as subordinate to society as to those in society they subordinate. Accordingly, it then follows that society's own habitus is that of its human membership, letting them unconsciously work to ensure its existence. After all, habitus is an historical product, creating and recreating singular (individual) and multiple (collective) practices and appreciation of practices in concurrence with the schemes produced by history, or the scheming of history. Hence, the scheming of society endlessly transformed through a dialectic with its human habitus environment, to replicate economic, social, and political societal structures.

It is through humans as habitus agents, both on a singular/multiple basis and as society's habitus, that services exist and are as they are. Within this context, services generally service human disadvantage, preying upon social inequality, its processes and reproduction, and habitus is front and centre or perhaps 'back' and centre within its covertness, on the crossing point of the individual and socially structured environment. Paradoxically, services also service human advantage, since the proclivity of habitus is to ensure 'action lines' towards maximum profit for agents, both symbolically and economically. Even though the habitus guides individuals towards particular acts and actions, aims and choices, of what is demanded by social conditions, there would be an element of spontaneous-ness within that, a spontaneity that is part of the habitus, but due to the nature of habitus, an unconscious part of the unconsciousness of it. A part that allows for a pure subjective, free from the objective society, state of being, an untainted sense of serviceable habitus, which may help keep society and its services a bit 'cleaner'.

Service Has the Final Word

How humans settle in place is a test of character, of (dis)position. Finding one's (dis)position is a site of struggle, especially when a 'settled' place is quite mature, as its structures, institutions, and services are already established and set in their ways and means, since the dogmatics of maturity can produce an inflexible temperament when encountering its spatial domain, The service structures are also not exempt from a certain inflexibility, hence the structural aspect of the settled place. However, the strongest and most durable structures are those that have an in-built designed flexibility, a flexibility of purpose and aim, and an ability to listen and observe effectively. From a certain perspective flexible services are the most welcomed varieties, as they are consumer based since their rationale is 'based' upon the agenda of the serviced, and the servicer agenda adapts accordingly to maximise the service of service.

From an inflexibility perspective, services can serve the purpose and aims of service owners. This is because the agendas, in their overt/covert formulation of these services, are for the advantage of the owners and not necessarily for the service users. To illustrate, these 'serviced' people are trained to think and act in certain ways, to reinforce the strength of 'their' specific service. An example is the services of religion, regardless of which religious belief system one follows, since it retains a dogmatic aspect within its belief systems. Thus, one has to hold a certain level of compliance to actually use a service and be a part of a service. Also, being a part of the service portfolio as a serviced individual can be overlooked, since doing so depends on the type of service one engages with, e.g. a service encounter may be a brief experience and limited to the basic level of 'use it and lose it'; a sense of fleetingness. Tourism is an illustration. One books their two-week tourist happening and lives the tourist life during that time and space, and then afterwards it is lost to time, except for the memories. Consequently, that service is stepped out of. Other services like welfare and government require a longer term commitment, sometimes by choice, other times by necessity.

Either way, societal manipulation is part of the process, progress, and procuress of service usage, because as one is an integral part of the societal performance, one is also an integral part of the societal service performance. It is extremely unlikely that any individual in society does not ever use a service during their lifespan. Or travel along life for a time without the necessity of doing the service experience, seeing as it would be problematic to survive without so doing. Similarly, where there are people demanding to be serviced, that demand is met by a service provider. So, for the service provider to survive, it also needs that connectivity and relationship with its serviced, a mutual breeding ground of fertile service provision. For example, where would politics be without the politicians and their associated parties having people to vote for them, lobby them, 'pay' for them, provide reasons for their policies, and oppose them with another political belief system. Therefore, all in the political field relationship contributes to that service and keeping it sustainable and vibrant.

Bordieuan application to how society is and how services can be analysed within that space, show that services retain various performance qualities. For example, an integral part of the service performance is communication, not the least of which is having a voice that provides opportunities to express one's position and disposition. Of course, by the very definition of communication, multiple voices are involved in the process, which may result in a power imbalance of articulate linguistics, i..e those who know how to 'speak' the specialised service language, of whatever type, and those who do not. Service speak operates in fields, political or otherwise, and it is these controlled and constructed spaces that dictate how services operate, their limitations, functionality, and structured processes. All these are powered by symbolic potency, consequently adding another layer of representation to sell the service, on top of the representational layers of the face-to-face service performance. From the communication and representations, that define these fields, emerges capital culturation as every service retains capacity of cultural capital, a capital badge of societal membership, and a sense of conformity and belonging. It is a building block of service, amongst many services, of which if all were added together would equate to society, structuring society, and being society's structure. Habitus supports the structuring structure that creates and sustains services, contributing to the fluidity of ongoing service existence and daily performance.

The relationship of service providers and users to the place of Alice Springs and its demographic, through Bordieuan filters, shows a service structure embedded with habitus of passion, energy, and an 'unconscious consciousness' to get the service work done. For example, through the service fields of religion, education, government, welfare, Indigenous, tourism, and politics, the linguistic inquiry of Alice Springs locals, both from a servicer and serviced platform, retain strong voices of how the place functions, its challenges, aspirations, aims, maintenance, capacity, and structuring structure. It is not coincidental that the fields engaged with emerged as the 'chosen' fields of investigation, it was not planned that way since involving a habitus unconscious planning, as that maybe is how the apparently random selected 'individual' service areas gravitated into like-minded services, to create the seven in the book. Accordingly, these are essentially what the 'society' of Alice Springs consists of in relation to its service capacity, and its society is defined by these services and helps define what those who dwell in the Alice think about the place, and hence its society as service offering.

When considering the word 'city' when describing Alice Springs, the Latin for 'city' was urbs and resident was civis. Subsequently urbs was supplanted by civitas. As civis and civitas sound similar to service, this is perhaps a relatedness, a recognition, even two thousand years ago, that society and service intertwine and enjoy an intimacy of performance. Consequently, service presence can be found throughout the structure of society, constantly tuning its performance, repairing or at least addressing societal defects, in essence a maintenance process. Ultimately, society needs its services and services require the place and spatial influences of society to be. It is how a human settlement place is constructed and structured, a procedure significantly influenced by the sociality of what humans generally are or purport to be. Afterall, humans are symbolic, social and cultural capital that generates the economic capital, both to serve and be serviced within society as service…or is that service as society!

References

Abel, T. 2007. "Cultural Capital in Health Promotion." In *Health and modernity: The role of theory in health promotion*, edited by D V. McQueen, I Kickbusch, L Potvin, J M Pelikan, L Balbo and T.H Abel, 43-73. New York, NY: Springer.

Accardo, A. and Corcuff, P. 1986. *La Sociologie de Pierre Bourdieu. Textes choisis et commentés*. Le Mascaret: Bordeaux.

Adkins, L, and Skeggs, B. (eds.) 2004. *Feminism after Bourdieu*. Oxford: Blackwell/The Sociological Review.

Alexander, J. C. 1995. *Fin de Siècle Social Theory*. London, UK: Verso.

Alice Springs. 1999. *Land Use Structure Plan December 1999 and Land Use Objectives*. Lands, Planning and Environment. N.T. Government: Darwin.

Alice Springs Regional Outline Structure Plan. 1985. Northern Territory Department of Lands: Darwin.

Alice Springs Urban Development Study. 1975. Agius, McNally, Holmwood Pty Ltd. Architects and Urban Design Consultants. Milsons Point: NSW.

Ambrasat, J., von Scheve, C., Schauenburg, G., Conrad, M., and Schroder, T. 2016. "Unpacking the Habitus: Meaning Making Across Lifestyles." *Sociological Forum* 31 (4):1-24.

American Heritage® *Dictionary of the English Language*, Fifth Edition. 2016. Houghton Mifflin Harcourt Publishing Company: USA.

Anheier, H. K., Gerhards, J., and Romo, F. P. 1995. "Forms of capital and social structure in cultural fields: Examining Bourdieu's social topography." *American Journal of Sociology* 100:859–903.

Arts Trail Project 2017. Tourism N.T. Corporate Website. *$100 million Arts Trail Project Progressing* 30/06/2017. https://www.tourismnt.com.au/en/news-and-media/latest-news/$100-million-arts-trail-project-progressing.

Atkinson, W. 2010. "Phenomenological Additions to the Bourdieusian Toolbox: Two Problems for Bourdieu, Two Solutions from Schutz." *Sociological Theory* 28 (1) March:1-19.

Australian Bureau of Statistics. 2011. *Census of Population and Housing*. ABS. www.abs.gov.au: Canberra.

Australian Bureau Statistics. 2016. *quick stats*. http://quickstats.censusdata.abs.gov.au/census_services/getproduct/census/2016/quickstat/LGA46090; LGA41330; SSC70302; LGA70200; UCL715007; LGA72200; LGA72800; LGA71000.

Australian Statistical Geography Standard (ASGS). 2016. https://www.abs.gov.au/websitedbs/D3310114.nsf/home/Australian+Statistical+Geography+Standard+(ASGS).

Bauder, H. 2008. "Citizenship as Capital: The Distinction of Migrant Labor." *Alternatives* 33:315–333.

Bendix, R. 1977. *Max Weber: an intellectual portrait*. University of California Press: Berkeley.

Bennett, T. and Silva, E. 2006. "Cultural Capital and Inequality – Policy Issues and Contexts." *Cultural Trends* 15 (2-3):87-106.

Blommaert, J. 1999. "The debate is open." In *Language ideological debates*, edited by J. Blommaert, 1-38. Berlin, New York: Mouton de Gruyter.

Blunt, E. J. 1982. "The Influence of World War II on the Development of the Northern Territory's Ground Transport Links." Bachelor's in Literature Thesis, University of New England.

Bourdieu, P. 1973. "Cultural Reproduction and Social Reproduction." In *Knowledge, Education, and Cultural Change*, edited by R. Brown, 71-112. London: Tavistock Publications Limited.

———. 1977. *Outline of a Theory of Practice*. Cambridge, UK: Cambridge University Press.

———. 1979. *Distinction. A social Critique of the Judgement of Taste*. Translated by R Nice. Cambridge, Massachusetts: Harvard University Press.

———. 1984. *Distinction: A Social Critique of the Judgement of Taste*. Translated by R Nice. Cambridge, Massachusetts: Harvard University Press.

———. 1985. "The Social Space and the Genesis of Groups." *Theory and Society*, 14 (6) November:723-744.

———. 1986. "Forms of capital." In *Sociology of Education: A Critical Reader*, edited by A. R. Sadovnik, 83-95. New York: Routledge.

———. 1986b. "The forms of capital." In *Handbook of theory and research for the sociology of education*, edited by J. G. Richardson, 241-258 (Chapter 1: 15-29). CT: Greenwood Press.

———. 1987. *Choses dites*. Paris: Euditions de Minuit.

———. 1987b. "Bourdieu What Makes a Social Class? On The Theoretical and Practical Existence Of Groups." *Berkeley Journal of Sociology*, 32:1-17.

———. 1989. "Social Space and Symbolic Power." *Sociological Theory*, 7 (1) Spring:14-25.

———. 1990a. *The Logic of Practice*. Cambridge: Polity Press.

———. 1990b. *In Other Words*. Cambridge, UK: Polity

———. 1990c. *Sociology in Question*. Cambridge: Polity Press

———. 1991. *Language and Symbolic Power*. Edited and Introduced by J B. Thompson. Translated by G Raymond and M Adamson. Cambridge: Polity Press.

———. 1993. *Sociology in Question*. London: SAGE.

———. 1994. *Raisons pratiques. Sur la théorie de l'action*. Paris: Seuil.

———. 1997a. *Méditations pascaliennes*. Paris: Seuil.

———. 1999. *The Weight of the World*. Stanford, CA: Stanford University Press.

———. 2000. *Les structures sociales de l'économie*. Paris: Seuil.

———. 2000a. *Pascalian Meditations*. Cambridge, UK: Polity.

———. 2001. *Langage et pouvoir symbolique*. Paris: Seuil.

———. 2002. *Distinction.: A Social Critique of the Judgment of Taste*. Translated by R Nice. Cambridge: Harvard University Press.

Bourdieu, P. and J-C. Passeron. 1977. *Reproduction in Education, Society, and Culture*. London: Sage.

Bourdieu, P. and Passeron, J. C. 1990. *Reproduction in education, society and culture*. London: Sage.

Bourdieu, P. and Wacquant, L. 1992. *An Invitation to Reflexive Sociology*. Cambridge: Polity.

Bowman, B. 1993. *A History of Central Australia 1930-1980, Volume 1*. Alice Springs: Alice Springs Library Collection.

Brolga Awards 2019. Tourism N.T. Corporate Website Brolga Awards. https://www. tourismnt.com.au/en/industry-toolkit/brolga-awards.

Bullock, A. and Trombley, S. (eds.) 1999. *The New Fontana Dictionary of Modern Thought* Third Edition. London: Harpercollins Pub Ltd.

Casey, K. L. 2005. *Defining Political Capital: A Reconsideration of Bourdieu's Interconvertibility Theory*. University of Missouri-St. Louis.

Census of the Commonwealth of Australia. 1954. *Population Recorded in each District: Northern Territory. Census 1947 and 1954 (Exclusive of full-blood Aboriginals).* Canberra: Commonwealth Bureau of Census and Statistics.

Central Australia the war years 1939-45. http://www.thewaryears.alicespringsrsl.com.au/military2.shtml.

Chamber of Commerce NT. 2019. chambernt.com.au.

Cheng, S. 2012. *Cultural Capital, Ecomic Capital, and Academic Achievemnet: Some Evidence from Taiwan.* A Dissertation. Submitted to Michigan State University.

China Ready 2019. Tourism N.T. Corporate Website China Ready. https://www.tourismnt.com.au/en/industry-toolkit/china-ready.

Chomsky, N. 1965. *Aspects of the Theory of Syntax.* Cambridge, Mass.: MIT Press.

Cockerham, W. C., Rutten, A., and Abel, T. 1997. "Conceptualizing contemporary health lifestyles: Moving beyond Weber." *Sociological Quarterly,* 38: 321–342.

Cornell Wagner Pty Ltd. 2002. *Alice Springs Central Area Draft Master Plan*: Alice Springs Collection, Alice Springs Town Library.

Crossley, N. 2001. *The Social Body.* London, UK: Sage.

de Saussure, F. 1974. *Course in General Linguistics.* Translated by W. Baskin. Glasgow: Collins.

de Saussure. F. (1916) 1983. *Course in General Linguistics.* London: Duckworth.

Department of Corporate and Information Services (DCIS). 2019. https://dcis.nt.gov.au/about.

DiMaggio, P. 1979. "Review Essay: On Pierre Bourdieu." *American Journal of Sociology* 84 (6):1460–1474. http://www.jstor.org/stable/2777906.

Domenico Pecorari and Associates Pty Ltd. 2005. *Conservation and Management Plan for the Seven Mile Aerodrome Alice Springs.* Vol. October. Alice Springs.

Durkheim, E. --1960: Montequieu and Rousseau: Forerunners of Sociology. Ann Arbor, Mich: University of Chicago Press.

Eagleton, T. 1990. *Ideology.* London: Verso.

Edgerton, J. D. and Roberts, L. W. 2014. "Cultural capital or habitus? Bourdieu and beyond in the explanation of enduring educational inequality." *Theory and Research in Education* 12 (2):1–28.

Exploring the Stuart Highway: further than the eye can see. 1997. West Beach, South Australia: Tourist Information Distributors Australia.

Gaventa, J. 2003. *Power after Lukes: a review of the literature.* Brighton: Institute of Development Studies.

Gibson-Graham, J.K. 1996 *The End of Capitalism (As We Knew It): A Feminist Critique of Political Economy.* Malden, Mass: Blackwell.

Gieseking, J.J. 2014. *The People, Place, and Space Reader.* Hoboken: Taylor and Francis.

Giles, A. 2015 May. *Our Territory. Budget 2015-16. Making your life Simpler, Safer, Smarter.* Public Information Leaflet.

Goldthorpe, J. H. 2007. "Cultural Capital: Some Critical Observations." Sociologica 2 (2):1–23.

Goodman, N. 1978. *Ways of Worldmaking.* USA: Hacking Publishing.

Gramsci, A. 1978. *Selections from Political Writings (1921-1926).* Translated by Q. Hoare. London: Lawrence & Wishart.

Grenfell, M. (ed.) 2008. *Bourdieu: Key Concepts.* Stocksfield: Acumen.

Hartwig, M. C. 1965. "The Progress of White Settlement in the Alice Springs District and its effects upon the Aboriginal Inhabitants, 1860-1894." PhD, University of Adelaide.

Harvey, D. 1989. *The Condition of Postmodernity.* Oxford: Blackwell.

Heidegger, M. 1962. *Being and Time.* New York: Harper and Row.

Jackson, P. 2008. "Pierre Bourdieu, the 'cultural turn' and the practice of international history." *Review of International Studies* 34: 155–181.

Jenkins, R. 1992. *Pierre Bourdieu*. London: Routledge.

Jenkins, R. 2002. *Pierre Bourdieu*, rev. ed. London, UK: Routledge.

Johnson, D. (2002-01-28). "Obituary: Pierre Bourdieu | Books". *The Guardian*.

Kennicott, P. 2004. "Bush's Capital, And Its Costs." *Washington Post*. com. 19 December 2004. http://www.washingtonpost.com/ wp-dyn/articles/A9478-2004Dec17.

Lareau A and Weininger EB 2003. "Cultural capital in educational research: A critical assessment." *Theory and Society* 32:567–606.

Lin, Nan. 2001. *Social Capital: Structural Analysis in the Social Sciences*. Cambridge: Cambridge University.

Lizardo, O. 2004. "The Cognitive Origins of Bourdieu's Habitus." *Journal for the Theory of Social Behavior* 34 (4):375–401.

Lloyd, C. 2008. "Australian Capitalism Since 1992: A New Regime of Accumulation?" *Journal of Australian Political Economy* 61 June:30-55.

Martin, J. L. 2003. "What is field theory?" *American Journal of Sociology* 109:1–49.

Marx, K, 1848 (1996). *The Communist Manifesto*. London; Chicago, Ill:Pluto Press.

Marx, K. 1867b. *Das Kapital: Kritik der politischen Ökonomie. Erstes Buch, Der Produktionsprozeß des Kapitals.* Hamburg: Verlag von Otto Meissner.

Marx, K. and Engles, F. 1867 (2001). *Werke. Band 23, 20.* Auflage. Berlin: Karl Dietz Verlag.

Marx, K. and Engels, F. 1953. *Die deutsche Ideologie*. Berlin: Karl Dietz Verlag.

McDonough, P. and Polzer, J. 2012. "Habitus, Hysteresis, and Organizational Change in the PublicSector." *Canadian Journal of Sociology/Cahierscanadiensde sociologie* 37(4):357-379.

McLennan, G. 1998. "Fin de Sociologie? The Dilemmas of Multidimensional Social Theory." *New Left Review* 230:58–90.

Moraru, M. 2016. *Bordieu, Multilingualism, and Immigration: Understanding how second-generation multilingual immigrants reproduce linguistic practices with non-autochthonous minority languages in Cardiff, Wales.* Thesis submitted for the degree of Doctor of Philosophy. School of Modern Languages Cardiff University.

Mustafa, E. and Johnson, V. 2008. "Bourdieu and organizational analysis." *Theory and Society* 37:1–44.

Navarro, Z. 2006. "In Search of Cultural Interpretation of Power." *IDS Bulletin* 37 (6):11-22.

Nicolaescu, A. C. 2010. "Dimitrie Cantemir Bourdieu – Habitus, Symbolic Violence, the Gift: "You give me/I give you" Principle." Christian University 1 (3) September:1-10.

Online Etymology Dictionary. 2019. https://www.etymonline.com/word/city.

Operational Plan 2018-19. Tourism NT. Department of Tourism, Sport and Culture. Northern Territory Government. https://dtsc.nt.gov.au/about-us.

Rawolle, S. 2005. "Cross-field effects and temporary social fields: a case study of the mediatization of recent Australian knowledge economy policies." *Journal of Education Policy* 20 (6):705-724.

Parkes, D. N., Burnley, I. H. and Walker, S. R. 1985. *Arid Zone Settlement in Australia: A Focus on Alice Springs.* Tokyo: The United Nations University.

Peillon, M. 1998. "Bourdieu's Field and the Sociology of Welfare." *Journal of Social Policy* 27 (2): 213–229.

Piaget, J. 1970. *Structuralism*. New York: Basic Books.

Pickel, A. 2005. "The Habitus Process: A Biopsychosocial Conception." *Journal for the Theory of Social Behaviour* 35 (4):437–461.

QuickStats 2016. Census Australia | Northern Territory | Indigenous Regions. Alice Springs.https://quickstats.censusdata.abs.gov.au/census_services/getproduct/census/2016/quickstat/IREG701?opendocument.

QuickStats 2016. Census Australia | Northern Territory | Local Government Areas. Alice Springs (T). https://quickstats.censusdata.abs.gov.au/census_services/getproduct/census/2016/quickstat/LGA70200

QuickStats 2016. Census Australia | Northern Territory | Statistical Area Level 3. Alice Springs. https://quickstats.censusdata.abs.gov.au/census_services/getproduct/census/2016/quickstat/70201?opendocument

Reay, D. 2004. "It's All Becoming a Habitus: Beyond the Habitual Use of Habitus in Educational Research." *British Journal of Sociology of Education* 25:431–44.

Sayer, A. 2005. *The Moral Significance of Class*. Cambridge, UK: Cambridge University Press.

Schinkela, W. and Noordegraaf, M. 2011. "Professionalism as Symbolic Capital: Materials for a Bourdieusian Theory of Professionalism." *Comparative Sociology* 10: 67–96.

Schwingel, M. 2003. *Pierre Bourdieu zur Einführung*. Hamburg: Junius-Verlag.

Searle, J. 1997. *The Construction of Social Reality*. New York: Free Press.

Shrapnel, P. 1970. *Northern Territory Growth of Alice Springs and Darwin. A Summary of a study on Past, Present and Potential Growth in Darwin and Alice Springs*: Philip Shrapnel and Co Ltd.

Silva, E. B. 2005. "Gender, home and family in cultural capital theory." *British Journal of Sociology* 56 (1):83–104.

Smith, A. 1991. *Convoys up the track: a history of 121st Australian General Transport Company (AIF), 1941-1946*. Plympton, South Australia.

Smith, B. A. 2005. *"Mort & Co (1849 - 1888)"*. Guide to Australian Business Records. www.gabr.net.au.

Street Ryan and Associates. 1999 February. *Alice Springs Economic Profile. Business and management*: Alice Springs Town Council. Department of Industries and Business.

Suellentrop, C. 2004. "America's New Political Capital." *Slate*. 30 November, 2004. www.slate.com.

Swartz, D. 1997. *Culture & Power: The Sociology of Pierre Bourdieu*. Chicago: University of Chicago Press.

The Free Dictionary. 2019. By Farlex. https://www.thefreedictionary.com/service

The Office of the Commissioner for Public Employment 2019. https://ocpe.nt.gov.au/.

Tourism N.T. Corporate Website. 2019. *Tourism NT Act 2012* N.T. Tourism N.T. Northern Territory Government. http://www.tourismnt.com.au/en/About-us.

TurboCharged Tourism. 2019. en/news-and-media/latest-news/turbocharged-tourism-hits-2-5-billion09/10/2019 https://www.tourismnt.com.au/en/news-and-media.

Vester, M. 2005. "Class and Culture in Germany." In *Rethinking Class, Cultures, Identities and Life-Styles*, edited by F Devine, M Savage, J Scott and R Crompton, 69–94. Basingstoke, UK: Palgrave Macmillan.

Wacquant, L. J. D. 2014. "Homines in Extremis: what fighting scholars teach us about habitus." *Body & Society* 20 (2): 3-17.

Webb, J., Schirato, T., and Danaher, G. 2002. Understanding Bourdieu. Series editors: Rachel Fensham and Terry Threadgold. *Cultural Studies*. Australia: Allen and Unwin.

Weber, M. 1985. *The Protestant Ethic and the Spirit of Capitalism*. London: Taylor and Francis Ltd.

Weininger, E. B. 2002. "Chapter 4. Pierre Bourdieu on Social Class and Symbolic Violence." In *Alternative Foundations of Class Analysis*, edited by E. O. Wright, 119-179.

Wilford, J. R. 2003. *Granites-Tanami Region Northern Territory*. Canberra, ACT: CRC Leme. GeoScience Australia.

www.ingramcontent.com/pod-product-compliance
Lightning Source LLC
Chambersburg PA
CBHW040931050426
42334CB00060B/3158